PEARSON

Lone Star College-Kingwood
American Government Reader

Custom Edition

Taken from:
American Government: Readings and Cases,
Nineteenth Edition
by Peter Woll

and

*Voices of Dissent: Critical Readings in
American Politics,* Eighth Edition
by William F. Grover and Joseph G. Peschek

Pearson Learning Solutions, 501 Boylston Street, Suite 900, Boston, MA 02116
A Pearson Education Company
www.pearsoned.com

Printed in the United States of America

1 2 3 4 5 6 7 8 9 10 XXXX 16 15 14 13 12 11

000200010270785889

JL/TB

ISBN 10: 1-256-33976-8
ISBN 13: 978-1-256-33976-2

Lone Star College-Kingwood American Government Reader

Contents

The Constitution

1   *Some Truths Are Not Self-Evident*

Howard Zinn

Writing during the bicentennial celebrations of 1987, historian and political scientist Howard Zinn makes a case that the Constitution is of minor importance in determining the degree of justice, liberty, and democracy in our society. While not denying the symbolic and moral weight of the Constitution, Zinn contends that social movements and citizen action have been far more significant in the realization of democratic values over the course of American history. He provides examples from the areas of racial equality, freedom of speech, economic justice, sexual equality, and questions of war and peace to support his claim that a "mere document" like the Constitution "is no substitute for the energy, boldness, and concerted action of the citizens."

This year [1987] Americans are talking about the Constitution but asking the wrong questions, such as, Could the Founding Fathers have done better? That concern is pointless, 200 years after the fact. Or, Does the Constitution provide the framework for a just and democratic society today? That question is also misplaced, because the Constitution, whatever its language and however interpreted by the Supreme Court, does not determine the degree of justice, liberty or democracy in our society.

The proper question, I believe, is not how good a document is or was the Constitution but, What effect does it have on the quality of our lives? And the answer to that, it seems to me, is, Very little. The Constitution makes promises it cannot by itself keep, and therefore deludes us into complacency about the rights we have. It is conspicuously silent on certain other rights that all human beings deserve. And it pretends to set limits on governmental powers, when in fact those limits are easily ignored.

I am not arguing that the Constitution has no importance; words have moral power and principles can be useful even when ambiguous. But, like other historic documents, the Constitution is of minor importance compared with the actions that

Reprinted from *The Nation* 245, no. 3, August 1987.

citizens take, especially when those actions are joined in social movements. Such movements have worked, historically, to secure the rights our human sensibilities tell us are self-evidently ours, whether or not those rights are "granted" by the Constitution.

Let me illustrate my point with five issues of liberty and justice:

First is the matter of racial equality. When slavery was abolished, it was not by constitutional fiat but by the joining of military necessity with the moral force of a great antislavery movement, acting outside the Constitution and often against the law. The Thirteenth, Fourteenth and Fifteenth Amendments wrote into the Constitution rights that extra-legal action had already won. But the Fourteenth and Fifteenth Amendments were ignored for almost a hundred years. The right to equal protection of the law and the right to vote, even the Supreme Court decision in *Brown v. Board of Education* in 1954 underlining the meaning of the equal protection clause, did not become operative until blacks, in the fifteen years following the Montgomery bus boycott, shook up the nation by tumultuous actions inside and outside the law.

The Constitution played a helpful but marginal role in all that. Black people, in the political context of the 1960s, would have demanded equality whether or not the Constitution called for it, just as the antislavery movement demanded abolition even in the absence of constitutional support.

What about the most vaunted of constitutional rights, free speech? Historically, the Supreme Court has given the right to free speech only shaky support, seesawing erratically by sometimes affirming and sometimes overriding restrictions. Whatever a distant Court decided, the real right of citizens to free expression has been determined by the immediate power of the local police on the street, by the employer in the workplace and by the financial limits on the ability to use the mass media.

The existence of a First Amendment has been inspirational but its protection elusive. Its reality has depended on the willingness of citizens, whether labor organizers, socialists or Jehovah's Witnesses, to insist on their right to speak and write. Liberties have not been given; they have been taken. And whether in the future we have a right to say what we want, or air what we say, will be determined not by the existence of the First Amendment or the latest Supreme Court decision but by whether we are courageous enough to speak up at the risk of being jailed or fired, organized enough to defend our speech against official interference and can command resources enough to get our ideas before a reasonably large public.

What of economic justice? The Constitution is silent on the right to earn a moderate income, silent on the rights to medical care and decent housing as legitimate claims of every human being from infancy to old age. Whatever degree of economic justice has been attained in this country (impressive compared with others, shameful compared with our resources) cannot be attributed to something in the Constitution. It is the result of the concerted action of laborers and farmers over the centuries, using strikes, boycotts and minor rebellions of all sorts, to get redress of grievances directly from employers and indirectly from legislators. In the future, as in the past, the Constitution will sleep as citizens battle over the distribution of the nation's wealth, and will be awakened only to mark the score.

On sexual equality the Constitution is also silent. What women have achieved thus far is the result of their own determination, in the feminist upsurge of the nineteenth and early twentieth centuries, and the more recent women's liberation movement. Women have accomplished this outside the Constitution, by raising female and male consciousness and inducing courts and legislators to recognize what the Constitution ignores.

Finally, in an age in which war approaches genocide, the irrelevance of the Constitution is especially striking. Long, ravaging conflicts in Korea and Vietnam were waged without following Constitutional procedures, and if there is a nuclear exchange, the decision to launch U.S. missiles will be made, as it was in those cases, by the President and a few advisers. The public will be shut out of the process and deliberately kept uninformed by an intricate web of secrecy and deceit. The current Iran/*contra* scandal hearings before Congressional select committees should be understood as exposing not an aberration but a steady state of foreign policy.

It was not constitutional checks and balances but an aroused populace that prodded Lyndon Johnson and then Richard Nixon into deciding to extricate the United States from Vietnam. In the immediate future, our lives will depend not on the existence of the Constitution but on the power of an aroused citizenry demanding that we not go to war, and on Americans refusing, as did so many G.I.s and civilians in the Vietnam era, to cooperate in the conduct of a war.

The Constitution, like the Bible, has some good words. It is also, like the Bible, easily manipulated, distorted, ignored and used to make us feel comfortable and protected. But we risk the loss of our lives and liberties if we depend on a mere document to defend them. A constitution is a fine adornment for a democratic society, but it is no substitute for the energy, boldness and concerted action of the citizens.

Discussion Questions

1. What is Zinn's main point about the relationship of the Constitution to political change and the expansion of democracy?

2. Identify the five issues of justice and liberty discussed by Zinn and explain how each relates to his main point about the Constitution.

2   *Federalist No. 15*

The Insufficiency of the Present Confederation to Preserve the Union
For the Independent Journal.
Alexander Hamilton

To the People of the State of New York.

IN THE course of the preceding papers, I have endeavored, my fellow-citizens, to place before you, in a clear and convincing light, the importance of Union to your political safety and happiness. I have unfolded to you a complication of dangers to which you would be exposed, should you permit that sacred knot which binds the people of America together be severed or dissolved by ambition or by avarice, by jealousy or by misrepresentation. In the sequel of the inquiry through which I propose to accompany you, the truths intended to be inculcated will receive further confirmation from facts and arguments hitherto unnoticed. If the road over which you will still have to pass should in some places appear to you tedious or irksome, you will recollect that you are in quest of information on a subject the most momentous which can engage the attention of a free people, that the field through which you have to travel is in itself spacious, and that the difficulties of the journey have been unnecessarily increased by the mazes with which sophistry has beset the way. It will be my aim to remove the obstacles from your progress in as compendious a manner as it can be done, without sacrificing utility to despatch.

In pursuance of the plan which I have laid down for the discussion of the subject, the point next in order to be examined is the "insufficiency of the present Confederation to the preservation of the Union." It may perhaps be asked what need there is of reasoning or proof to illustrate a position which is not either controverted or doubted, to which the understandings and feelings of all classes of men assent, and which in substance is admitted by the opponents as well as by the friends of the new Constitution. It must in truth be acknowledged that, however these may differ in other respects, they in general appear to harmonize in this sentiment, at least, that there are material imperfections in our national system, and that something is necessary to be done to rescue us from impending anarchy. The facts that support this opinion are no longer objects of speculation. They have forced themselves upon the sensibility of the people at large, and have at length extorted from those, whose mistaken policy has had the principal share in precipitating the extremity at which we are arrived, a reluctant confession of the reality of those defects in the scheme of our federal government, which have been long pointed out and regretted by the intelligent friends of the Union.

We may indeed with propriety be said to have reached almost the last stage of national humiliation. There is scarcely anything that can wound the pride or degrade the character of an independent nation which we do not experience. Are there engagements to the performance of which we are held by every tie respectable among men? These are the subjects of constant and unblushing violation. Do we owe debts to foreigners and to our own citizens contracted in a time of imminent peril for the preservation of our political existence? These remain without any proper or satisfactory provision for their discharge. Have we valuable territories and important posts in the possession of a foreign power which, by express stipulations, ought long since to have been surrendered? These are still retained, to the prejudice of our interests, not less than of our rights. Are we in a condition to resent or to repel the aggression? We have neither troops, nor treasury, nor government.[1] Are we even in a condition to remonstrate with dignity? The just imputations on our own faith, in respect to the same treaty, ought first to be removed. Are we entitled by nature and compact to a free participation in the navigation of the Mississippi? Spain excludes us from it. Is public credit an indispensable resource in time of public danger? We seem to have abandoned its cause as desperate and irretrievable. Is commerce of importance to national wealth? Ours is at the lowest point of declension. Is respectability in the eyes of foreign powers a safeguard against foreign encroachments? The imbecility of our government even forbids them to treat with us. Our ambassadors abroad are the mere pageants of mimic sovereignty. Is a violent and unnatural decrease in the value of land a symptom of national distress? The price of improved land in most parts of the country is much lower than can be accounted for by the quantity of waste land at market, and can only be fully explained by that want of private and public confidence, which are so alarmingly prevalent among all ranks, and which have a direct tendency to depreciate property of every kind. Is private credit the friend and patron of industry? That most useful kind which relates to borrowing and lending is reduced within the narrowest limits, and this still more from an opinion of insecurity than from the scarcity of money. To shorten an enumeration of particulars which can afford neither pleasure nor instruction, it may in general be demanded, what indication is there of national disorder, poverty, and insignificance that could befall a community so peculiarly blessed with natural advantages as we are, which does not form a part of the dark catalogue of our public misfortunes?

This is the melancholy situation to which we have been brought by those very maxims and councils which would now deter us from adopting the proposed Constitution; and which, not content with having conducted us to the brink of a precipice, seem resolved to plunge us into the abyss that awaits us below. Here, my countrymen, impelled by every motive that ought to influence an enlightened people, let us make a firm stand for our safety, our tranquillity, our dignity, our reputation. Let us at last break the fatal charm which has too long seduced us from the paths of felicity and prosperity.

It is true, as has been before observed that facts, too stubborn to be resisted, have produced a species of general assent to the abstract proposition that there exist material defects in our national system; but the usefulness of the concession, on the part of the old adversaries of federal measures, is destroyed by a strenuous opposition to a remedy, upon the only principles that can give it a chance of success. While they admit that the government of the United States is destitute of energy, they contend against conferring upon it those powers which are requisite to supply that energy. They seem still to aim at things repugnant and irreconcilable; at an augmentation of federal authority, without a diminution of State authority; at sovereignty in the Union, and complete independence in the members. They still, in fine, seem to cherish with blind devotion the political monster of an imperium in imperio. This renders a full display of the principal defects of the Confederation necessary, in order to show that the evils we experience do not proceed from minute or partial imperfections, but from fundamental errors in the structure of the building, which cannot be amended otherwise than by an alteration in the first principles and main pillars of the fabric.

The great and radical vice in the construction of the existing Confederation is in the principle of LEGISLATION for STATES or GOVERNMENTS, in their CORPORATE or COLLECTIVE CAPACITIES, and as contradistinguished from the INDIVIDUALS of which they consist. Though this principle does not run through all the powers delegated to the Union, yet it pervades and governs those on which the efficacy of the rest depends. Except as to the rule of appointment, the United States has an indefinite discretion to make requisitions for men and money; but they have no authority to raise either, by regulations extending to the individual citizens of America. The consequence of this is, that though in theory their resolutions concerning those objects are laws, constitutionally binding on the members of the Union, yet in practice they are mere recommendations which the States observe or disregard at their option.

It is a singular instance of the capriciousness of the human mind, that after all the admonitions we have had from experience on this head, there should still be found men who object to the new Constitution, for deviating from a principle which has been found the bane of the old, and which is in itself evidently incompatible with the idea of GOVERNMENT; a principle, in short, which, if it is to be executed at all, must substitute the violent and sanguinary agency of the sword to the mild influence of the magistracy.

There is nothing absurd or impracticable in the idea of a league or alliance between independent nations for certain defined purposes precisely stated in a treaty regulating all the details of time, place, circumstance, and quantity; leaving nothing to future discretion; and depending for its execution on the good faith of the parties. Compacts of this kind exist among all civilized nations, subject to the usual vicissitudes of peace and war, of observance and non-observance, as the interests or passions of the contracting powers dictate. In the early part of the present century there was an epidemical rage in Europe for this species of compacts, from which the politicians of the times fondly hoped for benefits which were never realized. With a view to establishing the equilibrium of power and the peace of that part of the world, all the resources of negotiation were exhausted, and triple and quadruple alliances were formed; but they were scarcely formed before they were broken, giving an instructive but afflicting lesson to mankind, how little dependence is to be placed on treaties which have no other sanction than the obligations of good faith, and which oppose general considerations of peace and justice to the impulse of any immediate interest or passion.

If the particular States in this country are disposed to stand in a similar relation to each other, and to drop the project of a general DISCRETIONARY SUPERIN-

TENDENCE, the scheme would indeed be pernicious, and would entail upon us all the mischiefs which have been enumerated under the first head; but it would have the merit of being, at least, consistent and practicable Abandoning all views towards a confederate government, this would bring us to a simple alliance offensive and defensive; and would place us in a situation to be alternate friends and enemies of each other, as our mutual jealousies and rivalships, nourished by the intrigues of foreign nations, should prescribe to us.

But if we are unwilling to be placed in this perilous situation; if we still will adhere to the design of a national government, or, which is the same thing, of a superintending power, under the direction of a common council, we must resolve to incorporate into our plan those ingredients which may be considered as forming the characteristic difference between a league and a government; we must extend the authority of the Union to the persons of the citizens, —the only proper objects of government.

Government implies the power of making laws. It is essential to the idea of a law, that it be attended with a sanction; or, in other words, a penalty or punishment for disobedience. If there be no penalty annexed to disobedience, the resolutions or commands which pretend to be laws will, in fact, amount to nothing more than advice or recommendation. This penalty, whatever it may be, can only be inflicted in two ways: by the agency of the courts and ministers of justice, or by military force; by the COERCION of the magistracy, or by the COERCION of arms. The first kind can evidently apply only to men; the last kind must of necessity, be employed against bodies politic, or communities, or States. It is evident that there is no process of a court by which the observance of the laws can, in the last resort, be enforced. Sentences may be denounced against them for violations of their duty; but these sentences can only be carried into execution by the sword. In an association where the general authority is confined to the collective bodies of the communities, that compose it, every breach of the laws must involve a state of war; and military execution must become the only instrument of civil obedience. Such a state of things can certainly not deserve the name of government, nor would any prudent man choose to commit his happiness to it.

There was a time when we were told that breaches, by the States, of the regulations of the federal authority were not to be expected; that a sense of common interest would preside over the conduct of the respective members, and would beget a full compliance with all the constitutional requisitions of the Union. This language, at the present day, would appear as wild as a great part of what we now hear from the same quarter will be thought, when we shall have received further lessons from that best oracle of wisdom, experience. It at all times betrayed an ignorance of the true springs by which human conduct is actuated, and belied the original inducements to the establishment of civil power. Why has government been instituted at all? Because the passions of men will not conform to the dictates of reason and justice, without constraint. Has it been found that bodies of men act with more rectitude or greater disinterestedness than individuals? The contrary of this has been inferred by all accurate observers of the conduct of mankind; and the inference is founded upon obvious reasons. Regard to reputation has a less active influence, when the infamy of a bad action is to be divided among a number than when it is to fall singly upon one. A spirit of faction, which is apt to mingle its poison in the deliberations of all bodies of men, will often hurry the persons of whom they are composed into improprieties and excesses, for which they would blush in a private capacity.

In addition to all this, there is, in the nature of sovereign power, an impatience of control, that disposes those who are invested with the exercise of it, to look with an evil eye upon all external attempts to restrain or direct its operations. From this spirit it happens, that in every political association which is formed upon the principle of uniting in a common interest a number of lesser sovereignties, there will be found a kind of eccentric tendency in the subordinate or inferior orbs, by the operation of which there will be a perpetual effort in each to fly off from the common centre. This tendency is not difficult to be accounted for. It has its origin in the love of power. Power controlled or abridged is almost always the rival and enemy of that power by which it is controlled or abridged. This simple proposition will teach us how little reason there is to expect, that the persons intrusted with the administration of the affairs of the particular members of a confederacy will at all times be ready, with perfect good-humor, and an unbiased regard to the public weal, to execute the resolutions or decrees of the general authority. The reverse of this results from the constitution of human nature.

If, therefore, the measures of the Confederacy cannot be executed without the intervention of the particular administrations, there will be little prospect of their being executed at all. The rulers of the respective members, whether they have a constitutional right to do it or not, will undertake to judge of the propriety of the measures themselves. They will consider the conformity of the thing proposed or required to their immediate interests or aims; the momentary conveniences or inconveniences that would attend its adoption. All this will be done; and in a spirit of interested and suspicious scrutiny, without that knowledge of national circumstances and reasons of state, which is essential to a right judgment, and with that strong predilection in favor of local objects, which can hardly fail to mislead the decision. The same process must be repeated in every member of which the body is constituted; and the execution of the plans, framed by the councils of the whole, will always fluctuate on the discretion of the ill-informed and prejudiced opinion of every part. Those who have been conversant in the proceedings of popular assemblies; who have seen how difficult it often is, where there is no exterior pressure of circumstances, to bring them to harmonious resolutions on important points, will readily conceive how impossible it must be to induce a number of such assemblies, deliberating at a distance from each other, at different times, and under different impressions, long to co-operate in the same views and pursuits.

In our case, the concurrence of thirteen distinct sovereign wills is requisite, under the Confederation, to the complete execution of every important measure that proceeds from the Union. It has happened as was to have been foreseen. The measures of the Union have not been executed; the delinquencies of the States have, step by step, matured themselves to an extreme, which has, at length, arrested all the wheels of the national government, and brought them to an awful stand. Congress at this time scarcely possess the means of keeping up the forms of administration, till the States can have time to agree upon a more substantial substitute for the present shadow of a federal government. Things did not come to this desperate extremity at once. The causes which have been specified produced at first only unequal and disproportionate degrees of compliance with the requisitions of the Union. The greater deficiencies of some States furnished the pretext of example and the temptation of interest to the complying, or to the least delinquent States. Why should we do more in proportion than those who are embarked with us in the same political voyage? Why should we consent to bear more than our proper share of the common burden? These were suggestions which human selfishness could not withstand, and which even speculative men, who looked forward to remote consequences, could not, without hesitation, combat. Each State, yielding to the persuasive voice of immediate interest or convenience, has successively withdrawn its support, till the frail and tottering edifice seems ready to fall upon our heads, and to crush us beneath its ruins.

PUBLIUS.

1.   "I mean for the Union."

Ideology and
Public Opinion

3   *Liberal Individualism and the Crisis Of Citizenship*

Robert N. Bellah, Richard Madsen, William M. Sullivan, Ann Swidler, and Steven M. Tipton

Sociologist Robert Bellah and his four collaborators suggest that the exaggerated importance placed on individualism in America undermines citizenship and a strong sense of political community. Drawing on in-depth interviews with middle-class Americans for their much-discussed 1985 book Habits of the Heart, *the authors contend that most of us are unable to find in political participation and public involvement elements of a good life. But this withdrawal into private pursuits leaves politics under the domination of those with the power and money to assert their organized interests. Writing more than a decade after the original publication of* Habits of the Heart, *Bellah draws on Robert Putnam's concept of "social capital" to argue that Americans face both a personal crisis and a social crisis that he calls a "crisis of civic membership." This crisis has been exacerbated by the success of neocapitalism, an ideology that sees markets and privatization as the solutions to social problems. In contrast, Bellah calls for a revival of civic- and community-oriented discourses that historically have been subordinate to liberal-capitalist individualism and asks us to critically question the materialistic basis of our notion of a just society.*

How ought we to live? How do we think about how to live? Who are we, as Americans? What is our character? These are questions we have asked our fellow citizens in many parts of the country. We engaged them in conversations about their lives and about what matters most to them, talked about their families and communities, their doubts and uncertainties, and their hopes and fears with respect to the larger society. We found them eager to discuss the right way to live, what to teach our children, and what our public and private responsibilities should be, but also a little dismayed by these subjects. These are important matters to those to whom we talked, and yet concern about moral questions is often relegated to the realm of private anxiety, as if it would be awkward or embarrassing to make it public. We hope this book will help transform this inner moral debate, often shared only with intimates, into public

Reprinted from *Habits of the Heart: Individualism and Commitment in American Life* (1996), by permission of University of California Press.

discourse. In these pages, Americans speak with us, and, indirectly, with one another, about issues that deeply concern us all. As we will see, many doubt that we have enough in common to be able mutually to discuss our central aspirations and fears. It is one of our purposes to persuade them that we do.

The fundamental question we posed, and that was repeatedly posed to us, was how to preserve or create a morally coherent life. But the kind of life we want depends on the kind of people we are—on our character. Our inquiry can thus be located in a longstanding discussion of the relationship between character and society. In the eighth book of the *Republic,* Plato sketched a theory of the relationship between the moral character of a people and the nature of its political community, the way it organizes and governs itself. The founders of the American republic at the time of the Revolution adopted a much later version of the same theory. Since for them, as for the Americans with whom we talked, freedom was perhaps the most important value, they were particularly concerned with the qualities of character necessary for the creation of a free republic.

In the 1830s, the French social philosopher Alexis de Tocqueville offered the most comprehensive and penetrating analysis of the relationship between character and society in America that has ever been written. In his book *Democracy in America,* based on acute observation and wide conversation with Americans, Tocqueville described the mores—which he on occasion called "habits of the heart"—of the American people and showed how they helped to form American character. He singled out family life, our religious traditions, and our participation in local politics as helping to create the kind of person who could sustain a connection to a wider political community and thus ultimately support the maintenance of free institutions. He also warned that some aspects of our character—what he was one of the first to call "individualism"—might eventually isolate Americans one from another and thereby undermine the conditions of freedom.

The central problem of our book concerns the American individualism that Tocqueville described with a mixture of admiration and anxiety. It seems to us that it is individualism, and not equality, as Tocqueville thought, that has marched inexorably through our history. We are concerned that this individualism may have grown cancerous—that it may be destroying those social integuments that Tocqueville saw as moderating its more destructive potentialities, that it may be threatening the survival of freedom itself. We want to know what individualism in America looks and feels like, and how the world appears in its light.

We are also interested in those cultural traditions and practices that, without destroying individuality, serve to limit and restrain the destructive side of individualism and provide alternative models for how Americans might live. We want to know how these have fared since Tocqueville's day, and how likely their renewal is.

While we focus on what people say, we are acutely aware that they often live in ways they cannot put into words. It is particularly here, in the tension between how we live and what our culture allows us to say, that we have found both some of our richest insights into the dilemmas our society faces and hope for the reappropriation of a common language in which those dilemmas can be discussed.

Taking our clue from Tocqueville, we believe that one of the keys to the survival of free institutions is the relationship between private and public life, the way in which citizens do, or do not, participate in the public sphere. We therefore decided to concentrate our research on how private and public life work in the United States: the extent to which private life either prepares people to take part in the public world or encourages them to find meaning exclusively in the private sphere, and the degree to which public life fulfills our private aspirations or discourages us so much that we withdraw from involvement in it.

The Crisis of Civic Membership

The consequences of radical individualism are more strikingly evident today than they were even a decade ago, when *Habits of the Heart* was published. In *Habits* we spoke of commitment, of community, and of citizenship as useful terms to contrast to an alienating individualism. Properly understood, these terms are still valuable for our current understanding. But today we think the phrase "civic membership" brings out something not quite captured by those other terms. While we criticized distorted forms of individualism, we never sought to neglect the central significance of the individual person or failed to sympathize with the difficulties faced by the individual self in our society. "Civic membership" points to that critical intersection of personal identity with social identity. If we face a crisis of civic identity, it is not just a social crisis, it is a personal crisis as well.

One way of characterizing the weakening of the practices of social life and civic engagement that we have called the crisis of civic membership is to speak of declining social capital. Robert Putnam, who has brought the term to public attention recently, defines social capital as follows: "By analogy with notions of physical capital and human capital—tools and training that enhance individual productivity—'social capital' refers to features of social organization, such as networks, norms, and trust, that facilitate coordination and cooperation for mutual benefits." There are a number of possible indices of social capital; the two that Putnam has used most extensively are associational membership and public trust.

Putnam has chosen a stunning image as the title of a recent article: "Bowling Alone: America's Declining Social Capital." He reports that between 1980 and 1993 the total number of bowlers in America increased by 10 percent, while league bowling decreased by 40 percent. Nor, he points out, is this a trivial example: nearly 80 million Americans went bowling at least once in 1993, nearly a third more than voted in the 1994 congressional elections and roughly the same as claim to attend church regularly. But Putnam uses bowling only as a symbol for the decline of American associational life, the vigor of which has been seen as the heart of our civic culture ever since Tocqueville visited the U.S. in the 1830s.

In the 1970s dramatic declines in membership began to hit organizations typically associated with women, such as the PTA and the League of Women Voters, in what has often been explained as the result of the massive entry of women into the workforce. In the 1980s falling membership struck traditionally male associations, such as the Lions, Elks, Masons, and Shriners, as well. Union membership has dropped by half since its peak in the middle 1950s. We all know of the continuing decline in the numbers of eligible voters who actually go the polls, but Putnam reminds us that the number of Americans who answer "yes" when asked whether they have attended a public meeting on town or school affairs in the last year has fallen by more than a third since 1973.

Almost the only groups that are growing are the support groups, such as twelve-step groups, that Robert Wuthnow has recently studied. These groups make minimal demands on their members and are oriented primarily to the needs of individuals: indeed, Wuthnow has characterized them as involving individuals who "focus on themselves in the presence of others," what we might call being alone together. Putnam argues that paper membership groups, such as the AARP (American Association of Retired Persons), which has grown to gargantuan proportions, have few or no civic consequences, because their members may have common interests but they have no meaningful interactions. Putnam also worries that the Internet, the electronic town meeting, and other much ballyhooed new technological devices are probably civically vacuous, because they do not sustain civic engagement. Talk radio, for instance, mobilizes private opinion, not public opinion, and trades on anxiety, anger, and distrust, all of which are deadly to civic culture. The one sphere that seems to be resisting the general trend is religion. Religious membership and church attendance have remained fairly constant after the decline from the religious boom of the 1950s, although membership in church-related groups has declined by about one-sixth since the 1960s.

What goes together with the decline of associational involvement is the decline of public trust. We are not surprised to hear that the proportion of Americans who reply that they trust the government in Washington only some of the time or almost never has risen steadily, from 30 percent in 1966 to 75 percent in 1992. But are we prepared to hear that the proportion of Americans who say that most people can be trusted fell by more than a third between 1960, when 58 percent chose that alternative, and 1993, when only 37 percent did?

The argument for decline in social capital is not one that we made in *Habits of the Heart*. *Habits* was essentially a cultural analysis, more about language than about behavior. We worried that the language of individualism might undermine civic commitment, but we pointed to the historically high levels of associational membership in America and the relative strength of such memberships here compared with those in other advanced industrial nations. Whether there has really been such a decline is still controversial, but we are inclined to believe that tendencies that were not yet entirely clear in the early 1980s when *Habits* was written are now discernible and disconcerting.

We believe that the culture and language of individualism influence these trends but that there are also structural reasons for them, many of which stem from changes in the economy we have already mentioned. The decline in social capital is evident in different ways in different classes. For example, the decline in civic engagement in the overclass is indicated by their withdrawal into gated, guarded communities. It is also related to the constant movement of companies in the process of mergers and breakups. Rosabeth Kanter has recently suggested some of the consequences of this movement:

For communities as well as employees this constant shuffling of company identities is confusing and its effects profound. Cities and towns rely on the private sector to augment public services and support community causes. There is a strong "headquarters bias" in this giving: companies based in a city tend to do more for it, contributing $75,000 a year on average more to the local United Way, than companies of similar size with headquarters elsewhere.

Kanter points out that the departure of a corporate headquarters from a middle-sized city can tear holes in the social fabric of that city. Not only are thousands of jobs lost but so is the civic leadership of the corporate executives. Local charities lose not only money but board members.

Corporate volatility can lead to a kind of placelessness at the top of the pyramid: "Cut loose from society the rich man can play his chosen role free of guilt and responsibility," observes Michael Lewis. "He becomes that great figure of American mythology—the roaming frontiersman. These days the man who has made a fortune is likely to spend more on his means of transportation than on his home: the private jet is the possession that most distinguishes him from the rest of us. . . . The old aristocratic conceit of place has given way to glorious placelessness." The mansions of the old rich were certainly expressions of conspicuous consumption, but they also encouraged a sense of responsibility for a particular place (city, state, region) where they were located. Wendell Berry has spoken of "itinerant professional vandals," who are perhaps not too different from Reich's "symbolic analysts," attached to no place at all and thus tempted to act more like an oligarchy than an establishment.

Moving to the opposite end of the income spectrum, Lee Rainwater, in his classic book *What Money Buys,* shows that poverty—income insufficient to maintain an acceptable level of living—operates to deprive the poor not only of material capital but of social capital as well. In traditional hierarchical societies, low levels of material well-being can be associated with established statuses that confer the benefits of clientship. In our kind of society, with its fundamentally egalitarian ideology and its emphasis on individual self-reliance, status—even personal identity—of those not-so-distant ancestors was one of vulnerable subordination, of being kicked around by people who told them what to do. Owning one's own home, taking vacations wherever one wants, being free to decide whom to see or what to buy once one has left the workplace—these are all freedoms that are especially cherished by those whose ancestors have never had them. The modest suburb is not the open frontier but it is, under the circumstances, a reasonable facsimile thereof.

Among the many ironies in the lives of at least a significant number of these middle Americans, however, is that labor union membership had much to do with their attainment of relative affluence and its attendant independence; yet for many of them the labor union has become one more alien institution from which they would like to be free. Middle Americans not only are suspicious of government, according to Gans, they don't like organizations of any kind. Relative to the upper middle class (the lower echelons of what we have been calling the overclass), they are not joiners, belonging to only one or two associations at the most, the commonest being a church. While continuing to identify strongly with the nation, they are increasingly suspicious of politics, which they find confusing and dismaying. Their political participation declines steadily.

As a consequence of tendencies that Gans is probably right in asking us to understand, middle Americans are today losing the social capital that allowed them to attain their valued independence in the first place. Above all this is true of the decline of the labor movement. This decline stems from legislative changes in the last twenty years that have deprived unions of much of their power and influence, and from congressional refusal since 1991 to raise the minimum wage from $4.25 an hour. But, as we see in France and other European countries, where loyalty to labor unions has survived, such attacks can be turned back. In America, union meetings, even where there are unions, are attended by 5 percent of the members at most. Lacking the social capital that union membership would provide, anxious-class Americans are vulnerable in new ways to the arbitrary domination they thought they had escaped. One may lose even one's home and one's recreational vehicle if one's job is downsized and the only alternative employment is at the minimum wage.

The decline of social capital in America becomes particularly distressing if we consider what has happened to our political participation. In *Voice and Equality* Sydney Verba and his colleagues have recently given us a comprehensive review of political participation in the United States. Although the data concerning trends over time are not unambiguous, they do indicate certain tendencies. During the last thirty years the average level of education of the American public has risen steadily, but the level of political participation, which is usually associated with education, has not. This fact can be taken as an indication that, controlling for education, political participation has declined. Even more significant is the nature of the changes. Political party identification and membership have declined, while campaign contributions and writing to congresspersons have increased. Both of these growing kinds of activities normally take place in the privacy of one's home as one writes a check or a letter. Verba and his associates note that neither generates the personal satisfactions associated with more social forms of political participation.

Further, making monetary contributions correlates highly with income and is the most unequal form of participation in our society. The increasing salience of monetary contributions as a form of political participation, as well as the general tendency for political participation to correlate with income, education, and occupation, leads to the summary conclusion of *Voice and Equality:*

> Meaningful democratic participation requires that the voices of citizens in politics be clear, loud, and equal: clear so that public officials know what citizens want and need, loud so that officials have an incentive to pay attention to what they hear, and equal so that the democratic ideal of equal responsiveness to the preferences and interests of all is not violated. Our analysis of voluntary activity in American politics suggests that the public's voice is often loud, sometimes clear, but rarely equal.

Although unequal levels of education, occupation, and income favor the originally advantaged in securing the resources for political participation, there is one significant exception. Verba and his associates note that:

[o]nly religious institutions provide a counterbalance to this cumulative resource process. They play an unusual role in the American participatory system by providing opportunities for the development of civic skills to those who would otherwise be resource-poor. It is commonplace to ascribe the special character of American politics to the weakness of unions and the absence of class-based political parties that can mobilize the disadvantaged—in particular, the working class—to political activity. Another way that American society is exceptional is in how often Americans go to church—with the result that the mobilizing function often performed elsewhere by unions and labor or social democratic parties is more likely to be performed by religious institutions.

To summarize the relationship of the decline of social capital to political participation we might consider how this relationship works out in the several social classes. Overall, with the exception of the activities centered in religious institutions, political participation has shifted away from those forms that require civic engagement to those that are essentially private, and above all to that of making monetary contributions. The unequal voice to which Verba and his associates point is an indication that the anxious class is seriously under-represented and the underclass scarcely represented at all. Even in the overclass, participation has shifted from more active forms of engagement to the more isolated forms of check- and letter-writing. Finally, Verba and his associates point out that the increasing importance of money in political life contributes to public cynicism: "In short, a participatory system in which money plays a more prominent role is one unlikely to leave either activists or the citizenry at large feeling better about politics."

Individualism and the American Crisis

Most Americans agree that things are seriously amiss in our society—that we are not, as the poll questions often put it, "headed in the right direction"—but they differ over why this is so and what should be done about it. We have sought for answers in the structural problems that we have described under the rubrics of the crisis in civic membership and the decline of social capital. What are some of the other explanations? Perhaps the most widespread alternative explanation locates the source of our problems in a crisis of the family. The cry that what our society most needs is "family values" is not one to be dismissed lightly. Almost all the tendencies we have been describing threaten family life and are often experienced most acutely within the family. Being unemployed and thus unable to get married or not having enough income to support an existing family due to downsizing or part-timing, along with the tensions caused by these conditions, can certainly be understood as family crisis. But why is the crisis expressed as a failure of family values?

It is unlikely that we will understand what is going on here unless we once again take into account the culture of individualism. If we see unemployment or reduced income because of downsizing as a purely individual problem rather than a structural problem of the economy, then we will seek to understand what is wrong with the unemployed or underemployed individual. If we also discern that such individuals are prone to have children out of wedlock, to divorce, or to fail to make child support payments, we may conclude that the cause is weakened family values. In *Habits of the Heart* we strongly affirmed the value of the family, and in both *Habits* and *The Good Society* we argued for renewed commitment to marriage and family responsibilities. But to imagine that problems arising from failures rooted in the structure of our economy and polity can primarily be traced to the failings of individuals with inadequate family values seems to us sadly mistaken. It not only increases the level of individual guilt, it also distracts attention from larger failures of collective responsibility.

The link between cultural individualism and the emphasis on family values has a further consequence. Families have traditionally been supported by the paid labor of men. Failure to support one's family may be taken as an indication of inadequate manhood. It is easy to draw the conclusion that if American men would only act like men, then family life would be improved and social problems solved. Some such way of thinking undoubtedly lies behind the movement known as Promise Keepers, as well as the Million Man March of 1995. While we share many of the values of these movements, we are skeptical that increased male responsibility will prove to be an adequate solution to our deep structural economic and political problems, or even that it will do more than marginally diminish the severe strains on the American family. The notion that if men would only be men then all would be well in our society seems to us a sad cultural delusion.

Another common alternative explanation of our difficulties is to explain them as the failure of community. This is indeed valid, we believe, but only if our understanding of community is broad and deep enough. In many current usages of the term, however, community means face-to-face groups formed by the voluntary efforts of individuals. Used in this way, failure of community as the source of our problems can be interpreted to mean that if only more people would volunteer to help in soup kitchens or Habitat for Humanity or Meals on Wheels, then our social problems would be solved. As in the case of family values, *Habits of the Heart* strongly affirms face-to-face communities and the valuable contributions voluntary groups can make to society. But we do not believe that the deep structural problems that we face as a society can be effectively alleviated by an increase in devotion to community in this narrow sense. We would agree that an increase in the voluntary commitments of individuals can over the long haul increase our social capital and thus add to the resources we can bring to bear on our problems. But to get at the roots of our problems these resources must be used to overcome institutional difficulties that cannot be directly addressed by voluntary action alone.

We see another difficulty in emphasizing a small-scale and voluntaristic understanding of community as the solution to our problems. As we noted in discussing the work of Verba and his colleagues, voluntary activity tends to correlate with income, education, and occupation. "Joiners" are more apt to be found in the overclass than in the underclass or the anxious class, again with the significant exception of religious groups. This means that voluntary activities are less often designed to help the most deprived, though we don't want to overlook those that are, than to serve the interests of the affluent. This is particularly true of political voluntarism, as Verba and his associates have shown conclusively. Thus, dismantling structures of public provision for the most deprived in hopes that the voluntary sector will take over is misguided in three important respects. First, the voluntary sector has by no means the resources to take up the slack, as churches, charities, and foundations have been pointing out repeatedly in recent years. The second reason is that our more affluent citizens may feel they have fulfilled their obligation to society by giving time and money to "making a difference" through voluntary activity without taking into account that they have hardly made a dent in the real problems faced by most Americans. The third reason is that, as we noted, the voluntary sector is disproportionately run by our better-off citizens and a good many voluntary activities do more to protect the well-to-do than the needy.

There is another sense of community that also presents difficulties if we think the solution to our problems lies in reviving community, and that is the notion of community as neighborhood or locality. *Habits of the Heart* encourages strong neighborhoods and supports civic engagement in towns and cities. But residential segregation is a fact of life in contemporary America. Even leaving aside the hyper-segregation of urban ghettos, segregation by class arising from differential housing costs is becoming increasingly evident in suburban America. Thus it is quite possible that in "getting involved" with one's neighborhood or even with one's suburban town one will never meet someone of a different race or class. One will not be exposed to the realities of life for people in circumstances different from one's own. One may even succumb to the natural human temptation to think that people who are different, particularly those lower in social status, are inferior. The anxious class does not want itself to be confused with the underclass. One of the least pleasant characteristics of the overclass, including its lower echelons in the educated upper middle class, is that they do not want to associate with middle Americans, with "Joe Six-Pack" and others who lack the proper cultural attributes. Even in the underclass, those who are not on welfare look down on those who are, and those who are on the dole briefly look down on those on it for a long time. Under such circumstances an exclusive emphasis on neighborhood solidarity could actually contribute to larger social problems rather than solving them.

What the explanations of our social problems that stress the failure of family values or the failure of community have in common is the notion that our problems are individual or in only a narrow sense social (that is, involving family and local community), rather than economic, political, and cultural. A related feature that these common explanations of our troubles share is hostility to the role of government or the state. If we can take care of ourselves, perhaps with a little help from our friends and family, who needs the state? Indeed, the state is often viewed as an interfering father who won't recognize that his children have grown up and don't need him anymore. He can't help solve our problems because it is in large measure he who created them.

In contrast, the market, in this mindset, seems benign, a mostly neutral theater for competition in which achievement is rewarded and incompetence punished. Some awareness exists, however, that markets are not neutral, that some people and organizations have enormous economic power and are capable of making decisions that adversely affect many citizens. From this point of view big business joins big government as the source of problems rather than their solution. Still, in America more than in most comparable societies, people are inclined to think that the market is fairer than the state.

Individualism and Neocapitalism

The culture of individualism, then, has made no small contribution to the rise of the ideology we called neocapitalism in Chapter 10 of *Habits*. There we drew a picture of the American political situation that has turned out not to be entirely adequate. We suggested that the impasse between welfare liberalism and its counter-movement, neocapitalism, was coming to an end and that two alternatives, the administered society and economic democracy, were looming on the scene. As it turned out, this incipient pair of alternatives did not materialize, or at least they are enduring a long wait. Instead, neocapitalism has grown ever stronger ideologically and politically. Criticism of "big government" and "tax-and-spend liberalism" has mounted even as particular constituencies, which in the aggregate include most citizens, favor those forms of public provision that benefit them in particular, while opposing benefits they do not receive.

We do not believe we were wrong in seeing ten years ago the severe strains that the neocapitalist formula was creating for the nation. Today those strains are more obvious than ever. But we clearly underestimated the ideological fervor that the neocapitalist position was able to tap—ironically for us, because so much of that fervor derives from the very source we focused on in our book: individualism. The neocapitalist vision is viable only to the degree to which it can be seen as an expression—even a moral expression—of our dominant ideological individualism, with its compulsive stress on independence, its contempt for weakness, and its adulation of success.

Discussion Questions

1. Bellah and his coauthors contend that the ideology of individualism—the foundation of our political beliefs—may well have grown "cancerous." Explain this disease in our belief system. Do you agree that this may be a serious problem today?

2. What is "social capital" and how does its depletion contribute to the "crisis of civic membership"?

3. Why do authors believe that explanations of our social problems that stress the failure of family values or the failure of community are inadequate?

4   *Excerpted from "Culture War? The Myth of a Polarized America"*

Morris P. Fiorina

Ever since University of Virginia sociologist James Davison Hunter published Culture Wars *in 1991, political commentators have been arguing about the breadth and depth of ideological divisions in the American electorate. Pepperdine University political scientist James Q. Wilson, for example, believes that the disagreements that divide the "blue" and "red" states are not only numerous but deep. Wilson identifies a particularly disturbing trend: Conservatives and liberals not only disagree with one another but also begin to distrust and even hate each other. In the present work, however, Stanford political scientist Morris Fiorina insists that while radicals on both ends of the spectrum gain much attention, most of the population is genuinely moderate. Political realignments, particularly in the South—which has gone from solidly Democratic to solidly Republican—make the extent of polarization in the United States much less potent than it appears.*

Culture War?

There is a religious war going on in this country, a cultural war as critical to the kind of nation we shall be as the Cold War itself, for this war is for the soul of America.[1]

With those ringing words insurgent candidate Pat Buchanan fired up his supporters at the 1992 Republican National Convention. To be sure, not all the assembled delegates cheered Buchanan's call to arms, which was at odds with the "kinder, gentler" image that incumbent President George H. W. Bush had attempted to project. Indeed, Republican professionals expressed concern about the "family values" emphasis of the convention in general, and Buchanan's remarks in particular.[2] Their concerns proved well founded: elections analysts later included negative reaction to the convention and Buchanan's fiery words among the factors contributing to the defeat of President Bush, albeit factors of lesser importance than

---

Reprinted from *Culture War? The Myth of a Polarized America* (2006), Pearson Education, Inc.

the struggling economy and repudiation of his "Read my lips, no new taxes" pledge.[3]

Political campaigns encourage fiery rhetoric, of course, most of which dies down after the campaign. So, too, did talk of a culture war wax and wane during the mid-1990s. Buchanan seemed vindicated in 1994 when the Republicans captured Congress in the "year of the angry white male." The story line held that white men under economic pressure were livid about gays, guns, immigration, affirmative action, and Hillary, and turned in frustration to the Gingrich Republicans. But in 1996 talk of a culture war waned as hapless Republican presidential candidate Robert Dole demanded of a satisfied country "where's the outrage?" Then in 1998 discussion of the culture war erupted anew, fueled by the Monica Lewinsky scandal. And except for a brief period in the aftermath of 9/11 the flames have not diminished since.

The "culture war" refers to a displacement of the classic economic conflicts that animated twentieth-century politics in the advanced democracies by newly emergent moral and religious ones. The literature generally attributes Buchanan's inspiration to a 1991 book, *Culture Wars*, by sociologist James Davison Hunter, who divided Americans into the culturally "orthodox" and the culturally "progressive" and argued that increasing conflict was inevitable.[4] In a later book provocatively titled *Before the Shooting Begins*, Hunter writes,

> ... when cultural impulses this momentous vie against each other to dominate public life, tension, conflict, and perhaps even violence are inevitable.[5]

Not surprisingly, no one has embraced the idea of the culture war more enthusiastically than the journalistic community, ever alert for subjects that have "news value." Conflict, of course, is high in news value. Disagreement, division, polarization, battles, and war make better copy than agreement, consensus, moderation, cooperation, and peace. Thus, the culture war frame fits the news values of journalists who cover American politics. Their reports tell us that contemporary voters are deeply divided on moral issues:

> ... the real emotional splits in the country lie in gut-level social issues: They are the topics that move Americans in their everyday lives, and the ones that actually draw the lines separating the two parties today.[6]
>
> The divide went deeper than politics. It reached into the nation's psyche ... It was the moral dimension that kept Bush in the race.[7]

And close elections do not reflect indifferent, uncertain, or ambivalent voters; rather, close elections reflect a standoff between two large blocs of deeply committed partisans:

> When George W. Bush took office, half the country cheered and the other half seethed.[8]
>
> Such political divisions cannot easily be shifted by any president, let alone in two years, because they reflect deep demographic divisions.... The 50-50 nation appears to be made up of two big, separate voting blocks, with only a small number of swing voters in the middle.[9]

The 2000 election brought pictorial representation of the culture war in the form of the red and blue map of the United States. Vast areas of the southern and midwestern heartland emerged from the election as Republican red. But the huge expanses of red territory contained relatively few people per square mile. The much smaller areas of Democratic blue contained the more populous cosmopolitan states of the east and west coasts and the Great Lakes. Often commentators accompanied such colorful maps with polling factoids intended to illustrate the cultural divide: the probability that a white, gun-toting, born-again, rural southern male voted for Al Gore was about as tiny as the probability that a feminist, agnostic, professional, urban northern female voted for George W. Bush, although few asked how many Americans fell into such tightly bounded categories. For the most part pundits reified the different colors on the map, treating them as *prima facie* evidence of deep cultural divisions:

> Bush knew that the landslide he had wished for in 2000 … had vanished into the values chasm separating the blue states from the red ones.[10]
>
> You see the state where James Byrd was lynch-dragged behind a pickup truck until his body came apart—it's red. You see the state where Matthew Shepard was crucified on a split-rail fence for the crime of being gay—it's red. You see the state where right-wing extremists blew up a federal office building and murdered scores of federal employees—it's red. The state where an Army private who was thought to be gay was bludgeoned to death with a baseball bat, and the state where neo-Nazi skinheads murdered two African Americans because of their skin color, and the state where Bob Jones University spews its anti-Catholic bigotry: they're all red too.[11]

Claims of deep national division were standard after the 2000 elections, and few commentators challenged them.[12] On the contrary, the belief in a fractured nation continued to be expressed even by high-level political operatives:

> We have two massive colliding forces. One is rural, Christian, religiously conservative. [The other] is socially tolerant, prochoice, secular, living in New England and the Pacific coast.[13]
>
> You've got 80 percent to 90 percent of the country that look at each other like they are on separate planets.[14]

A November 2003 report of the Pew Research Center for the People & the Press led a prominent journalist to comment:

> The red states get redder, the blue states get bluer, and the political map of the United States takes on the coloration of the Civil War.[15]

While Andrew Kohut, director of the Pew Center, reportedly commented that

> … the anger level is so high that if the demonstrators of 1968 had felt like this there would have been gunfire in the streets.[16]

Political commentators saw a continuation, if not an intensification of the culture war as the 2004 election approached.

> The culture war between the Red and Blue Nations has erupted again—big time—and will last until Election Day next year. Front lines are all over, from the Senate to the Pentagon to Florida to the Virginia suburbs where, at the Bush-Cheney '04 headquarters, they are blunt about the shape of the battle: "The country's split 50–50 again," a top aide told me, "just as it was in 2000."[17]

After the 2004 elections much of the commentary continued in this vein. Instant post-election analysis attributed President Bush's reelection to the higher turnout and increased support of Evangelical Christians (wrongly as it turned out). In response, bitterly disappointed Democratic commentators slammed the denizens of red states, whose votes reflected "fundamentalist zeal, a rage at secularity, religious intolerance, fear of and hatred for modernity"—attitudes more common "in the Muslim world, in Al Qaeda, in Saddam Hussein's Sunni loyalists" than in other democracies.[18] And,

> Listen to what the red state citizens say about themselves, the songs they write, and the sermons they flock to. They know who they are—they are full of original sin and they have a taste for violence. The blue state citizens make the Rousseauvian mistake of thinking humans are essentially good, and so they never realize when they are about to be slugged from behind.[19]

Even mainstream media commentators saw a "national fissure" that "remains deep and wide," and "Two Nations Under God."[20]

In sum, many contemporary observers of American politics believe that old disagreements about economics now pale in comparison to new divisions based on sexuality, morality, and religion, divisions so deep as to justify fears of violence and talk of war in describing them.[21]

The sentiments expressed in the previously quoted pronouncements of scholars, journalists, and politicos range from simple exaggeration to sheer nonsense. Such assertions both reflect and contribute to a widespread mythology about contemporary American politics. The simple truth is that there is no culture war in the United States—no battle for the soul of America rages, at least none that most Americans are aware of. Certainly, one can find a few faux-warriors who engage in noisy skirmishes. Many of the activists in the political parties and the various cause groups do, in fact, hate each other and regard themselves as combatants in a war. But their hatreds and battles are not shared by the great mass of the American people—certainly nowhere near to "80–90 percent of the country"—who are for the most part moderate in their views and tolerant in their manner.[22] Most Americans are somewhat like the unfortunate citizens of some third-world countries who try to stay out of the crossfire while left-wing guerrillas and right-wing death squads shoot at each other.

The myth of a culture war rests on misinterpretation of election returns, a lack of comprehensive examination of public opinion data, systematic and self-serving misrepresentation by issue activists, and selective coverage by an uncritical media more concerned with news value than with getting the story right. There is little evidence that Americans' ideological or policy *positions* are more polarized today than they were two or three decades ago, although their *choices* often seem to be. The explanation is that the political figures Americans evaluate are more polarized. A polarized political class makes the citizenry appear polarized, but it is largely that—an appearance.

Endnotes

[1] This quotation appears in slightly different forms throughout the literature, probably because it was written up differently by journalists who covered the speech and/or read slightly different versions of it. This version is quoted in Nancy Davis and Robert Robinson, "A War for America's Soul?" In Rhys Williams, ed., *Cultural Wars in American Politics* (New York: Aldine de Gruyter, 1997): 39.

[2] Andrew Rosenthal, "The 1992 Campaign: Issues—'Family Values,'" *New York Times*, September 21, 1992: 1.

[3] Paul Abramson, John Aldrich, and David Rohde, *Change and Continuity in the 1992 Elections*. (Washington, DC: CQ Press, 1994): 43–44, 137. For a detailed analysis of the association between family values issues and the 1992 voting see Laura Arnold and Herbert Weisberg, "Parenthood, Family Values, and the 1992 Presidential Election." *American Politics Quarterly* 24(1996): 194–220.

[4] *Culture Wars*: *The Struggle to Define America* (New York: Basic Books, 1991).

[5] *Before the Shooting Begins*: *Searching for Democracy in America's Culture War* (New York Free Press.1998 : 88.

[6] John Harwood and Shailagh Murray, "Split Society: Year After Year, The Big Divide In Politics Is Race." *Wall Street Journal*, December 19, 2002: A1.

[7] David Broder, "One Nation, Divisible; Despite Peace, Prosperity, Voters Agree to Disagree," *Washington Post*, November 8, 2000: A1.

[8] Jill Lawrence, "Behind Its United Front, Nation Divided As Ever," *USA Today*, February 18, 2002: A1.

[9] "On His High Horse," *The Economist*, November 9, 2002: 25.

[10] John Kenneth White, *The Values Divide* (New Jersey: Chatham House, 2003): 171.

[11] Clinton advisor Paul Begala, as quoted in Bob Clark, "As You Were Saying … It's Time for Gore's Pit Bull to Practice What He Preaches," *Boston Herald*, November 18, 2000: 16.

[12] For a notable exception see Robert Samuelson, "Polarization Myths," *Washington Post*, December 3, 2003: A29.

[13] Republican pollster Bill McInturff, as quoted in "One Nation, Fairly Divisible, Under God," *The Economist*, January 20, 2001: 22.

[14] Matthew Dowd, Bush reelection strategist. Dowd was explaining why Bush had not tried to expand his electoral base. Quoted in Ron Brownstein, "Bush Falls to Pre-9/11 Approval Rating," *Los Angeles Times*, October 3, 2003: A1.

[15] E. J. Dionne Jr., "One Nation Deeply Divided," *Washington Post*, November 7, 2003: A31.

[16] Quoted in John Leo, "Splitting Society, Not Hairs," *US News and World Report Science & Society*, December 15, 2003: 66. Kohut may be too young to remember, but there *was*

sporadic gunfire in the streets and on college campuses during the 1960s *"time of troubles."* We have more to say about the Pew Report in chapter 4.

[17]Howard Fineman, "Election Boils Down to a Culture War: Abortion Issue is First Skirmish in the Battle for White House." *Newsweek*, October 22, 2003: http://msnbc.msn.com/id/3225677, accessed December 12, 2003.

[18]Gary Wills, "The Day the Enlightenment Went out," *New York Times*, November 4, 2004, nytimes.com.

[19]Jane Smiley, "The unteachable ignorance of the red states," slate.msn.com/id/2109218/

[20]Ronald Brownstein, "The National Fissure Remains Deep and Wide," www.latimes.com, November 3, 2004. Thomas Friedman, "Two Nations Under God," *New York Times*, November 4, 2004, nytimes.com.

[21]Of course, there is nothing new about cultural conflict in the United States—it has been a common element of our politics since the beginning of the Republic. It only seems new to today's generation of political commentators because such issues were relatively muted from the late-1930s until the mid-1960s.

[22]On the whole our conclusions support the earlier findings of Alan Wolfe, *One Nation, After All* (New York: Viking, 1998). Some critics have dismissed Wolfe's findings as reflecting only the views of 200 middle class suburban families. The chapters that follow report similar findings based on an examination of the views of tens of thousands of Americans questioned in national surveys.

Questions

1.   On what particular issues does America appear to be most polarized?

2.   To what extent is America's "culture war" merely a "culture dispute"?

3.   President Bush's strategy of mobilizing religious conservatives is often said to have artificially created a culture war environment. To what extent are the President's policies to blame for whatever culture war exists?

Mass Media

5   *It's The Media, Stupid*

Robert W. McChesney and John Nichols

During the 1992 presidential election, candidate Bill Clinton's campaign team hung a now-famous sign in their headquarters that read "It's the economy, stupid." The sign served as a reminder to link all discussions of policy issues to the faltering economy, thereby constantly connecting issues to a central critique of President George Bush's handling of the economy. In this article, Robert McChesney, a media scholar and activist, and John Nichols, a journalist, similarly seek to draw constant attention to the central importance of connecting all discussions about reforming American democracy to the need for media reform. They begin by emphasizing the important connection between the free flow of information and a healthy democratic society. Then they outline the problem in straight-forward terms: by 2000, fewer than ten giant media conglomerates dominated the mass media of the United States, with firms like Disney, AOL-Time Warner, SONY, and GE leading the way. This level of corporate control over what we see and hear as "news" guarantees that the values of profit-maximizing and commercialism will guide the U.S. media system, to the detriment of news that truly informs the public on the crucial issues of the day. The result is news that does not challenge the world-view of elite interests, nor offer a broad range of competing perspectives, thus greatly diminishing the quality of democracy. Or as the authors put it, corporate media has fanned the flames of a "crisis for democracy." To address this crisis, McChesney and Nichols offer an ambitious agenda for media reform aimed at strengthening democratic participation and citizenship. For the authors contend that what is needed in the twenty-first century is nothing short of a "broad crusade for democratic renewal in America."

Participatory self-government, or democracy, works best when at least three criteria are met. First, it helps when there are not significant disparities in economic wealth and property ownership across the society. Such disparities undermine the ability of citizens to act as equals. Second, it helps when there is a sense of community and a notion that an individual's well-being is determined to no small extent by the community's well-being. This provides democratic political culture with a substance that cannot exist if everyone is simply out to advance narrowly defined self-interests, even if those interests might be harmful to the community as a whole. Third, democracy requires that there be an effective system of political communication, broadly construed, that informs and engages the citizenry, drawing people meaningfully into the polity. This becomes especially important as societies grow larger and more complex, but has been true for all societies dedicated toward self-government. While democracies by definition must respect individual freedoms, these freedoms can only be exercised in a meaningful sense when the citizenry is informed, engaged, and participating. Moreover, without this, political debate can scarcely address the central issues of power and resource allocation that must be at the heart of public deliberation in a democracy. As James Madison noted, "A popular government without popular information, or the means of acquiring it, is but a prologue to a farce or a tragedy, or perhaps both."

These three criteria are related. In nondemocratic societies those in power invariably dominate the communication systems to maintain their rule. In democratic societies the manner by which the media system is structured, controlled and subsidized is of central political importance. Control over the means of communication is an integral aspect of political and economic power. In many nations, to their credit, media policy debates have been and are important political issues. In the U.S., to the contrary, private commercial control over communication is often regarded as innately democratic and benevolent, and therefore not subject to political discussion. Government involvement with media or communication is almost universally denigrated in the U.S. as a direct invitation to tyranny, no matter how well intended. The preponderance of U.S. mass communications is controlled by less than two dozen enormous profit-maximizing corporations, which receive much of their income from advertising placed largely by other huge corporations. But the extent of this media ownership and control goes generally unremarked in the media and intellectual culture, and there appears to be little sense of concern about its dimensions among citizenry as a whole.

.   .   .

It was the rainiest, wettest, coldest April morning Washington had seen in a long time. And still they came—thousands of mostly young activists determined to mount a nonviolent but noisy protest outside the spring 2000 meetings of the World Bank and the International Monetary Fund (IMF). As they reached a key intersection near the World Bank building, they were blocked by armed battalions of riot police and National Guardsmen. The authorities stood their ground, but the Mobilization for Global Justice activists refused to back down.

This was the sort of standoff to which even the most jaded television assignment editors dispatched their crews—despite the fact that the weather made for some fogged-up camera lenses. On the street, a reporter for one Washington television station pulled aside a young woman who was soaking wet, and announced to the cameraman that it was time to do a live shot. When the signal came that they were on air, the reporter started to make small talk with the activist about the miserable weather. "I really want to talk about the policies of the World Bank and the IMF," the young woman said. "Their structural adjustment policies are causing real harm in specific countries around the world. . . ." The reporter pulled the microphone back, looked to the camera and said, "Well, everybody has an opinion. Let's go back to the anchor desk."

That same afternoon, as young people who had attended teach-ins, listened to debates and read literature and books in preparation for the demonstration continued to face down the police in the streets, conservative commentator Tony Snow was attacking the protestors on Washington radio as ignorant and uninformed. The next morning, *The Wall Street Journal* referred to them as "Global Village Idiots." The supposedly liberal *Washington Post* and *New York Times* editorial pages both dismissed the protests as not much more than a waste of police resources and everyone else's time. And, despite the fact that at least 150 activists were still in jail, and that people in Washington, across the nation and indeed, around the world, were buzzing about a new era of activism, television news programs went back to broadcasting the usual mix of commercials and vapid "news you can use."

Molly Ivins put it rather succinctly when she observed, a few days later, that "for reasons unclear to me, the mainstream media seem to have decided that anyone who questions any aspect of globalization is an extremist nut, despite the rather obvious fact that global poverty is growing under the kind auspices of the World Bank, the International Monetary Fund, and the World Trade Organization."

In our view, the reasons for this are clear. The closer a story gets to examining corporate power the less reliable our corporate media system is as a source of information that is useful to the citizens of a democracy. And on issues like the global capitalist economy, the corporate media are doubly unreliable, because they rank as perhaps the foremost beneficiaries of Wall Street-designed trade deals like NAFTA, and of the machinations of the three multilateral agencies developed to shape the global economy to serve corporate interests: the World Bank, the IMF and the World Trade Organization (WTO). Moreover, almost all the favored mainstream sources for coverage of global economic affairs are strident advocates for a corporate-driven vision of globalization. Thus, corporate journalists—even those low enough on the pecking order to be dispatched to stand in the rain on a Washington street corner—generally will find arguments against the status quo incomprehensible.

Just as the media dropped the ball in Washington in April 2000, it blew a chance to cover an even more dramatic story of citizens speaking truth to power in the fall of 1999, when the WTO met in Seattle. As one of the most significant challenges to global economics in decades was playing out—a challenge so powerful that the WTO meetings were actually shut down for a time and ultimately failed to launch a new round of trade liberalization, a challenge so intense that President Clinton felt compelled to assert his agreement on a variety of issues with those protesting in the streets—the broadcast media treated the story as an event of secondary importance. There was no round-the-clock coverage, as was seen only four months earlier when John F. Kennedy Jr.'s fatal plane crash reshaped the broadcast schedules of CNN, the Fox News Channel, and every other cable TV news service for two full weeks. During the WTO meetings and demonstrations—which dealt with arguably the most important political issues of our age—no attempt was made to provide comprehensive coverage. One night, as demonstrators filled the streets of Seattle and ministers of finance battled through the night over the most fundamental questions of how the global economy would be structured, as the President of the U.S. hunkered down in a hotel surrounded by armed troops, the Fox News Channel interrupted its scheduled programming for a live special report . . . not from Seattle, but from the scene of the latest doings of the parents of JonBenet Ramsey.

What happened in Seattle sums up the crisis for democracy that occurs when the media system is set up primarily to maximize profit for a handful of enormous self-interested corporations. An Orwellian disconnect is created. The news required for a functional democracy—the news that empowers citizens to act in their own interest and for the good of society—is discarded to make way for the trivial, sensational, and salacious. How many Americans have come home from a school board meeting, a city council session, a local demonstration or a mass national rally to discover the vital issues they had just addressed are being ignored or distorted? The flow of information that is the lifeblood of democracy is being choked by a media system that every day ignores a world of injustice and inequality, and the growing resistance to it . . .

Back in 1992, Bill Clinton's campaign strategists hung a sign in the war room of their Little Rock headquarters that read, "It's the economy, stupid." The point of the sign was to remind campaign workers to circle every discussion of election issues around to the subject of the sagging economy. In many senses, this book is like that sign. We are here to argue that it's time to point out the connections between media reform and democratic renewal. To sound a wake up call reminding us that access to communications is a nonnegotiable demand in a democratic society, and that scoring real victories for labor, the environment, and social justice will be made all the more possible by opening up the democratizing the media. Meanwhile, when the corporate press comes looking for a soundbite on what the ruckus is all about, tell them, "It's the media, stupid."

.   .   .

Americans devour media at a staggering rate; in 1999 the average American spent almost twelve hours per day with some form of media. We are also in the midst of an unprecedented technological revolution—based around digital technologies, typified by the Internet—that looks to weave media and electronic communication into nearly every waking moment of our lives. In conventional parlance, these developments are presented as benign; they are all about liberating individuals, investors, and consumers from the constraints of time and space while offering a cornucopia of exciting new options and possibilities. This, however, is a superficial and misleading perspective on what is happening. Indeed, when one lifts the hood, so to speak, to see what is driving the media revolution, a very different picture emerges. It is instead a world where highly concentrated corporate power is pulling the strings to dominate our existence so as to maximize return to shareholders, and to protect the corporation's role—and corporate power in general—from being subjected to the public scrutiny and political debate it so richly deserves. It is a poison pill for democracy.

Yet in our American democracy the issue of media barely registers. The structures of our media, the concentration of its ownership, the role that it plays in shaping the lives of our children, in commercializing our culture, and in warping our elections, has been off-limits. When we examine the reality of media in the year 2000, however, it becomes clear that this circumstance must shift. The case for making media an issue is made, above all, by a survey of the contemporary media landscape.

In 2000, the U.S. media system is dominated by fewer than ten transnational conglomerates: Disney, AOL-Time Warner, News Corporation, Viacom, Seagram (Universal), Sony, Liberty (AT&T), Bertelsmann, and General Electric (NBC). Their media revenues range from roughly $8 billion to $30 billion per year. These firms tend to have holdings in numerous media sectors. AOL-Time Warner, for example, ranks among the largest players in film production, recorded music, TV show production, cable TV channels, cable TV systems, book publishing, magazine publishing, and Internet service provision. The great profit in media today comes from taking a movie or TV show and milking it for maximum return through spin-off books, CDs, video games, and merchandise. Another twelve to fifteen firms, which do from $2 or $3 billion to $8 billion per year in business, round out the system. These firms—like Comcast, Hearst, New York Times, Washington Post, Cox, Advance, Tribune Company, Gannett—tend to be less developed conglomerates, focusing on only two or three media sectors. All in all, these two dozen or so firms control the overwhelming percentage of movies, TV shows, cable systems, cable channels, TV stations, radio stations, books, magazines, newspapers, billboards, music, and TV networks that constitute the media culture that occupies one-half of the average American's life. It is an extraordinary degree of economic and social power located in very few hands.

It has not always been this way. Much of this concentration has taken place in the past few decades, as technology and market imperatives made concentration and conglomeration far more attractive and necessary. Today it is impossible for the small, independent firm to be anything but a marginal player in the industries mentioned above. Most important, the flames of media concentration were fanned by a collapsing commitment on the part of the federal government to serious antitrust prosecution, a diminution of the federal standards regarding fairness, and government "deregulation," most notably the 1996 Telecommunications Act. Congressional approval of the Telecommunications Act, after only a stilted and disengaged debate, was a historic turning point in media policy making in the United States, as it permitted a consolidation of media and communication ownership that had previously been unthinkable.

A surface survey of the statistics regarding media ownership, while deeply disturbing in what it reveals, fails to convey the full depth of the concentration of media ownership. Not only are media markets dominated by a handful of conglomerates with "barriers to entry," making it nearly impossible for newcomers to challenge their dominance, but they are also closely linked to each other in a manner that suggests almost a cartel-like arrangement. Some of the largest media firms own parts of the other giants; Liberty, for example, is the second largest shareholder in News Corporation and among the largest shareholders in AOL Time Warner. Moreover, the media giants employ equity joint ventures—where two competing firms share ownership in a single venture—to an extent unknown almost anywhere else in the economy. These joint ventures work to reduce competition, lower risk, and increase profits. By 1999 the nine largest media giants had an equity join venture with six, on average, of the other eight giants; often a media giant would have multiple joint ventures with another firm. In sum, this is a tightly knit community of owners, dominated by some of the wealthiest individuals in the world. Indeed, thirteen of the hundred wealthiest individuals in the world—all of whom are worth over $4 billion— are media magnates.

Such concentration of media ownership is clearly negative by any standard that cherishes free speech and diversity in the marketplace of ideas. But concentration in media ownership is not the sole cause of the problems with the media, and in some cases it is not a significant factor at all. Concentration is important to a large extent because it magnifies the limitations of a commercial media system, and makes those limitations less susceptible to redress by the market. But this sounds very abstract, so let's cut to the bone: the problem with concentrated media is that it accentuates the two main problems of commercial media, hypercommercialism and denigration of public service. These are really two sides of the same coin. As massive media corporations are better able to commercially carpet bomb society, their ability or willingness to provide material with editorial and creative integrity declines. It is not that the individuals who run these firms are bad people; the problem is that they do destructive things by rationally following the market cues they are given. We have a media system set up to serve private investors first and foremost, not public citizens.

No better example of how this process works can be found than in the U.S. radio industry. Since deregulation of ownership in 1996, some one-half of U.S. stations have been sold. A few massive giants, owning hundreds of stations—as many as eight in each market—have come to dominate the industry. As profits shoot through the roof, low-budget standardized fare has nearly eliminated the local content, character, and creativity that were once features of this relatively inexpensive electronic medium. "A huge wave of consolidation has turned music stations into cash cows that focus on narrow playlists aimed at squeezing the most revenue from the richest demographics," the trade publication *Variety* observed in 1999. "Truth be told, in this era of megamergers, there has never been a greater need for a little diversity on the dial."

The radio example points to the one other crucial group, aside from media owners, that gets treated with love and affection by corporate media executives: the corporate advertising community. Businesses spent some $214 billion in the U.S. on advertising in 1999—some 2.4 percent of the GDP—and almost all of this money ended up in the hands of some media firm. Though journalists and civics teachers bristle at the notion, those media that depend upon advertising for the lion's share of their income—radio, TV, newspapers, magazines—are, in effect, part of the advertising industry. Throughout the 1990s the media giants used their market power to pummel their customers with ads and to bend over backward to make their media attractive to Madison Avenue. By 1999 the four major TV networks, for example, were providing nearly sixteen minutes per hour of commercials during prime time, an enormous increase from just a decade earlier. A conglomerate like Time Warner was able to sign a $200 million advertising deal with General Motors that "crosses most of the entertainment company's divisions," so that "GM will have a first-look option on all automobile marketing opportunities within Warner Bros. operations." Not content with traditional advertising, media firms are now working on "virtual ads," whereby "a marketer's product can be seamlessly inserted into live or taped broadcasts." With ads so inserted during actual programs, viewers will be unable to avoid the commercials through zapping. Advertising has also been plugged into new venues, such as video games. But this does not capture the full spread of commercialism. In television, for example, the new growth area for revenues is selling merchandise that is shown on its programs. It barely caused a ripple when Tommy Hilfiger hired the Viacom-owned cable channel VH1, rather than an ad agency, to produce a series of TV ads, because VH1 is so effective at selling. In sum, the entire U.S. media experience increasingly resembles an infomercial.

Nowhere is the commercial marination of the American mind more apparent than in the case of children, where the advertising assault was increased exponentially in the 1990s. There are now four full-time cable channels (owned by the four largest U.S. media firms) bombarding children with commercial programming twenty-four hours per day. Advertisers have targeted the youth market as arguably the most important in the nation. Girls between the ages of seven and fourteen spend some $24 billion per year and influence parental decisions worth another $66 billion. Commercial indoctrination of children is crucial to corporate America. One study revealed that when eight-year-olds were shown two pictures of identical shoes, one with the Nike logo and the other with the Kmart logo, they liked both equally. The response of twelve-year-olds was "Kmart, are you kidding me?" This desire to indoctrinate fuels the commercial drive into education and suggests that the moral foundation for coming generations may be resting on a dubious base. Nobody knows what the exact consequence of this commercial blitzkrieg upon children will be, but the range of debate extends from "pretty bad" to "absolutely terrible." The only thing we know for certain is that the media giants and advertisers who prosper from it do not care and cannot care. It is outside their frame of reference.

In this light, it is worth considering the status of the long-standing conflict between "church and state" in media; this refers to the ability of journalists and creative workers to conduct their affairs without having output determined by what serves the immediate interests of advertisers, or owners for that matter. In conventional wisdom, the U.S. media system has been at its best when the divider between "church and state"—especially though not exclusively in journalism—has been pronounced and respected. That way media users can regard the articles and news and entertainment programs they read, see, and hear in the media as reflecting the best judgment of media workers, not the surreptitious bribe of a commercial interest. Nowhere has the collapse of editorial integrity been more pronounced than in magazine publishing. As the late Alexander Liberman, legendary editorial director of Condé Nast, noted in 1999, advertisers "have too much power. They determine, if not specifically, then generally what magazines are now." A series of scandals in the late 1990s affirmed what has been suspected: Advertisers have tremendous control over the editorial copy in U.S. magazines, and editors who are discomfited by this had best find employment elsewhere. "They're glitz bags," Norman Mailer said of magazines in 1999. "They are so obviously driven by the ads that the ads take prominence over the stories."

Hollywood films have so thoroughly embraced commercial values that *Variety* now writes of the "burgeoning subfield of Product Placement Cinema." Conglomerate control of films and music and television (all of the TV networks, all of the main studios but the floundering MGM, and all four of the firms that dominate the U.S. music scene are owned by the eight largest media firms) has opened the floodgates to commercialism and has proven deadly for creativity. "A movie studio is part of this huge corporate cocoon," Peter Bart, editor of *Variety* and former head of Paramount, writes, "and therefore, theoretically, a studio should be willing to take bigger risks because one bad movie . . . won't erode the value of the [parent company's] shares. But the way it works out, the studios are if anything more risk averse. They are desperate to hedge their bets. It's the nature of bureaucratic self-protection. . . .The pressure is reflected in the sort of movies that get made . . . the sort of pablum that studios chewed on for ten years, that's gone through endless rewrites, has been pretested by endless focus groups, and is successful—if insipid." Or as an executive at Time Warner's "independent" studio New Line Pictures puts it, "We're very marketing-driven as a company. I'm instructed not to greenlight a project if I can't articulate how to sell it." As Bart concludes, this is "not exactly a recipe for art."

This said, we are not attempting to make a blanket indictment of everything produced by the corporate media system. We are not suggesting that every article or broadcast segment is foul, nor that they are all tainted, nor even that some material that is tainted cannot also be good. There are extremely talented people employed in the commercial media system, and the pressure to satisfy audiences does indeed sometimes promote excellent fare. But corporate and commercial pressures greatly undermine the overall quality of the system and skew it in ways that are not at all the result of audience demand. In the world of corporate media, the key is to attract the preferred target audience while spending as little money as possible. In the battle for consumer attention, this strongly promotes a rehashing of tried-and-true formulae, as well as the use of sex, violence, and what is termed "shock" or "gross-out" fare. In a world where people are surrounded by innumerable media options (albeit owned by numerable firms), sex and violence are proven attention getters.

Corporate control and hypercommercialism are having what may be their most devastating effects in the realm of journalism. There is no need to romanticize the nature of U.S. professional journalism from the middle of the century into the 1980s; in many respects it was deeply flawed. Yet whatever autonomy and integrity journalism enjoyed during that time of Bob Woodward, Carl Bernstein, and *Lou Grant* is now under sustained and unyielding attack by corporate owners in the hunt for profit. No more striking evidence for this exists than the results of a 1999 Pew Research Center poll of journalists concerning their profession. Until the 1990s, journalists tended to be stalwart defenders of the media system, and most scholarship emphasized journalists' hypersensitivity to criticism of their field. No more. The Pew poll found that "at both the local and national level, majorities of working journalists say the increased bottom-line pressure is hurting the quality of coverage." "This past year," David Halberstam wrote in 1999, "has been, I think, the worst year for American journalism since I entered the profession forty-four years ago." Bob Woodward, the Watergate investigator who has enjoyed one of the most successful and prestigious media careers of the era, says that in these days of hypercommercialism and hypercompetition, "No one is the keeper of the conscience of journalism."

The brave new world of corporate journalism manifests itself in many ways. The primary effects of tightened corporate control are a serious reduction in staff, combined with pressure to do vastly less expensive and less controversial lifestyle and feature stories. Where there is "news," it often takes the form of canned crime reports that foster unrealistic and unnecessary fears. This is the magic elixir for the bottom line. Sometimes the new world of corporate journalism is typified by blatant corporate censorship of stories that might hurt the image of the media owner. But the maniacal media baron as portrayed in James Bond films or profiles of Rupert Murdoch is far less a danger than the cautious and compromised editor who seeks to "balance" a responsibility to readers or viewers with a duty to serve his boss and the advertisers. In media today, even among journalists who entered the field for the noblest of reasons, there is an internalized bias to simply shy away from controversial journalism that might enmesh a media firm in a battle with powerful corporations or government agencies. True, such conflicts have always been the stuff of great journalism, but they can make for very bad business, and in the current climate business trumps journalism just about every time.

The most common and noticeable effect of the corporate noose on journalism is that it simply allows commercial values to redirect journalism to its most profitable position. So it is that relatively vast resources are deployed for news pitched at a narrow business class, and suited to their needs and prejudices; it is predominant in newspapers, magazines, and television. Likewise, news for the masses increasingly consists of stories about celebrities, royal families, athletes, natural disasters, plane crashes, and train wrecks. Political coverage is limited to regurgitating what some politician says, and "good" journalism is practiced when a politician from the other side of the aisle is given a chance to respond. But that is not journalism; it is stenography. Perhaps the strongest indictment of corporate journalism is that the preponderance of it would be compatible with an authoritarian political regime. So it is that China has few qualms about letting most commercial news from the U.S. inside its borders; it can see that this low caliber of journalism is hardly a threat to its rule. It is the BBC, with its regrettable penchant for covering politics seriously, that draws the commissar's ire.

There is also intense pressure for journalism to contribute immediately and directly to the bottom line. One Tennessee TV station received adverse publicity for offering to do TV news "puff pieces" on local businesses in exchange for $15,000 payments. It is important to note, however, that the mistake made by that Tennessee station was not the spirit of the offer—it well reflects the pattern across the news media—but, rather, the baldness of it. Firms also use the news to hype their other programming, as in 1996 when NBC *Nightly News* made the Summer Olympics its most covered news story that year, even though none of the other networks had the Olympics ranked on their top-ten lists. Why? Because NBC was airing the Olympics that summer—and reaping the attendant financial rewards. The fall of 1999 saw a huge debate erupt in newspaper circles after the *Los Angeles Times* devoted the entire editorial space in an edition of its 164-page Sunday magazine to articles, photos and graphics describing downtown Los Angeles' new Staples Center sports arena. The newspaper did not reveal at the time of the magazine's publication, however, that it would be dividing the $2 million in revenues generated by the section with the owners of the arena. So dark was the scenario that the former publisher of the *Los Angeles Times*, Otis Chandler, sent a letter to the staff describing the new management's move as "unbelievably stupid and unprofessional."

Above all, however, the *Los Angeles Times* was blatant. It allowed the corrupting linkage between advertisers and the media to be clearly identified. More often than not, a measure of subtlety keeps controversies under wraps.

In addition to triviality and craven commercialism, the willingness or capacity of U.S. journalism to challenge elite assumptions or to question the status quo—never especially great in the best of times—has shriveled. So it was, for example, that the preponderance of media coverage of the 1999 war in Kosovo lamely reflected elite opinion in the U.S., when even the rudimentary application of traditional journalism standards would point to severe discrepancies in the official story line.

All told, this creates a crisis for democracy. Alexis de Tocqueville rightly celebrated the role that a free and diverse media plays not only in greasing the wheels of electoral systems but in maintaining the very structures of civil society. The nineteenth-century surveyor of the American public landscape went so far as to say of news organizations, "They maintain civilization." Who would seriously attempt to make such a statement about today's media?

.   .   .

What is necessary, in the end, is for media reform to be advanced as part of a progressive platform for democratic reform across society. The foundation of a broader progressive platform will be the demand for social justice and an attack upon social inequality and the moral stench of a society operated purely along commercial lines. In the U.S. today, the richest one percent of the population has as much money to spend as the poorest 100 million Americans, double the ratio for just twenty years earlier. The political system reinforces this inequality by being, as is now roundly acknowledged, a plaything for big business where the interests of the balance of society have been pushed to the margins if not forgotten. The corporate media system reinforces this inequality and rule of the market and limits the possibility of democratic reform. In sum, media reform is inexorably intertwined with broader democratic reform; they rise and fall together.

Hence we return to the point that emerged forcefully in the analysis of media reform around the world: the importance of political parties to provide necessary leadership and to force the issue into the political arena. In the U.S., both the Republican and Democratic Parties, with only a few prominent exceptions, have been and are in the pay of the corporate media and communication giants. It is unlikely that any breakthroughs can be expected there until much spadework is done. The logical place to begin that spadework ought to be the small parties and factions of the left in America, the New Party, the Greens, the Labor Party, Democratic Socialists of America, Americans for Democratic Action, and U.S. Action. In our view, all of these groups need to incorporate media reform issues into their platforms and their visions. Ideally, these organizations, which have remarkably similar stances on a host of issues, might adopt a shared vision—perhaps as a step toward building the sort of labor, left, green, feminist, people of color coalitions seen in New Zealand's Alliance Party, Iceland's Alliance, and other Third Left groupings. In Wisconsin, already, the Greens and New Party activists are working together on joint projects. In Washington, D.C., the Greens have merged with the D.C. Statehood Party.

Sadly, however, these new left parties have dropped the ball concerning media so far, with only one or two exceptions. As U.S. Rep. Bernie Sanders, the Vermont independent who is the only socialist member of the U.S. House of Representatives, and who has made media reform a central issue for over a decade has noted: "This is an issue that is absolutely vital to democracy, and that only the left can address. The New Party, the Green Party, the Labor Party, progressive Democrats should be all over this issue. But, for most of the left, it's not even on the agenda." This has to change, and change soon, both for the sake of media reform and for the sake of these parties and progressive politics in the United States. It is difficult for us to imagine a better place to build trust and cooperation across these left groupings than with a shared response to media, which has been so devastatingly dismissive of third-party initiatives, save those of billionaire hot dogs Ross Perot and Donald Trump.

Who would contribute to the shaping of a progressive media reform platform? Ideally, it would be shaped as similar platforms in Sweden, Finland, Canada, and other lands have been. Local and national groups working on media reform would participate. There would also be significant input from media unions, such as the Newspaper Guild, the National Writers Union, and the American Federation of Television and Radio Artists. We believe these groups could get the ball rolling by coming together in support of a set of basic principles not unlike those advanced by Britain's Campaign for Press and Broadcast Freedom.

There is every reason to believe that these groups could ultimately agree on an agenda that calls for basic reforms, such as:

*   Expansion of funding for traditional public-service broadcasting with an eye toward making it fully noncommercial and democratically accountable. In particular, substantial new funding should be provided for the development of news and public affairs programming that will fill the gap created by the collapse of serious newsgathering by the networks and their local affiliates.
*   Development of noncommercial, community-run, public-access television and radio systems that are distinct from public-service broadcasting and that are deeply rooted in local communities. As part of this initiative, the federal government should remove barriers to the development of microradio initiatives. Seed money, similar to that provided by government and foundations for economic development in low-income and minority communities, should be targeted toward groups seeking to develop microradio.
*   Setting far stricter standards for commercial broadcasters in exchange for granting them broadcast licenses. For example, why not ban or strictly limit advertising on childrens' programs and on news broadcasts? Why not take a percentage of the broadcasters' revenues and set it aside for creative people and journalists to control time set aside for children's shows and newscasts? Why not make a condition of receiving a broadcast license that the broadcaster will not carry any paid political advertising during electoral campaigns? And that they will provide free time to all, liberally defined, viable candidates?

- Creation of a broad initiative to limit advertising in general, using regulation and taxation to prevent commercial saturation.
- Reassertion of anti-trust protections in order to limit the amount of media that can be owned by one firm. Why not, for example, limit radio stations to one per owner? The benefits of concentrated ownership accrue entirely to owners, not to the public. Make it government policy to encourage diversity of ownership and diversity of editorial opinions, as was intended by the First Amendment. There should, as well, be a reassertion of traditional restrictions on cross-ownership of media within particular communities.
- Renewing the commitment of the U.S. government to develop incentives aimed at encouraging and protecting minority ownership of broadcast and cable outlets.
- Promotion of newspaper and magazine competition through the use of tax deductions or subsidies. One approach might allow taxpayers to deduct the cost of a limited number of newspaper and magazine subscriptions—as some professionals and academics now do. Such an initiative would boost the circulations of publications from across the ideological spectrum, but would be particularly helpful to publications that target low-income, working-class, and elderly citizens, as well as students. Significantly lowered postal fees for nonprofit publications that have minimal advertising might also be appropriate.
- Strengthen the position of media unions by encouraging the development of a stronger role for workers in determining the editorial content of news publications and broadcast news. As in European countries, union protections in the U.S. should be strengthened in order to assure that working journalists are free to perform their duties with an eye toward serving the public interest.
- Develop a new national program of subsidies for film and cultural production, particularly by members of ethnic and racial minority groups, women, low-income citizens, and others who frequently have a hard time finding market support for their artistic expressions.
- Use tax breaks and subsidies to promote creation of publishing and production cooperatives and other arts and culture vehicles designed to provide noncommercial outlets for writers and artists to bring meaningful, controversial, and substantive work to mass audiences. One proposal put forth by economist Dean Baker would let any American redirect $150 from their tax payments to any nonprofit medium of their choice. This could funnel as much as $25 billion into nonprofit media and create a very healthy competition among new and revitalized outlets for democratic and cultural expression. All this could be done without any government official gumming up the works.

In combination, these proposals would go a long way toward creating a strong democratic sector on the rapidly commercializing Internet, as every medium today has a web component almost by definition. By the same token, media reformers must demand that there be formal hearings and public deliberations on the future of digital communication systems. At present the crucial technical decisions are being made quietly behind closed doors to the benefit of the corporate community. That has to be stopped.

.   .   .

We believe that a media reform movement with clear goals and a clear strategy for achieving them will be a fundamental building block of a broad crusade for democratic renewal in America—a bold, powerful and ultimately successful initiative that has the potential to make this nation's promise for democracy real. It will be a movement that takes an issue too long neglected and pushes that concern to the center of the national debate. It will be a movement that gives us an answer to the powers-that-be who seek constantly to divert us from issues of consequence. It will be a movement that empowers us to respond to their distractions and deceits by laughing in their faces and saying: "It's the media, stupid."

Discussion Questions

1. Identify and reflect on McChesney and Nichols's three criteria of participatory self-government.

2. In what ways do the consolidation of corporate control over the media and growing media commercialism represent a threat both to democracy and to journalism?

3. Identify the key elements of McChesney and Nichols's progressive media reform agenda. How might support for this agenda be built?

6   *News Content and Illusion: Four Information Biases That Matter*

W. Lance Bennett

Debates about the quality of news coverage in the United States often revolve around assertions that the mass media are either too liberal or too conservative, depending on the politics of the critic. In this article, taken from his popular book News: The Politics of Illusion, political scientist W. Lance Bennett argues that this liberal versus conservative controversy about journalistic bias is a "dead-end debate." Rather than focusing on the ideological slant of the news, Bennett asks us to consider "universal information problems" that lead journalists to frame stories in such a way that familiar political narratives come to replace hard-hitting investigative coverage. These "information biases" transcend ideology, debasing the quality of public information while contributing to the transformation of news into a "mass-produced consumer product." The four characteristics of the news include personalization, dramatization, fragmentation, and the authority-disorder bias. They developed as an outgrowth of the connection between evolving communications technologies and the profit motive that drives the corporate media. Taken together, while these four traits heighten the dramatic tension of news reports, they also feed the public's disenchantment with the news, accentuating already rampant public cynicism and furthering the distance between citizens and their leaders. Ultimately, Bennett contends, democracy is weakened by the way news stories are presented—the information biases inherent in the dominant news format—regardless of any ideological tilt that may or may not actually exist. Coupled with the forgoing analysis of McChesney and Nichols, the troubling issue we are left to ponder is whether our cherished notion of the "free press" retains any semblance of reality in the twenty-first century.

It is a writer's obligation to impose narrative. Everyone does this. Every time you take a lump of material and turn it into something you are imposing a narrative. It's a writer's obligation to do this. And, by the same token, it is apparently a journalist's obligation to pretend that he never does anything of the sort. The journalist claims to believe that the narrative emerges from the lump of material, rises up and smacks you in the face like marsh gas.

—Nora Ephron

Reprinted from *News: The Politics of Illusion,* Fifth Edition (2003), Pearson Education, Inc.

When George W. Bush announced his presidential candidacy a breathtaking seventeen months before the 2000 presidential election, he did so on a movie-set stage in Iowa, surrounded by bales of hay and a shiny red forklift behind him. The day's news coverage anointed him the front-runner. As if to prove their point, reporters noted that Bush attracted by far the greatest press entourage, even though three other prominent candidates were also campaigning in the state that day. Mr. Bush wittily acknowledged that news organizations have choices about where they assign reporters, as he took the microphone on his campaign plane shortly after it took off for Iowa that morning. He quipped to the crowd of reporters on board: "Thanks for coming. We know you have a choice of candidates when you fly, and we appreciate you choosing Great Expectations." Great Expectations was the nickname he gave the plane as part of a larger spin effort to defuse the typical pattern of news building up expectations about candidates only to dramatize their next fall. Mr. Bush again played flight attendant when he asked the reporters to "Please stow your expectations securely in your overhead bins, as they may shift during the trip and can fall and hurt someone—especially me."

This campaign 2000 story was written more in an entertainment format than as a means to deliver serious political information; it was personality-centered, well-scripted, and set as a comedy scene in which Mr. Bush played a flight attendant doing the pre-takeoff announcement. The story was also artificial in the sense of being disconnected from larger questions about the race, the issues, or Mr. Bush's qualifications for being president. Most importantly, there was no clear basis on which the Washington press had decreed him the front-runner. True, the ability to deliver clever lines may be some qualification for being president, but the readers of the news story would be unable to know if Mr. Bush uttered that monologue spontaneously or if it was scripted as part his advisors' communication strategy to win over a skeptical press pack. Perhaps, in the mediated reality of contemporary politics, the distinction between an innate ability to think on one's feet and learning to deliver a scripted performance no longer matters.

A closer look at this front-runner story and the campaign news that surrounded it reveals one tangible political condition mentioned in passing that might explain why journalists granted Mr. Bush the early lead: money. Mr. Bush had already set a record for early campaign fund-raising. Raising the largest amount of money makes a candidate front-runner in the eyes of political insiders, as well as in the story lines of the prominent national journalists who cover politics from the perspectives of insiders. Pegging the political fortunes of candidates to the sizes of their war chests is not an idle measure of potential electoral success. It is money, after all, that indicates the strength of business and interest group belief that a candidate will support their political goals. And it takes money to bring a candidate's political messages to voters who are more expensive to reach than ever before. Yet one of the reasons that people are hard to reach is that they tend not to trust politicians or the journalists who cover them. And one of the reasons that people mistrust the political establishment is money. Both polls and public interest groups often identify money as one of the ills of politics.

The insider view that politics is bitter, partisan, personalized, manipulative and money-driven may be a defensible perspective (it is the inside view, after all), but this does not make it the only choice that news organizations have about how to cover government. This is not to argue that topics such as money should be ignored in campaign coverage. To the contrary, the question is how news organizations decide to play those topics in their stories.

Consider the choices that news organizations have in how to frame a campaign story in which money is a potential plot element. *Framing involves choosing a broad organizing theme for selecting, emphasizing, and linking the elements of a story such as the scenes, the characters, their actions, and supporting documentation.* For example the framing of the previous story might have been shifted from the *horse race* to the *money chase,* with a serious investigation of the interests to which Mr. Bush and the other candidates might be indebted. Yet the above story and hundreds more that followed it throughout the campaign told the tale of the horse race one more time. In the horse race plot, money is generally left poorly developed in the background, requiring us to decode the reasons why George W. Bush may be the leading candidate. Also typical of many political stories, this dramatized news fragment was implicitly negative. Money has become a code for what ails our public life, a disruptive or disordering principle in the democratic order of things.

The opening of the Bush presidential campaign thus displayed the information biases of many political news stories: (1) it was personality oriented, (2) with dramatic staging and scripting, (3) that left it fragmented or disconnected from underlying political issues and realities (such as Mr. Bush's issue positions or other qualifications for being named the leading candidate), and (4) its implicit message (about money in this case) is typically negative, suggesting threats to the normal order of things. The result is that while people may tune in to news for its entertainment value, they also find reason in many stories to doubt or dismiss politics in general.

This communication system appears to contribute to a public that is increasingly cynical and disillusioned with politics and government. The paradox is that journalists complain about the over-scripted campaigns, and, more generally, the staged events they cover, but they seem unable to find other ways to write stories or to replace the cynical tone with perspectives that might help citizens become more engaged. As a result of these and other factors, large numbers of people actively avoid politics, while watching the media spectacle with a mixture of disbelief and disapproval. Meanwhile more people escape from public affairs and political participation into ever more personalized media worlds that one observer has likened to the gated communities and suburban enclaves into which many people have physically migrated in society.

Let's move from the opening story of the 2000 election to the dramatic conclusion. To make a long story short, the *Bush as front-runner* story (with minor variations) swept through the news media for a time until it was replaced by other campaign *horse race* dramas, often with Mr. Gore as front-runner, each creating an episode to advance a long running story that must (if we are to call it news) continue to develop. Thus Mr. Bush and Democratic front-runner Al Gore jockeyed through the primaries, walked through heavily-scripted conventions, see-sawed through the debates, and finally headed to the finish line in one of the closest contests in American history. In an unexpected twist, the story was jarred from its predictable ending (an election night winner) because the electoral vote count was so close that it did not decide the result. The dispute over a handful of votes in Florida was eventually ended by a Supreme Court ruling that left many on both sides angry at the process that determined the result.

Did this photo finish in the presidential horse race of 2000 draw a large crowd of excited spectators? Hardly. The voter turnout reached a new modern era low beneath 50 percent. Continuous weekly polling of voters by *The Vanishing Voter,* a Harvard project led by Thomas Patterson and Marvin Kalb, revealed that a majority of voters did not become interested in the election until after it was over and the dispute in Florida broke out.

The point here is not to place the blame for civic disengagement on the news media. Journalists complained throughout the campaign that they had little to work with. How much more could they say about Al Gore's woodenness or George Bush's feeble grasp of foreign policy? Yet this begs the question: Why were journalists acting like movie critics giving barely passing reviews to all those poorly-scripted and repetitively-acted political performances? Why was there so little innovative coverage that might stimulate citizen engagement with the election either on the level of the candidates (for example, the political and economic interests that they represented) or on the level of stirring involvement beyond the momentary act of voting in the most important democratic ritual in the civic culture?

It is remarkable that the leading news organizations not only converged in their horse race and campaign strategy coverage, but they stuck with those narrative choices in the face of clear voter disinterest. Even in the final weeks of the contest, stories with standardized dramatized framings such as the *horse race,* the *war room,* and other military metaphors outnumbered stories on all the issues in the race, combined, by a wide margin. For example, a study of *The Washington Post* and *The New York Times* in the final two weeks of the campaign showed that dramatized framings of the race or the strategic conflict outnumbered all policy issue stories by a margin of 69 to 45 in the *Post,* while the *Times'* melodrama-to-issue gap was even greater at 93 to 63. *Consider the possibility that the choices of such narrative framings of politics contain information biases that are far more serious and at the same time more difficult for the average person to detect than ideological biases.*

A Different Kind of Bias

This [article] takes a close look at news content. The concern is with information biases that make news hard to use as a guide to citizen action because they obscure the big picture in which daily events take place, and, in addition, they often convey a negative or cynical tone about politics that undermines citizen motivation for digging deeper to learn more or to become engaged. . . . Most debates about journalistic bias are concerned with the question of ideology. For example, does the news have a liberal or conservative, a Democratic or Republican, drift? To briefly review the argument, some variations in news content or political emphasis may occur, but they can seldom be explained as the result of journalists routinely injecting their partisan views into the news. To the contrary, the avoidance of political partisanship by journalists is reinforced, among other means, by the professional ethics codes of journalists, by the editors who monitor their work, and by the business values of the companies they work for.

Another important point to recall is that people who see a consistent ideological press bias (that is, across most stories or over extended periods of time) are seeing it with the help of their own ideology. This generalization is supported by opinion research showing that people in the middle see the press as generally neutral, whereas those on the left complain that the news is too conservative, and those on the right think the news has a left-leaning bias. There are at least two ironies in this ongoing and inherently unre-solvable debate about ideological bias. First, even if neutrality or objectivity could be achieved, citizens with strong views on particular issues would not recognize it. Second, even if the news contained strong ideological or issue biases, people with a point of view (who are most likely to detect bias in the first place) would be well equipped to defend themselves against such biases. Indeed many nations favor a partisan press system as the best way to conduct public debates and to explore issues . . .

So, many Americans are caught up in dead-end debates about a kind of news bias that is at once far less systematic and much less dangerous than commonly assumed. In the meantime, and this may be the greatest irony of all, these preoccupations with the politics of journalists detract attention from other information bias that really are worth worrying about. A more sensible approach to news bias is to look for those universal information problems that hinder the efforts of citizens, whatever their ideology, to take part in political life.

The task [of this article] is to understand the U.S. public information system at a deeper level than the endless debates over ideological bias. Fortunately most of the pieces to the news puzzle are right in front of us. For all of its defects, the news continues to be largely a public production, with government press offices, media organizations, and popular tastes all available for inspection. . . .

In turning to the workings of this system, it is important to understand that the news biases examined here have evolved over a long period of time. Their roots can be traced to the transition from a partisan to a commercial press in the 1800s. . . . It is thus helpful to think of the biases that we see at any point in time as historical prod-ucts of the changing system of relations between people, press, and politicians. These relations continually shape and construct news and contribute to its evolving forms.

Four Information Biases That Matter: An Overview

Our expectations about the quality of public information are rather high. Most of us grew up with history books full of journalistic heroism exercised in the name of truth and free speech. We learned that the American Revolution was inspired by the polit-ical rhetoric of the underground press and by printers' effective opposition to the British Stamp Act. The lesson from the trial of Peter Zenger has endured through time: *the truth is not libelous.* The goal of the history book journalists was as unswerv-ing as it was noble: to guarantee for the American people the most accurate, critical, coherent, illuminating, and independent reporting of political events. Yet Peter

Zenger would probably not recognize, much less feel comfortable working in, a modern news organization.

Like it or not, the news has become a mass-produced consumer product, bearing little resemblance to history book images. Communication technologies, beginning with the wire services and progressing to satellite feeds and digital video, interact with corporate profit motives to create generic, "lowest-common-denominator" information formats. Those news story formulas often lack critical perspectives and coherent or useful organizing principles. . . . The illusions of coherence, diversity, and relevance have been achieved through packaging the news to suit the psychological tastes of different segments of the market audience. It is necessary to look beyond ideology and the packaging of our favorite news source in order to see the remarkable similarities that run through most mainstream news content. In particular, there are four characteristics of news that stand out as reasons why public information in the United States does not do as much as it could to advance the cause of democracy: *personalization, dramatization, fragmentation,* and the *authority-disorder bias.*

Personalization

If there is a single most important flaw in the American news style, it is the overwhelming tendency to downplay the big social, economic, or political picture in favor of the human trials, tragedies, and triumphs that sit at the surface of events. For example, instead of focusing on power and process, the media concentrate on the people engaged in political combat over the issues. The reasons for this are numerous, from the journalist's fear that probing analysis will turn off audiences to the relative ease of telling the human-interest side of a story as opposed to explaining deeper causes and effects.

It is easy for the news audience to react for or against the actors in these personalized human-interest stories. When people are invited to take the news personally, they can find a wide range of private, emotional meanings in it, however, the meanings inspired by personalized news may not add up to the shared critical and analytical meanings on which a healthy democracy thrives. Personalized news encourages people to take an egocentric rather than a socially concerned view of political problems. The focus on personalities encourages a passive spectator attitude among the public. Moreover, the common media focus on flawed political personalities at the center of mistakes and scandals invites people to project their general anger and frustration at society or in their private lives onto the distant symbolic targets of politics. Either way, whether the focus is on sympathetic heroes and victims or hateful scoundrels and culprits, the media preference for personalized human-interest news creates a "can't-see-the-forest-for-the-trees" information bias that makes it difficult to see the big (institutional) picture that lies beyond the many actors crowding center stage who are caught in the eye of the news camera.

The tendency to personalize the news would be less worrisome if human-interest angles were used to hook audiences into more serious analysis of issues and problems. Almost all great literature and theater, from the Greek dramas to the modern day, use strong characters to promote audience identifications and reactions in order to draw people into thinking about larger moral and social issues. American news often stops at the character development stage, however, and leaves the larger lessons and social significance, if there is any, to the imagination of the audience. As a result, the main problem with personalized news is that the focus on personal concerns is seldom linked to more in-depth analysis. What often passes for analysis are opaque news formulas such as "he/she was a reflection of us," a line that was used in the media frenzies that followed the deaths of Britain's Princess Diana and America's John Kennedy, Jr. Even when large portions of the public reject personalized news formulas, as in the case of the year-long journalistic preoccupation with whether President Clinton's personal sexual behavior undermined his leadership, the personalization never stops. This systematic tendency to personalize situations is one of the defining biases of news.

Dramatization

Compounding the information bias of personalization is a second news property in which the aspects of events that are reported tend to be the ones most easily dramatized in simple "stories." As noted above, American journalism has settled overwhelmingly on the reporting form of stories or narratives, as contrasted, for example, to analytical essays, political polemics, or more scientific-style problem reports. Stories invite dramatization, particularly with sharply drawn actors at their center.

News dramas emphasize crisis over continuity, the present over the past or future, conflicts and relationship problems between the personalities at their center, and the impact of scandals on personal political careers. News dramas downplay complex policy information, the workings of government institutions, and the bases of power behind the central characters. Lost in the news drama (*melodrama* is often the more appropriate term) are sustained analyses of the persistent problems of our time, such as inequality, hunger, resource depletion, population pressures, environmental collapse, toxic waste, and political oppression. Serious though such human problems are, they just are not dramatic enough on a day-to-day level to make the news.

Important topics do come up, of course, such as when natural disasters strike, nuclear waste contaminates air or water supplies, or genocide breaks out in a distant land. Chronic conditions generally become news only when they reach astounding levels that threaten large-scale cataclysm through famine, depression, war, or revolution. But then the stories go away, again leaving the origins of and the solutions for those problems little-discussed in all but the biggest of stories. Most of these seemingly sudden "crises" are years in the making: deforestation that worsens flooding, neglected nuclear dumps festering in the Arctic or in Washington State, or bandit governments in African nations undermining the hope for civil society. With a steady flow of information provided by experts and issue advocacy organizations, these stories could be kept in the news as reminders to publics and politicians that there may be more important things than the glitzy media event of the day or the routine political skirmishing in Washington.

Crises, not the slow buildups to them, are the perfect news material, meaning that they fit neatly into the dramatization bias. The "crisis cycle" portrayed in the news is classic dramatic fare, with rising action, falling action, sharply drawn characters, and, of course, plot resolutions. By its very definition, a crisis is something that will subside on its own or reach dramatic closure through clean-up efforts or humanitarian relief operations. Unfortunately the crisis cycles that characterize our news system only reinforce the popular impression that high levels of human difficulty are inevitable and therefore acceptable. Crises are resolved when situations return to "manageable" levels of difficulty. Seldom are underlying problems treated and eliminated at their source. The news is certainly not the cause of these problems, but it could become part of the solution if it substituted illumination of causes for dramatic coverage of symptoms.

As in the case of personalization, dramatization would not be a problem if it were used mainly as an attention-focusing device to introduce more background and context surrounding events. Drama can help us engage with the great forces of history, science, politics, or human relations. When drama is used to bring analysis into mind, it is a good thing. When drama is employed as a cheap emotional device to focus on human conflict and travail, or farce and frailty, the larger significance of events becomes easily lost in waves of immediate emotion. The potential advantages of drama to enlighten and explain are sacrificed to the lesser tendencies of melodrama to excite, anger, and further personalize events. Thus the news often resembles real-life soap operas, only with far more important consequences than the ones on entertainment TV.

One of the things that makes the news dramatic—indeed, that may even drive news drama—is the use of visuals: photos, graphics, and live-action video. These elements of stories not only make the distant world seem more real, they make the news more believable. In many ways, particularly for television, the pictures may not only tell the stories but help editors and reporters decide which stories to tell and how to tell them.

In principle, there is nothing wrong with the emphasis on sights in news production. In fact one might argue that thinking visually is the best way to engage the senses more fully in communicating about society and politics. Yet there is often a tension between not reporting important stories that are hard to picture and reporting possibly unimportant stories simply because they offer great visual images. . . . The economics of audience attention often shade editorial decisions in the direction of starting with the pictures and then adding the words.

It is important to worry about the bases of such editorial decisions because in many ways they distinguish between good and bad uses of news drama. When stories are selected more for visuals than for larger political significance and context, the scripting of the story may bend information rather badly to suggest that the pictures do, in fact, reflect the larger situation. And since there is more than a grain of truth to the old adage that "seeing is believing," people may be compelled to see aspects of society that simply are not there or that are not there in the ways they are dramatically portrayed in the news. The visually graphic coverage of crime on TV is an example of this. . . . At the very least, the selection of news stories primarily because they offer dramatic images is one of several important reasons why the news is often so fragmented or disconnected from larger political or economic contexts that would provide other ways to tell the story.

Fragmentation

The emphasis on personal and dramatic qualities of events feeds into a third information characteristic of the news: the isolation of stories from each other and from their larger contexts so that information in the news becomes fragmented and hard to assemble into a big picture. The fragmentation of information begins by emphasizing individual actors over the political contexts in which they operate. Fragmentation is then heightened by the use of dramatic formats that turn events into self-contained, isolated happenings. The fragmentation of information is further exaggerated by the severe space limits nearly all media impose for fear of boring readers and viewers with too much information.

Thus the news comes to us in sketchy dramatic capsules that make it difficult to see the causes of problems, their historical significance, or the connections across issues. It can even be difficult to follow the development of a particular issue over time as stories rise and fall more in response to the actions and reactions of prominent public figures than to independent reporting based on investigation of events. In addition, because it is difficult to bring historical background into the news, the impression is created of a world of chaotic events and crises that appear and disappear because the news picture offers little explanation of their origins.

The Authority-Disorder Bias

Passing for depth and coherence in this system of personalized, dramatized, and fragmented information is a fourth news tendency in which the authoritative voices of officials take center stage in many political news dramas to interpret the threatening and confusing events that threaten the order of social life. There is bias in placing so much news focus on the largely emotional questions of Who's in charge? and Will order be restored? (As opposed, for example, to What is the problem?, Why is it a problem?, What are the alternative explanations beyond the official ones?, and What can citizens do to make the situation better?)

It may be tempting to say that government, after all, is centrally about authority and order, so why shouldn't these concerns be central preoccupations of the news? The problem comes when journalists build themes about authority and order into the news as core dramatic emotional plot elements, rather than letting them pass through the news gates more formally when they arise in public debate, much the way partisan political views are generally reported. Instead, the focus on authority and order is often driven by considerations of what makes for bigger, more dramatic, more emotional stories.

Whether the world is returned to a safe, normal place, or the very idea of a normal world is called in question, the news is preoccupied with order, along with related questions of whether authorities are capable of establishing or restoring it. It is easy to see why these generic plot elements are so central to news: They are versatile and tireless themes that can be combined endlessly within personalized, dramatized, and fragmented news episodes. When the dramatic balance between order and disorder is not a plausible focus for an event, the news quickly turns the plot pair around and challenges authority itself, perhaps by publicizing the latest scandal charge against a leader or by opening the news gates to one politician willing to attack another.

In the past, it could be argued that the news more often resolved the authority-order balance in favor of official pronouncements aimed at "normalizing" conflicted situations by creating the appearance of order and control. A classic scenario of politics, according to political scientist Murray Edelman, is for authorities to take central stage to respond to crises (sometimes after having stirred them up in the first place) with emotionally reassuring promises that they will be handled effectively. Today's authorities still play out their parts, but the news increasingly finds ways to challenge either the pronouncements of officials or the presumption of order in society, or both. In short, the biggest change in portrayals of authority and order in the news . . . is that the dominant news focus has shifted away from trusted authorities providing reassuring promises to restore chaotic situations to a state of order or normalcy. Such stories continue to appear, of course, but the growing news trend is to portray unsympathetic, scheming politicians who often fail to solve problems, leaving disorder in their wake.

What is the evidence for the proposition that news is more negative and less likely to paint reassuring pictures of the return to normalcy following dramatic crises and scandals? . . . For reasons having more to do with the news business than with external realities, the following changes have been charted in news content in recent years:

- increased levels of mayhem (crime, violence, accidents, health threats, freeway chases, and other images of social chaos)
- greater volume of criticism of government, politicians, and their policies, and less focus on the substance of policies
- higher journalistic tone of cynicism and negativity.

Many of these order-challenging news patterns are relatively subtle, reflecting the "hidden hand" of economic decisions within news organizations. For example, . . . the news recorded great increases in crime stories in the 1990s during a period in which officially reported rates of most violent crimes actually declined. This suggests that images of social disorder may be based on little more than choosing stories for their attention-getting effects. Images of disorder can be further amplified through subtle emphases in news writing. For example, is the traditional American family *threatened* by the increase in single-parent and two working-parent households, or is the family in America simply *changing* in these ways as part of the normal course of social change?

The reason for thinking about authority and order as separable but related aspects of many news stories is that they are often set at odds with each other to create the dramatic tension in stories. Thus it would be too simple to say that authorities are almost always challenged and that disorder most often prevails. As news organizations take greater dramatic license with news plots, the two elements are mixed to achieve the greatest dramatic effect. A classic news plot represents authorities such as police, fire, and health officials as forces of good battling to restore order against social evils such as crime, violence, or disease. In one variation on this formula, crime or the latest health threat may seem to be running out of control, but officials appear in the news to tell us how we can be safe. Given the levels of mayhem and disorder in much of the news, the presence of at least some reassuring line of authority is a necessary dramatic counterpoint. Moreover, the question of what actually happened in a particular incident is often unclear at the time that news teams arrive. So we encounter the familiar news formula that goes: "The police aren't exactly sure what happened here yet, but their investigation is in progress, and we expect a report soon."

When authorities are anchoring a scene, dramatic speculation about levels of disorder may soar in news scripts. A typical example comes from a local newscast in Orlando, Florida, where Channel 6 announced an "exclusive" and promised a report from their "live truck" at the scene. The newscast opened with the anchor describing "A shocking scene in a Lake Mary neighborhood tonight. A home surrounded by crime-scene tape. A death police are calling 'suspicious.'" As the anchor spoke, the screen flashed the words "Neighborhood Shocker." Cut to the reporter live from the scene who further dramatized the death of a sixty-six-year-old woman by saying that police did not know what happened. As if to document this claim, the reporter interviewed a police officer who said that there were no signs of violence, forced entry, or robbery. Although this statement could easily have supported either an order or a disorder plot for the story, the local news format clearly favored playing the murder mystery/shocker plot. The reporter announced that the police planned an autopsy the next day and did not know what they would find. The live feed ended with the reporter saying that, in the mean time, they "want to keep a very tight lid on what happened. . . . Live in Lake Mary, Nicole Smith, Channel 6 News." The next day, it turned out that the woman had died naturally of a heart attack. So much for the "Neighborhood Shocker." As one observer noted, "Journalism Shocker" would have been a more appropriate on-screen warning.

By contrast, other dramatic plot formulas challenge authority either by focusing on alleged personal failings of politicians or by finding examples of government failures. The political poster story of the 1990s was about wasteful government spending. Many news organizations, both local and national, have run prominent features on "How government is wasting your tax dollars." The lure of such dramatic accounts over more representative news descriptions is illustrated in a *Los Angeles Times* investigative series on government spending on computers in different agencies. Even though the investigation turned up many positive examples of taxpayer dollars well spent, here is how the story opened:

> WASHINGTON—After pumping $300 billion into computer systems in the last two decades, the federal government has compiled a record of failure that has jeopardized the nation's welfare, eroded public safety and squandered untold billions of dollars.

Whether or not most events fit the authority-disorder plot, it is easy enough to make them fit. A news show with a regular feature on government waste will, of course, find some alleged example of waste every time the feature is scheduled. Also, since there are few features on good things the government is doing, examples of government thrift (other than those forced by budget cuts) are less likely to be news.

•   •   •

Consider the picture so far: Each day news consumers are bombarded by dozens of compartmentalized, unrelated dramatic capsules. Some emotional satisfaction can be derived from forming strong identifications with or against the actors who star in these mini-dramas. But what about facts? What about knowledge and practical information? Unless the consumer has an existing interest or perspective on the subject, recalling facts from the news resembles a trivia game played alone. Most people cannot remember three-fourths of the stories in a TV news broadcast immediately after watching it, and information recall about the remembered quarter is sketchy at best.

Communication scholars have developed considerable empirical support for these four information biases in the news. There is now a sizable literature that reads like an inventory of these problems. The tendencies toward personalization, dramatization, and fragmentation have all been remarkably enduring over time, although they may have become more exaggerated with the economic pressures of the business. . . . While the focus on authority and order is also an enduring defining feature of the news, the shifting balance from order to mayhem and the unreflectively negative tone toward officials has left many observers puzzled and concerned. Indeed many politicians say they have left government because of the relentlessly negative media scrutiny, while others have surrounded themselves by legions of media consultants and handlers. At the same time that many journalists criticize their own product in these terms, they confess being helpless to change it under the current system of profit- and ratings-driven business values.

Discussion Questions

1. Identify and explain the four information biases that Bennett explores. How do these biases affect what we see and hear as news? Can you think of ways any recent news stories have been influenced by these four biases?

2. In what way(s) is the quality of democracy imperiled by the continued consumption of news framed by information biases? Do you think that citizens would feel a stronger attachment to the political world if the news they received delved more honestly, analytically, and historically into the problems we face as a society?

Parties

7   *Party Government*

E. E. Schattschneider

The Convention at Philadelphia provided a constitution with a dual attitude: it was proparty in one sense and antiparty in another. The authors of the Constitution refused to suppress the parties by destroying the fundamental liberties in which parties originate. They or their immediate successors accepted amendments that guaranteed civil rights and thus established a system of party tolerance, i.e., the right to agitate and to organize. This is the proparty aspect of the system. On the other hand, the authors of the Constitution set up an elaborate division and balance of powers within an intricate governmental structure designed to make parties ineffective. It was hoped that the parties would lose and exhaust themselves in futile attempts to fight their way through the labyrinthine framework of the government, much as an attacking army is expected to spend itself against the defensive works of a fortress. This is the antiparty part of the Constitution scheme. To quote Madison, the "great object" of the Constitution was "to preserve the public good and private right against the danger of such a faction [party] and at the same time to preserve the spirit and form of popular government."

In Madison's mind the difference between an autocracy and a free republic seems to have been largely a matter of the precise point at which parties are stopped by the government. In an autocracy parties are controlled (suppressed) at the source; in a republic parties are tolerated but are invited to strangle themselves in the machinery of government. The result in either case is much the same, sooner or later the government checks the parties but *never do the parties control the government*. Madison was perfectly definite and unmistakable in his disapproval of party government as distinguished from party tolerance. In the opinion of Madison, parties were intrinsically bad, and the sole issue for discussion was the means by which bad parties might be prevented from becoming dangerous. What never seems to have occurred to the authors of the Constitution, however, is that parties might be used as beneficent instruments of popular government. It is at this point that the distinction between the modern and the antique attitude is made.

The offspring of this combination of ideas was a constitutional system having conflicting tendencies. The Constitution made the rise of parties inevitable yet was incompatible with party government. This scheme, in spite of its subtlety, involved a miscalculation. Political parties refused to be content with the role assigned to them. The vigor and enterprise of the parties have therefore made American political history the story of the unhappy marriage of the parties and the Constitution, a remarkable

Reprinted from *Party Government* (1942), Thomson Learning.

variation of the case of the irresistible force and the immovable object, which in this instance have been compelled to live together in a permanent partnership. . . .

The Raw Materials of Politics

People who write about interests sometimes seem to assume that all interests are special and exclusive, setting up as a result of this assumption a dichotomy in which the interests on the one side are perpetually opposed to the public welfare on the other side. But there are common interests as well as special interests, and common interests resemble special interests in that they are apt to influence political behavior. The raw materials of politics are not all antisocial. Alongside of Madison's statement that differences in wealth are the most durable causes of faction there should be placed a corollary that the common possessions of the people are the most durable cause of unity. To assume that people have merely conflicting interests and nothing else is to invent a political nightmare that has only a superficial relation to reality. The body of agreement underlying the conflicts of a modern society ought to be sufficient to sustain the social order provided only that the common interests supporting this unity are mobilized. Moreover, not all differences of interest are durable causes of conflict. Nothing is apt to be more perishable than a political issue. In the democratic process, the nation moves from controversy to agreement to forgetfulness; politics is not a futile exercise like football, forever played back and forth over the same ground. The government creates and destroys interests at every turn.

There are, in addition, powerful factors inhibiting the unlimited pursuit of special aims by an organized minority. To assume that minorities will stop at nothing to get what they want is to postulate a degree of unanimity and concentration within these groups that does not often exist in real life. If every individual were capable of having only one interest to the exclusion of all others, it might be possible to form dangerous unions of monomaniacs who would go to great extremes to attain their objectives. In fact, however, people have many interests leading to a dispersion of drives certain to destroy some of the unanimity and concentration of any group. How many interests can an individual have? Enough to make it extremely unlikely that any two individuals will have the same combination of interests. Anyone who has ever tried to promote an association of people having some special interest in common will realize, first, that there are marked differences of enthusiasm within the group and, second, that interests compete with interests for the attention and enthusiasm of every individual. Every organized special interest consists of a group of busy, distracted individuals held together by the efforts of a handful of specialists and enthusiasts who sacrifice other matters in order to concentrate on one. The notion of resolute and unanimous minorities on the point of violence is largely the invention of paid lobbyists and press agents.

The result of the fact that every individual is torn by the diversity of his own interests, the fact that he is a member of many groups, is *the law of the imperfect political mobilization of interests*. That is, it has never been possible to mobilize any interest 100 percent. . . .

It is only another way of saying the same thing to state that conflicts of interests are not cumulative. If it were true that the dividing line in every conflict (or in all major conflicts) split the community identically in each case so that individuals who are opposed on one issue would be opposed to each other on all other issues also, while individuals who joined hands on one occasion would find themselves on the same side on all issues, always opposed to the same combination of antagonists, the cleavage created by the cumulative effect of these divisions would be fatal. But actually conflicts are not cumulative in this way. In real life the divisions are not so clearly marked, and the alignment of people according to interests requires an enormous shuffling back and forth from one side to the other, tending to dissipate the tensions created.

In view of the fact, therefore, (1) that there are many interests, including a great body of common interests, (2) that the government pursues a multiplicity of policies and creates and destroys interests in the process, (3) that each individual is capable of having many interests, (4) that interests cannot be mobilized perfectly, and (5) that conflicts among interests are not cumulative, it seems reasonable to suppose that the government is not the captive of blind forces from which there is no escape. There is nothing wrong about the raw materials of politics.

The Party Model of Government

The framers of the Constitution believed in mixed government and at every point stressed the importance of limiting majority rule, which they essentially relegated to the House of Representatives. The "evil" factions of *Federalist 10* included, in modern terms, parties as well as interest groups. The framers' goal was deliberative, not democratic, government. Ultimately, the consent of the people, in Lockean terms, checked government, but popular consent was different than participation. A balanced and deliberative government would be more capable of acting in the national interest, thereby more likely to achieve the consent of all of the people, than would a process controlled by a popular majority or dominated by special interests.

Mixed government is the eighteenth-century model, while the idea of democratic government became ascendant in the nineteenth century. Madison and Hamilton in *The Federalist* admired and cited the mixed government of Rome as their paradigm. By the middle of the nineteenth century, Athenian democracy supported the emerging nineteenth-century democratic and party model of government. Gary Wills has pointed out in his brilliant treatise, *Lincoln at Gettysburg,* that "America as a second Athens was an idea whose moment had come in the nineteenth century. This nation's founders first looked to Rome, not to Greece, for their model. Like most men of the eighteenth century, they thought of Athens as ruled by mobs. . . . The 'mixed government' of Rome—not Athens' direct democracy—was the model invoked in debates over the proper constitution for the United States."★

The party model of government transforms the consent of the people into the rule of the majority. Majority rule can only be accomplished through *aggregative* parties.

★Gary Wills, Lincoln at Gettysburg (Touchstone: 1992), p. 42.

Party as well as balanced government is a deliberative process, but, in eighteenth-century terms, party deliberations are aimed at achieving not the national interest but the selfish or factional interests of the party organization and its members. Electoral victory by whatever means becomes the primary goal of parties.

Proponents of party government push aside eighteenth-century skepticism of faction and democracy. The only politically viable way to define the national interest, party proponents argue, is through aggregative parties that give the electorate a choice between programs that will determine what the government will do.

In contrast to the eighteenth century, democratic and party government is based on a belief in the rationality of man, and therefore the viability of a "government by discussion" through the mechanisms of political parties.* The framers were skeptical of raw politics and political incentives, which they viewed as more likely to be selfish than altruistic.

Woodrow Wilson expressed the ideas of the nineteenth century in his classic work, *Congressional Government,* written when he was a graduate student at Johns Hopkins University and published in 1885. He observed, "Whatever intention may have controlled the compromises of constitution-making in 1787, their result was to give us, not government by discussion, which is the only tolerable sort of government for a people which tries to do its own governing, but only legislation by discussion, which is no more than a small part of government by discussion."† Wilson admired the party government of Great Britain, and he bemoaned the lack of leadership and discipline in American political parties. Lack of leadership, he wrote, "gives to our national parties their curious, conglomerate character. It would seem to be scarcely an exaggeration to say that they are homogeneous only in name. Neither of the two principal parties is of one mind with itself. Each tolerates all sorts of difference of creed and variety of aim within its own ranks. Each pretends to the same purposes and permits among its partisans the same contradictions to those purposes."‡

Proponents of party government echoed Woodrow Wilson's views on many occasions long after he wrote. During much of the twentieth century, political scientists and pundits called for stronger political parties, arguing that our weak party system is a major deficiency and barrier to effective democratic leadership.

The Role of Parties in Government by Discussion

While arguably democracy and democratic theory originated with the Greeks, Aristotle being the supreme democratic theorist, democratic theory and practice inevitably changed over the centuries. The democratic politics of Athens in the fourth century B.C. was entirely different from the nineteenth century, which saw the

---

*See Sir Ernst Barker, Reflections on Government (London: Oxford University Press, 1942).
†Woodrow Wilson, Congressional Government (New York: Meridian Books, Inc., 1956, from the original edition published in 1885), pp. 197–198.
‡Ibid, p. 210.

expansion of the franchise and the development of political parties as democratic movements became firmly established in Great Britain and the United States.

In the nineteenth century, Great Britain not only ruled the waves but also defined democracy in theory and practice. Political parties emerged that reflected the major class divisions, and Tories and Whigs went to the hustings to present their programs to the electorate. In the two-party system, government changed hands when the majority party could no longer win electoral support. The opposition party then took over the reins of government. In a parliamentary system such as Britain and its commonwealth nations, the majority party in parliament elects the prime minister and cabinet. In the United States, under the separation of powers, separate constituencies choose the president, House of Representatives, and the Senate.

Democratic theory posits rational choice by the electorate after discussion of conflicting party programs. In this way, the parties help bridge the gap between the government and the people. The following is a classic reading that defines democracy as government by discussion, a process in which political parties are key actors.

8   *What's The Matter With America?*

Thomas Frank

In this selection from his best selling book What's the Matter with Kansas? *author Thomas Frank explores what he considers the "preeminent question of our times," namely why ever-increasing numbers of working class and average income Americans vote for conservative politicians whose policies intensify the economic hardships faced by those very same Americans. Frank attributes this "derangement" to the "Great Backlash," a cultural anger that emerged in the 1960s to be harnessed by Republican politicians who appeal to socially and culturally conservative issues in the service of economic ends that advance the fortunes of corporations and the wealthy. Or as Frank characterizes it, "The leaders of the backlash may talk Christ, but they walk corporate." The result has been a boon to the Republican party. As they attract more angry, disaffected former Democrats with anti-abortion, anti-gay, anti-Hollywood, and other appeals central to the culture wars of our era, their economic agenda worsens the plight of those voters, whose anger intensifies even more, enhancing the power of Republicans in a kind of self-fulfilling spiral. While Frank views this political transformation through its impact on his home state of Kansas, this same "panorama of madness" pervades the entire nation. Indeed, it is the hallmark of party politics in the U.S. today.*

The poorest county in America isn't in Appalachia or the Deep South. It is on the Great Plains, a region of struggling ranchers and dying farm towns, and in the election of 2000 the Republican candidate for president, George W. Bush, carried it by a majority of greater than 80 percent.

This puzzled me when I first read about it, as it puzzles many of the people I know. For us it is the Democrats that are the party of workers, of the poor, of the weak and the victimized. Understanding this, we think, is basic; it is part of the ABCs of adulthood. When I told a friend of mine about that impoverished High Plains county so enamored of President Bush, she was perplexed. "How can anyone who has ever worked for someone else vote Republican?" she asked. How could so many people get it so wrong?

Her question is apt; it is, in many ways, the preeminent question of our times. People getting their fundamental interests wrong is what American political life is all about. This species of derangement is the bedrock of our civic order; it is the foundation on which

Reprinted from *What's the Matter with Kansas?* (2004), Henry Holt and Company, Inc.

all else rests. This derangement has put the Republicans in charge of all three branches of government; it has elected presidents, senators, governors; it shifts the Democrats to the right and then impeaches Bill Clinton just for fun.

If you earn over $300,000 a year, you owe a great deal to this derangement. Raise a glass sometime to those indigent High Plains Republicans as you contemplate your good fortune: It is thanks to their self-denying votes that you are no longer burdened by the estate tax, or troublesome labor unions, or meddling banking regulators. Thanks to the allegiance of these sons and daughters of toil, you have escaped what your affluent forebears used to call "confiscatory" income tax levels. It is thanks to them that you were able to buy two Rolexes this year instead of one and get that Segway with the special gold trim.

Or perhaps you are one of those many, many millions of average-income Americans who see nothing deranged about this at all. For you this picture of hard-times conservatism makes perfect sense, and it is the opposite phenomenon—working-class people who insist on voting for liberals—that strikes you as an indecipherable puzzlement. Maybe you see it the way the bumper sticker I spotted at a Kansas City gun show puts it: "A working person that *supports* Democrats is like a chicken that *supports* Col. Sanders!"

Maybe you were one of those who stood up for America way back in 1968, sick of hearing those rich kids in beads bad-mouth the country every night on TV. Maybe you knew exactly what Richard Nixon meant when he talked about the "silent majority," the people whose hard work was rewarded with constant insults from the network news, the Hollywood movies, and the know-it-all college professors, none of them interested in anything you had to say. Or maybe it was the liberal judges who got you mad as hell, casually rewriting the laws of your state according to some daft idea they had picked up at a cocktail party, or ordering your town to shoulder some billion-dollar desegregation scheme that they had dreamed up on their own, or turning criminals loose to prey on the hardworking and the industrious. Or perhaps it was the drive for gun control, which was obviously directed toward the same end of disarming and ultimately disempowering people like you.

Maybe Ronald Reagan pulled you into the conservative swirl, the way he talked about that sunshiny, Glenn Miller America you remembered from the time before the world went to hell. Or maybe Rush Limbaugh won you over, with his daily beat-down of the arrogant and the self-important. Or maybe you were pushed; maybe Bill Clinton made a Republican out of you with his patently phony "compassion" and his obvious contempt for average, non-Ivy Americans, the ones he had the nerve to order into combat even though he himself took the coward's way out when his turn came.

Nearly everyone has a conversion story they can tell: how their dad had been a union steelworker and a stalwart Democrat, but how all their brothers and sisters started voting Republican; or how their cousin gave up on Methodism and started going to the Pentecostal church out on the edge of town; or how they themselves just got so sick of being scolded for eating meat or for wearing clothes emblazoned with the State U's Indian mascot that one day Fox News started to seem "fair and balanced" to them after all.

Take the family of a friend of mine, a guy who came from one of those midwestern cities that sociologists used to descend upon periodically because it was supposed to be so "typical." It was a middling-sized industrial burg where they made machine tools, auto parts, and so forth. When Reagan took office in 1981, more than half the working population of the city was employed in factories, and most of them were union members. The ethos of the place was working-class, and the city was prosperous, tidy, and liberal, in the old sense of the word.

My friend's dad was a teacher in the local public schools, a loyal member of the teachers' union, and a more dedicated liberal than most: not only had he been a staunch supporter of George McGovern, but in the 1980 Democratic primary he had voted for Barbara Jordan, the black U.S. Representative from Texas. My friend, meanwhile, was in those days a high school Republican, a Reagan youth who fancied Adam Smith ties and savored the writing of William F. Buckley. The dad would listen to the son spout off about Milton Friedman and the godliness of free-market capitalism, and he would just shake his head. *Someday, kid, you'll know what a jerk you are.*

It was the dad, though, who was eventually converted. These days he votes for the farthest-right Republicans he can find on the ballot. The particular issue that brought him over was abortion. A devout Catholic, my friend's dad was persuaded in the early nineties that the sanctity of the fetus outweighed all of his other concerns, and from there he gradually accepted the whole pantheon of conservative devil-figures: the elite media and the American Civil Liberties Union, contemptuous of our values; the la-di-da feminists; the idea that Christians are vilely persecuted—right here in the U.S. of A. It doesn't even bother him, really, when his new hero Bill O'Reilly blasts the teachers' union as a group that "does not love America."

His superaverage midwestern town, meanwhile, has followed the same trajectory. Even as Republican economic policy laid waste to the city's industries, unions, and neighborhoods, the townsfolk responded by lashing out on cultural issues, eventually winding up with a hard-right Republican congressman, a born-again Christian who campaigned largely on an anti-abortion platform. Today the city looks like a miniature Detroit. And with every bit of economic bad news it seems to get more bitter, more cynical, and more conservative still.

This derangement is the signature expression of the Great Backlash, a style of conservatism that first came snarling onto the national stage in response to the partying and protests of the late sixties. While earlier forms of conservatism emphasized fiscal sobriety, the backlash mobilizes voters with explosive social issues—summoning public outrage over everything from busing to un-Christian art—which it then marries to pro-business economic policies. Cultural anger is marshaled to achieve economic ends. And it is these economic achievements—not the forgettable skirmishes of the never-ending culture wars—that are the movement's greatest monuments. The backlash is what has made possible the international free-market consensus of recent years, with all the privatization, deregulation, and deunionization that are its components. Backlash ensures that Republicans will continue to be returned to office even when their free-market miracles fail and their libertarian schemes don't deliver and their "New Economy" collapses. It makes possible the policy pushers' fantasies of "globalization" and a free-trade empire that are foisted upon the rest of the world with such self-assurance. Because some artist decides to shock the hicks by dunking Jesus in urine, the entire planet must remake itself along the lines preferred by the Republican Party, U.S.A.

The Great Backlash has made the laissez-faire revival possible, but this does not mean that it speaks to us in the manner of the capitalists of old, invoking the divine right of money or demanding that the lowly learn their place in the great chain of being. On the contrary; the backlash imagines itself as a foe of the elite, as the voice of the unfairly persecuted, as a righteous protest of the people on history's receiving end. That its champions today control all three branches of government matters not a whit. That its greatest beneficiaries are the wealthiest people on the planet does not give it pause.

In fact, backlash leaders systematically downplay the politics of economics. The movement's basic premise is that culture outweighs economics as a matter of public concern—that *Values Matter Most*, as one backlash title has it. On those grounds it rallies citizens who would once have been reliable partisans of the New Deal to the standard of conservatism. Old-fashioned values may count when conservatives appear on the stump, but once conservatives are in office the only old-fashioned situation they care to revive is an economic regimen of low wages and lax regulations. Over the last three decades they have smashed the welfare state, reduced the tax burden on corporations and the wealthy, and generally facilitated the country's return to a nineteenth-century pattern of wealth distribution. Thus the primary contradiction of the backlash: it is a working-class movement that has done incalculable, historic harm to working-class people.

The leaders of the backlash may talk Christ, but they walk corporate. Values may "matter most" to voters, but they always take a backseat to the needs of money once the elections are won. This is a basic earmark of the phenomenon, absolutely consistent across its decades-long history. Abortion is never halted. Affirmative action is never abolished. The culture industry is never forced to clean up its act. Even the greatest culture warrior of them all was a notorious cop-out once it came time to deliver, "Reagan made himself the champion of 'traditional values,' but there is no evidence he regarded their restoration as a high priority," wrote Christopher Lasch, one of the most astute analysts of the backlash sensibility. "What he really cared about was the revival of the unregulated capitalism of the twenties: the repeal of the New Deal."

This is vexing for observers, and one might expect it to vex the movement's true believers even more. Their grandstanding leaders never deliver, their fury mounts and mounts, and nevertheless they turn out every two years to return their right-wing heroes to office for a second, a third, a twentieth try. The trick never ages; the illusion never wears off. *Vote* to stop abortion; *receive* a rollback in capital gains taxes. *Vote* to make our country strong again; *receive* deindustrialization. *Vote* to screw those politically correct college professors; *receive* electricity deregulation. *Vote* to get government off our backs; *receive* conglomeration and monopoly everywhere from media to meatpacking. *Vote* to stand tall against terrorists; *receive* Social Security privatization. *Vote* to strike a blow against elitism; *receive* a social order in which wealth is more concentrated than ever before in our lifetimes, in which workers have been stripped of power and CEOs are rewarded in a manner beyond imagining.

Backlash theorists, as we shall see, imagine countless conspiracies in which the wealthy, powerful, and well connected—the liberal media, the atheistic scientists, the obnoxious eastern elite—pull the strings and make the puppets dance. And yet the backlash itself has been a political trap so devastating to the interests of Middle America that even the most diabolical of string-pullers would have had trouble dreaming it up. Here, after all, is a rebellion against "the establishment" that has wound up abolishing the tax on inherited estates. Here is a movement whose response to the power structure is to make the rich even richer; whose answer to the inexorable degradation of working-class life is to lash out angrily at labor unions and liberal workplace-safety programs; whose solution to the rise of ignorance in America is to pull the rug out from under public education.

Like a French Revolution in reverse—one in which the sans-culottes pour down the streets demanding more power for the aristocracy—the backlash pushes the spectrum of the acceptable to the right, to the right, farther to the right. It may never bring prayer back to the schools, but it has rescued all manner of right-wing economic nostrums from history's dustbin. Having rolled back the landmark economic reforms of the sixties (the war on poverty) and those of the thirties (labor law, agricultural price supports, banking regulation), its leaders now turn their guns on the accomplishments of the earliest years of progressivism (Woodrow Wilson's estate tax; Theodore Roosevelt's antitrust measures). With a little more effort, the backlash may well repeal the entire twentieth century.

As a formula for holding together a dominant political coalition, the backlash seems so improbable and so self-contradictory that liberal observers often have trouble believing it is actually happening. By all rights, they figure, these two groups—business and blue-collar—should be at each other's throats. For the Republican Party to present itself as the champion of working-class America strikes liberals as such an egregious denial of political reality that they dismiss the whole phenomenon, refusing to take it seriously. The Great Backlash, they believe, is nothing but crypto-racism, or a disease of the elderly, or the random gripings of religious rednecks, or the protests of "angry white men" feeling left behind by history.

But to understand the backlash in this way is to miss its power as an idea and its broad popular vitality. It keeps coming despite everything, a plague of bitterness capable of spreading from the old to the young, from Protestant fundamentalists to Catholics and Jews, and from the angry white man to every demographic shading imaginable.

It matters not at all that the forces that triggered the original "silent majority" back in Nixon's day have long since disappeared; the backlash roars on undiminished, its rage carrying easily across the decades. The confident liberals who led America in those days are a dying species. The New Left, with its gleeful obscenities and contempt for the flag, is extinct altogether. The whole "affluent society," with its paternalistic corporations and powerful labor unions, fades farther into the ether with each passing year. But the backlash endures. It continues to dream its terrifying dreams of national decline, epic lawlessness, and betrayal at the top regardless of what is actually going on in the world.

Along the way what was once genuine and grassroots and even "populist" about the backlash phenomenon has been transformed into a stimulus–response melodrama with a plot as formulaic as an episode of "The O'Reilly Factor" and with results as predictable—and as profitable—as Coca-Cola advertising. In one end you feed an item about, say, the menace of gay marriage, and at the other end you generate, almost mechanically, an uptick of middle-American indignation, angry letters to the editor an electoral harvest of the most gratifying sort.

From the air-conditioned heights of a suburban office complex this may look like a new age of reason, with the Web sites singing each to each, with a mall down the way that every week has miraculously anticipated our subtly shifting tastes, with a global economy whose rich rewards just keep flowing, and with a long parade of rust-free Infinitis purring down the streets of beautifully manicured planned communities. But on closer inspection the country seems more like a panorama of madness and delusion worthy of Hieronymous Bosch: of sturdy blue-collar patriots reciting the Pledge while they strangle their own life chances; of small farmers proudly voting themselves off the land; of devoted family men carefully seeing to it that their children will never be able to afford college or proper health care; of working-class guys in midwestern cities cheering as they deliver up a landslide for a candidate whose policies will end their way of life, will transform their region into a "rust belt," will strike people like them blows from which they will never recover.

Discussion Questions

1. Frank argues that backlash conservatism creates numerous contradictions. Explore some of the contradictions. Why does he view them as "self-damaging"?

2. At one point Frank offers the following semi-humorous contention: "With a little more effort, the backlash may well repeal the entire twentieth century." Explain what he means by that.

3. The thrust of Frank's argument rests on the belief that while backlash conservatism offers cultural issues to motivate voters, subsequent economic policy ruins the livelihoods of those same voters. In essence, he thinks economics should be more fundamental than social issues. Do you agree? Is it "deranged" for voters to allow concern for divisive social/cultural issues to trump economic concerns?

9 Just Democracy: The Crisis and Opportunity in American Elections

Katrina vanden Heuvel

Competitive political parties and frequent elections are part of the backbone of democracy. In this article, Katrina vanden Heuvel, Editor and Publisher of The Nation *magazine, surveys the health of democracy in America as the fall 2008 presidential election approaches. She finds some encouraging signs—millions of new voters registered and turnout in the spring 2008 presidential primaries at record levels in many states. She also sees rising hope and enthusiasm, generated in large part by the candidacy of Illinois Senator Barack Obama and his epic Democratic primary battle with New York Senator Hillary Clinton. Obscuring these bright spots, however, are ominous dark clouds of crisis, and vanden Heuvel highlights several key flash points in the electoral process, some relatively new, others long entrenched in the system. In order to address and hopefully overcome these dilemmas, vanden Heuvel then outlines an array of reforms—part of a "holistic democracy agenda"—that attempt to revive the promise of our electoral system, including changes in how we elect our leaders and how we fund their campaigns. The entire plan comes down to an effort to build a Just Democracy movement that aims to inspire peoples' confidence in our beleaguered political system—making an informed, engaged citizenry more likely.*

Democracy in America made a surprising—and welcome—comeback this spring. Many of us assumed the front-loaded primary season meant the contest would be less democratic than ever, but instead Barack Obama and Hillary Clinton were forced to fight the longest and most nationally inclusive race for a presidential nomination in history. About 3.5 million new voters registered and cast ballots, boosting participation among young people and people of color to new highs. More people voted in the Democratic primaries in North Carolina and Indiana than turned out for John Kerry in those states during the 2004 presidential race. The previously untapped

Reprinted from *The Nation* 287, no. 3, July 2008.

potential of our democracy was on full display.

No candidate has spoken to this potential more directly than Obama. Millions of Americans embraced the presumptive Democratic nominee's "firm conviction . . . that working together we can move beyond some of our old racial wounds, and that in fact we have no choice if we are to continue on the path of a more perfect union."

Obama's audacious hope is intoxicating, but that hope must be sustained by a vision of what a more perfect union would look like.

Essential to realizing that vision in the twenty-first century is a transformation that doesn't rank high in any poll or list of probable reforms.

If we are to realize the potential the primary season has revealed and begin moving toward that more perfect union, if we are to finally transcend our downsized politics of excluded alternatives, progressives will have to drive a bold agenda to invigorate democracy at home and capture greater power for the people. There may never be a better time than the next few years.

Some in Washington have touted the export of democracy abroad (often with disastrous results) while they neglect our own. The terrible irony is that they would not grant unconditional funding to a country whose democratic design looks like ours. The machinery of American democracy is broken: mistakes, chicaneries, snafus and disasters debilitate almost every race everywhere, every two years, with the result that an increasing number of Americans report feeling alienated by the voting process.

There are clear signs of the decline of our democracy: registration and voter turnout lag far behind other democracies; ever larger numbers of citizens are disenfranchised; the cost of running for office is spiraling out of control, excluding citizens of average means from participating in government; and our media, the forum for the healthy debate so essential to any democracy, are increasingly incapable of acting in the public interest.

This decline predates the 2000 presidential contest. Some of its roots are found in the invidious history of racial discrimination of which Senator Obama (all too briefly) reminded us. That unresolved election focused attention on our increasingly dysfunctional electoral system and the larger problems of our democracy. The past seven years of extremist Republican rule have stymied every effort to address the flaws that the 2000 election revealed.

Pollsters tell us that "process reforms" don't galvanize voters. Candidates slight them. Pundits often scorn them, assuming that money will always dominate and that corruption is simply a fact of nature. But the primary season just past—which saw Americans of every background and political persuasion becoming experts on superdelegates and tuning in to a live broadcast of the Democratic Party's rules and bylaws committee meeting—suggests that Americans do care about how our elections are run, and that they want them to be fair and functional. Obama—and, for that matter, Republican John McCain, who made his reputation as an election reformer—should, in this election year, address the concerns of millions of Americans about a broken system. And in 2009 progressives should recognize that it is vital to break from cynicism and advance a vision of government that is, in fact, of the people, by the people and for the people. It's time for Just Democracy.

The Crisis

American representative democracy is in trouble. New flash points arise daily; others have been with us for years:

- The Supreme Court recently upheld Indiana's harsh new law requiring voters to present a photo ID or be denied their right to vote, despite its potential to disenfranchise many people. That was a green light for building new barriers to voting.
- The Brennan Center for Justice at the New York University School of Law recently declared Florida to be "the most hostile state in the nation to new voters—particularly in traditionally underserved communities that might otherwise see record-breaking participation in this presidential election year." The number of registered voters in Florida has actually dropped seven percentage points since 2004, to only 65 percent of those eligible.
- Roughly one-third of all eligible Americans, 64 million people, are not registered to vote. This percentage is even higher for African-Americans (30 percent) and Hispanics (40 percent). Shockingly, for those between the ages of 18 and 24, it climbs to 50 percent. Registration rates are directly correlated with income: about 80 percent of those who make $75,000 or more a year are registered to vote, while only about 55 percent of those who make between $15,000 and $24,999 are registered. It's unacceptable for this country's registration rate to be so low.
- The United States is the only democracy in the world that strips the right to vote from citizens who have done time in prison. Fourteen states permanently disenfranchise some citizens; in 2004, these laws stripped 5.3 million Americans with felony convictions—disproportionately but by no means solely African-American and Latino—of the right to vote, even after they had paid their debt to society.
- Many Americans who are registered to vote don't make it to the polls. With only a single day on which to cast their ballot, working people often find themselves without the time to participate in the most basic ritual of our democracy.

Turnout is further suppressed by the increasing obstacles voters face when they try to cast their ballots: whether it's simply the failure to provide enough machines for voting to proceed quickly and efficiently, false notices instructing people to vote on the wrong day or at the wrong place, or bogus robo-calls to voters spreading disinformation and challenges at the polls—primarily targeting African-Americans—we confront a disturbing number of efforts to corrupt our democratic process.

The laws allowing voter challenges are the product of historic efforts to disenfranchise African-Americans. In Ohio the State Assembly first allowed challenges at polling places in 1831; by 1859 possessing a "visible admixture of African blood" was enough to endanger someone's right to vote. Florida allowed challenges for the first time just a year after federal law overruled a state law denying African-American men the right to vote. If these statutes and others like them have been purged of their overt racist bias, they still allow voters of any color to be excluded from the democratic process on the slimmest of pretexts.

Despite much of the mainstream media's eagerness to declare our elections since 2000 a success, too many of the problems that emerged during the 2000 debacle are still with us. In Columbus, Ohio, in 2004 African-American voters waited in line for hours before they could cast their ballots, while voters in white areas voted quickly and easily. In 2006 voters in one predominantly minority jurisdiction in Tennessee waited in line for as long as five and a half hours because of an insufficient number of voting machines. Similar reports were heard from states as diverse as Maryland, Colorado, Georgia, Ohio, Pennsylvania, Illinois, Utah and Massachusetts.

Even when voters are able to cast ballots, they do so without the confidence that their votes will be counted or, ultimately, count. Legitimate fears of easily hacked voting machines that leave no paper trail are exacerbated by a Supreme Court that ordered votes not to be counted in 2000.

That there have been so few serious efforts at the federal level to reform the Electoral College, which played a determining role in the 2000 selection of George W. Bush—who had fewer popular votes than Al Gore—is a disturbing sign that our democracy is unable to respond to the most basic consensus. In the aftermath of the Supreme Court's *Bush v. Gore* decision, which decided the election by awarding Florida's electoral votes to Bush, a Gallup poll summed up fifty years' worth of polling with the judgment that "a majority of Americans have continually expressed support for the notion of an official amendment of the U.S. Constitution that would allow for direct election of the president."

How we wound up with such a convoluted electoral process is a complicated story, but one of the key elements was the desire of the slaveholding states to preserve the influence they had gained through the infamous three-fifths compromise, in which slaves were counted as three-fifths of a person for the purpose of apportioning Representatives to the House. The Electoral College allowed those states to exert that same influence over the selection of the President.

Slavery is long gone, but time has done little to rid the Electoral College of its biases. Whether you live in the District of Columbia (whose citizens are denied voting rights in Congress) or New York City, Los Angeles or Chicago, the Electoral College blatantly privileges the votes of some citizens over others.

How much your vote counts should never depend on where you live. In a country where many of us live in "safe states"—states that aren't contested by the major-party candidates so voting can feel pointless— it is not surprising that in a worldwide survey of voter turnout for national elections since 1945, the United States placed 139th.

As Michael Waldman, executive director of the Brennan Center, observes in his new book, *A Return to Common Sense: Seven Bold Ways to Revitalize Democracy*, "In the United States, a typical off-year election sees turnout at 47 percent. Even in a presidential race, in recent years roughly four out of ten voting-age citizens haven't made it to the polls." Given the partisan divide among the voters who ultimately do make it to the polls, the President is often the choice of no more than a third of eligible American voters. This is not majority rule; it is plurality rule.

In a real democracy voters have a real choice. Under the Constitution, Congress was designed to reflect the diversity of the public, but now the power of incumbency limits the choices available to the people. In the 2004 House elections, only seven of the 399 incumbents running lost their seats. Subtract the four incumbent Texas Democrats whose districts were infamously dismantled by Texas Republican Tom DeLay, and only three incumbents lost—a North Korean-style 99 percent re-election rate. Four of the five national elections between 1996 and 2006 saw more than 98 percent of incumbents hang onto their seats. Even the "blue wave" of 2006 saw just twenty-nine seats in the House change hands. The power of incumbency has calcified our government into a duopoly.

Incumbents derive much of their staying power from the redistricting process, which has increasingly become a bipartisan farce in which the parties collaborate to draw district lines that will preserve their power (or, as DeLay demonstrated, gut the other guy).

Meanwhile, the citadels of incumbency are defended by arsenals of campaign cash. Even in a change election like 2006, the Center for Responsive Politics declared, "money was a clear winner." In 407 of 435 contests for the House, and twenty-four of thirty-three Senate contests, the winner simply outspent the loser. Given the recognition that incumbents already enjoy, they hold a massive advantage over challengers in fundraising; in the past three election cycles Congressional incumbents have raised hundreds of millions more than their opponents. At its source, the money flooding into our campaigns reflects unchecked and overwhelming corporate power; a recent study by the Campaign Finance Institute suggests that "bundlers," who will probably provide more than half the 2008 presidential candidates' staggering campaign contributions, represent only three industries: finance, law and real estate.

For too long, our politicians have been more focused on mobilizing money than the masses. Last November one analyst projected that the 2008 campaign would burn through $5 billion; we are already approaching the $2.5 billion mark.

At the same time, by creating an Internet-based infrastructure that has the potential to bypass the big-money establishment, Obama's campaign has revolutionized the way money is raised for elections. Its extraordinary ability to tap small donors, amassing more than 1.5 million individual donors, 90 percent of whom have given $100 or less, promises to upend old, corrupt ways and make him (and other candidates) less mortgaged to wealthy special interests (even so, 55 percent Obama raised comes from large donors). And commendably, the campaign has cut off lobbyist donations to the Democratic National Committee and discouraged donors from helping "527" shadow operations, named after a provision in the tax code that allows groups to bypass restrictions on spending that is coordinated with parties or candidates. Still, Obama's decision in June to opt out of the public financing system for the general election is likely to boost the role of big special-interest contributions in the campaign.

Despite Obama's challenge to the old order, the system remains entrenched in other ways. The cost of television advertising is one of the most powerful engines of the money chase. Between 2002 and 2006 the already vast sums thrown at television advertising during elections nearly doubled, from $995.5 million to $1.7 billion. Broadcasters took that to the bank: spending on political ads accounted for half their revenue growth in 2001–02 and a jaw-dropping 80 percent of that growth in 2003–04. Not too long ago broadcasters were expected to operate as a public trust;

they had a civic duty to promote public debate. Now elections seem to present little more than an opportunity for the networks to cash in on the crisis of our democracy.

The steadiest opposition to reforming a broken campaign finance system comes from big media companies, particularly those that own television stations, which now derive more than 12 percent of their income in election years from political advertising. As increasingly consolidated media dumb down political coverage—and, in the case of local elections, simply eliminate it—they enable a system in which information about candidates and campaigns comes only in the form of paid propaganda.

The Opportunity

This is not the first time it's been clear that our electoral process demands renewal.

The Nation published clarion calls for change in 2001 and 2004. Now comes a confluence of events that offers an immense opportunity for reform. There's a chance that Obama will become President in 2009, and as a constitutional lawyer with a long record of teaching and action on electoral reform and voting rights, he may well be the best prepared President since the founders to take on the electoral process. And he could have a Congress in 2009 that is particularly well suited to act in alliance with a progressive administration.

Just a century ago progressive forces brought about a flurry of constitutional amendments, including women's suffrage and direct election of senators. We have a similar opportunity to pass the reforms that will build a more just democracy. A prodemocracy movement already has the grassroots and netroots in place, as well as the principles and concrete proposals. It will take political will, savvy strategy and hard-nosed organizing. That organizing should be integrated into the 2008 campaign, and it should continue after this year's voting is done.

The first challenge such a prodemocracy movement faces is crafting an agenda for people to rally behind, one to which they can hold their representatives accountable and one that captures the popular imagination. All too often democracy reformers find themselves fighting separate battles—over voting, campaign finance and media, to name a few—that are really part of a single war. When these issues are isolated from one another, arguments over policy quickly turn them into an insiders' fight—a fight that reformers have a tough time winning. Instead of repeatedly waging the same battles on ever narrower ground and debating the minutiae of policy, reformers must mobilize a popular movement that sees the links between these issues.

By developing a holistic democracy agenda, the larger public-interest and progressive community can unify and amplify particular issues—healthcare, the environment, an end to reckless wars and economic injustice. Of course, we all know how hard it is to break out of our silos. But if we are going to be stronger than the sum of our parts, it's crucial that we recognize our common stake in revitalizing our democratic process. That will free all of us to take on and defeat the powerful interests that dominate our broken democracy.

We need leaders like elder statesmen Bill Moyers and Al Gore as well as younger activists like Van Jones, Majora Carter and Stephanie Moore, who have emerged from a generation committed to a principled and participatory politics. We also need tough-minded commitment by activists on the ground and on the web to drive this agenda into the debate and out to the people, and the willingness to challenge the progressive organizations we've supported for years, our most trusted champions, to devote resources and energy to this cause and then use their power to hold politicians accountable.

All these measures are critical to changing our political landscape. And they are more possible in an era when tools like the Internet can promote change and connections among reformers. For a start, new online-offline combinations, using social networking, can create communities that would have been impossible to tap just a few years ago. Internet dynamo Lawrence Lessig's new group Change Congress (change-congress.org) has the potential to organize in new and pathbreaking ways. Linked to the online-offline strategy of building new communities and tapping into existing ones, building Just Democracy should be an integral part of the work done by a broad range of groups, from the NAACP to the League of Conservation Voters to the AFL-CIO to the League of Young Voters to Media Matters. Candidates who block reform should be challenged. We need an idealistic movement and a savvy operation with a long-term strategy.

What would a core agenda be? How about Just Democracy—a program to ensure that every voter can vote, that every vote gets counted, that money talks no louder than the many and that every challenger gets to make his or her case? Media reform is a piece of the puzzle, of course, as Robert McChesney and John Nichols have outlined in our pages. So too is party reform: how can a party that calls itself "Democratic" make unelected superdelegates defining players in its nominating process? There is no need to separate those necessary reforms, but my focus here is on the most important elements of a program to revitalize our electoral process.

Many of them are embodied in legislative proposals that have already been introduced in Congress. The long work of perfecting our democracy begins here.

Count Every Vote

The Help America Vote Act (HAVA) was intended to assuage Americans' fears that their votes might not be counted. Passed in 2002, it ranks somewhere between a disappointment and a fiasco. HAVA was a step in the right direction of establishing national standards—from voting machines to provisional ballots to paper trails to poll-worker training and voter protection—but it was not empowered to enforce crucial reforms, and it lacked a federal commitment to help states pay for elections.

There have been many legislative attempts to address the shortcomings of HAVA—including Senator Clinton and Representative Stephanie Tubbs Jones's Count Every Vote Act. So far, however, there has been no real movement on the issue. A new Congress, working with a committed President and an energized popular movement, could push through this legislation and, with it, genuine election reform.

Fix Black-Box Voting

Understandably, many prodemocracy advocates who make up the self-described Election Integrity Movement have focused their attention on the unreliability of voting machines manufactured by Diebold, Sequoia, ES&S and other corporations.

HAVA supported states in updating voting machines (without specifying the type of machine) and provided funding to reach that goal. But in a glaring omission, it was left to the states to mandate a paper trail confirming for voters that their ballots had been cast as intended.

In December Ohio's new Secretary of State, Jennifer Brunner, issued a report declaring that "critical security failures" "could impact the integrity of elections in the Buckeye State." And she made some good recommendations for how to proceed. Most important, Brunner—as California Secretary of State Debra Bowen and Minnesota Secretary of State Mark Ritchie have already done—supports switching from touch-screens to optical-scan machines, which read ballots voters mark by hand like a standardized test. Optical scans are far more trustworthy and cost-effective than touch-screens—and they provide a record of each vote. A significant number of states still use touch-screen voting machines that do not produce paper trails—indispensable records that can be audited to double-check the results recorded by the computers. These systems are simply too unreliable to trust, given what we know about electronic voting. It's long past time for states and the federal government to standardize one publicly reviewed open-source hardware and software design for all voting machines and to end the grip of the corporate voting machine cartel on our elections.

We need a secure paper trail on all votes cast. As Representative Rush Holt points out, election results for six states and those for counties in another fourteen states could not be audited if the election were held today. His Emergency Assistance for Secure Elections Act (HR 5036) deserves support. It is an optional program that would allow states or jurisdictions to be reimbursed for the expense of providing paper ballots and/or conducting audits of election results. Despite initial bipartisan support for the bill, some of the same Republican Representatives who voted to release it from committee turned around and voted against the bill when it reached the House floor, in a gross display of the obstructionism with which the GOP has met nearly every effort at reform.

Holt has also proposed the Voter Confidence and Increased Accessibility Act (HR 811, with 216 sponsors—nearly half the House, including at least twenty Republicans), which would require all voting systems to provide a voter-verified paper trail to serve as the official ballot for recounts and audits, a valuable short-term measure worthy of support. The ultimate solution to the problem of electronic voting is a national law requiring voter-verified paper records, which should be the primary source for tabulating votes, backed up by mandatory recounts. This is Just Democracy.

Every bit as important as our unreliable voting systems is the relatively low-tech measure of ensuring that every polling place has an adequate number of machines and poll workers. That anyone should have to wait in line for five and a half hours is a disgrace. States should establish formulas for voting machine and poll worker allocation that take into account a variety of demographic and voting factors, not just the number of registered voters at some arbitrary cut-off date.

End the 'Voter Fraud' Fraud

For too many years, American politics has been divided between two types of people: those who want more people to vote and those who want fewer people to vote.

Recently the Bush-packed Supreme Court issued a disturbing ruling in favor of the kind of law we've become all too familiar with. This time the offending legislation was from Indiana, which has mandated that voters present an official ID at the polls, putting even more obstacles in the way of people who simply want to cast a ballot.

Not surprisingly, the Bush Administration's Justice Department sided with this thinly-veiled attempt to discourage election day turnout by folks believed to skew Democratic: the poor, the elderly, the young and minority voters. Arguing in support of the State of Indiana, the Administration claimed that "a state need not wait to suffer harm; it can adopt prophylactic measures to prevent it from occurring in the first place."

Talking loosely about "voter fraud" when we really mean election fraud helps reinforce the impression that the former is widespread. It is not. Voter fraud—the impersonation of a voter by another person—is extremely rare in the United States. Proposals to institute forms of voter identification, such as Arizona's requirement that people present proof of citizenship in order to register, do very little to curtail fraud. They can, however, do an excellent job of disenfranchising the 11 percent of citizens—more than 21 million people—who do not have a government-issued photo ID. The cost of acquiring such identification essentially constitutes an insidious poll tax. That's why we need a Summer 2008 project to get picture IDs to poor, elderly and minority voters.

The resurgence of election fraud rooted in the racist practices of the past is a far more imminent threat. A new Congress should pass Obama's Deceptive Practices and Voter Intimidation Prevention Act (S 453, with one Republican and nineteen Democratic sponsors). Passed in the House in June of last year as HR 1281, this legislation would not only make the dirty-trick politics of voter intimidation and misinformation illegal but, just as important, it would require election administrators to work with the community to ensure that corrected information is disseminated to voters in the affected area.

Passing this legislation would begin to redress the shameful neglect of civil rights shown by the Bush Administration. From 2001 to 2006, the voting section of the civil rights division of Bush's Justice Department brought only two voting discrimination cases on behalf of African-American voters, one of which was initiated during the Clinton years. A prodemocracy White House must appoint officials committed to protecting the right to vote.

Re-enfranchise Citizens

In the twenty-first century, the other America is behind bars, literally and figuratively: with one of every 100 Americans in prison, we are establishing a perverse parallel America—a predominantly nonwhite one—and making it permanent by stripping those consigned there of the right to vote. It's a hopeful sign that a growing number of states are re-enfranchising ex-felons. Vermont, Maine and Puerto Rico never deny citizens the right to vote and even allow prisoners to vote from jail, while sixteen other states as well as the District of Columbia allow citizens to vote who are on probation or parole or who have been released from prison. Recognizing the right of ex-felons to vote would grant them the power to contest this status for others and help reintegrate them into society.

There are other second-class citizens in our country. Most egregiously, the mostly African-American population of the District of Columbia is denied representation in Congress. While the House voted in 2007 to allow the District a voting Representative in that chamber, the motion failed to pass the Senate by three votes.

Popularly Elect Our Presidents

The President is the only elected official whose office is intended to embody the will of the people as a whole. And yet we still maintain the Electoral College, which can override the people's will. We may have consigned the three-fifths compromise to history, but the Electoral College means that some people's votes count less than others'. Reform is long overdue, and the presidential election process has vast potential for transformative change right now.

The transpartisan push for a National Popular Vote for President is gaining traction. It would allow for the nationwide popular election for President to be implemented without amending the Constitution. States would pass identical laws by which they agree to award all their electoral votes to the presidential candidate who receives the most popular votes in all states and the District of Columbia. This interstate compact would go into effect only when it has been enacted by enough states—that is, those possessing a majority (currently 270) of the electoral votes. NPV has been endorsed by leading Republicans and Democrats, newspapers like the *New York Times* and *Los Angeles Times* and hundreds of legislators in forty states. In April 2007 Maryland became the first state to pass the legislation; since then, Illinois, New Jersey and Hawaii have followed suit. Eight states have passed NPV legislation in at least one chamber of their legislature. In June Florida Senator Bill Nelson proposed legislation to abolish the Electoral College. FairVote's executive director, Rob Richie, who has championed NPV, believes "we'll have it by 2012"—finally modernizing what he calls "an eighteenth-century way of structuring elections."

This bold step into the twenty-first century would redraw and expand the horizons of the possible, immediately bringing in millions of voters routinely ignored when candidates focus on a few battleground states—sixteen in 2004—that increasingly settle modern presidential campaigns. Passage of NPV could also be the catalyst that advances many of the other proposals suggested here. For the first time in history, votes would be counted across state lines, providing further impetus for reform at the federal level.

Guarantee the Right to Vote

The right to vote is a rallying cry for a prodemocracy movement. Most Americans don't realize that the right to vote is not enshrined in our Constitution. Nor do they understand that our voting system is a shocking patchwork of rules. As Representative Jesse Jackson Jr. has written in *The Nation*: "Our voting system's foundation is built on the sand of states' rights and local control. We have fifty states, 3,141 counties and 7,800 different local election jurisdictions. All separate and unequal."

In the long term, a constitutional amendment guaranteeing every citizen the right to vote would finally place our democracy on a sturdy foundation. With the passage of such an amendment, citizens could use the courts to demand equal protection of that right— it would be an invaluable tool for establishing national standards for voting systems, fighting disenfranchisement and ultimately ensuring that every vote counts and is counted correctly. The organizing campaign around a constitutional amendment could also provide a valuable long-term strategy for achieving Just Democracy.

Say Farewell to Katherine Harris

Even as our right to vote has slowly been eroded, it has become increasingly evident that our system of election administration is riddled with flaws. That any state's top election official could also be the state chair for a presidential campaign—as was infamously the case in Florida in 2000 with Katherine Harris and in Ohio in 2004 with Kenneth Blackwell—is a gross conflict of interest that should be illegal. Election officials should be barred from participating in campaigns, and we need to establish strict conflict-of-interest laws. It's exciting that some recently elected secretaries of state are among the democracy movement's savviest allies. For example, Minnesota's Mark Ritchie, who ran the nonpartisan voter registration and mobilization group National Voice in 2003, won in 2006 on an inventive platform designed to repair—not exploit—the vulnerabilities of our electoral system.

Adopt Election Day Registration

Many voters are in effect stripped of their right to vote by our voter registration system. They discover only when they arrive at the polls that they're not on the rolls, or they're forced by bureaucratic bungling to cast a provisional ballot that isn't guaranteed to be counted. And yet local governments have little difficulty sending out notices for jury duty. Why don't we have the same capacity to register citizens to vote?

Under any opt-in system, even with the most comprehensive outreach plans, there will be citizens who neglect to register, to say nothing of botched registrations. Minnesota's Ritchie has a good idea: make registration at Departments of Motor Vehicles an opt-out process rather than opt-in. That is, you must check a box if you do *not* want to be registered to vote; if you don't check the box, you'll automatically be registered. Most states didn't even require voters to register before the 1870s; they instituted registration as new waves of immigrants arrived on our shores and former slaves joined the electorate. Many of the world's democracies practice universal registration, which assumes that it is the duty of the state to promote the involvement of its citizens, who are therefore automatically registered when they reach voting age. This idea isn't entirely foreign to the United States—while it's alone among the states, North Dakota has the distinction of not even requiring registration to vote. There's no reason this shouldn't be true in the other forty-nine states.

Steven Hill, director of the Political Reform Program with the centrist New America Foundation, projects that universal registration could give 50 million Americans the chance to vote. "Voting is a right, not a privilege," the Brennan

Center's Michael Waldman observes. "We should recognize that individuals ought not to be charged with figuring out how to register and stay registered. And we should commit to the idea that in a democracy, the government has a duty, moral and legal, to make it possible for every eligible citizen to be able to vote." Waldman argues that universal registration could be the basis for a "grand bargain" between progressives and conservatives, simultaneously addressing the former's demand for access and the latter's desire for security (by making the government responsible for a national voter list). And while we're at it, let's lower the age for registering to vote to 16. We could even preregister young voters to ensure that they have the chance to make their voices heard. If we can register them for Selective Service, we can certainly register them to elect those who represent them in office. And how about retrieving Jesse Jackson's idea of every public high school student graduating with "a diploma in one hand and a voter card in the other"? It could start this fall, with the public school systems and their elected leaders, principals and union officials taking the lead on it this summer.

Short of abolishing registration entirely, allowing citizens to register up until—and even on—election day is one of the few measures guaranteed to boost turnout. Just over half the states cut off registration at least twenty-five days before an election, barring otherwise eligible voters from participating just when competition between candidates (and media coverage) intensifies.

Election Day Registration clearly demonstrates that many people who hope to vote on Election Day wind up being turned away at the polls. For more than twenty-five years, states with EDR have consistently boasted higher turnout than states without it. In 2004 average turnout was 12 percent higher in states with EDR than in those without it; in 2006 the seven states with EDR averaged a 10 percent greater turnout. Senators Russ Feingold and Amy Klobuchar, with Representative Keith Ellison, have introduced legislation to allow EDR for all elections to federal office. Should the bill pass, the lack of EDR at the local and state level will be that much harder to justify.

And finally, why should Election Day be on Tuesday? That day was originally chosen because it was convenient; it gave a nation of farmers time to get to the polls without interfering with the three days of worship. We're no longer a nation of farmers, and having to go to the polls in the middle of a workweek is far from convenient. One possible solution would be to finally declare Election Day a national holiday. Such a "deliberation day," as one proposal has dubbed it, would not only ease crowds at the polls but also provide a powerful reaffirmation of the importance of voting and our commitment to democracy. Instead of making voting one more item on a list of errands, we could make it the most important act of a day devoted to democracy.

End the Party Duopoly

For the first time in nearly a century more than a quarter of American voters are not registered as either Republicans or Democrats. During the 2004 presidential campaign, one poll suggested 57 percent of voters thought candidates besides Bush and Kerry should be included in the debates. In the latest biannual survey from Harvard's Institute of Politics of 18- to 24-year-olds, 37 percent of young voters agreed that there was a need for a third party.

If majority rule is to be more than a hollow slogan and third parties more than "spoilers," we need to experiment with more accurate ways to represent the diversity of backgrounds, perspectives and opinions of the American people. Proportional representation—in which 10 percent of the vote wins 10 percent of the seats—is one way. But the United States is an outlier when it comes to PR. We're one of the few "advanced" democracies that don't use it in national elections. But PR isn't as alien as it might seem: Cambridge, Massachusetts, has used a proportional voting scheme to elect its City Council for seven decades. Illinois used a similar system to elect its lower house from 1870 to 1980, and it enjoys broad bipartisan support. As opposed to our winner-take-all system, in which a mere plurality of voters can carry an election, full representation allows for the expression of a broader range of interests.

The Democrats' use of proportional representation in their nominating process gives a sense of what it means: every vote counts, no matter how lopsided the result might be in any district or state.

Although not as radical a departure as proportional representation, instant runoff voting (IRV)—in which low-scoring candidates are eliminated and their supporters' second-choice votes are added to those that remain, until one candidate wins a majority—is another way to challenge the duopoly while protecting majority rule for all.

Backed by groups like FairVote and the New America Foundation, IRV also has the support of McCain and Obama, along with Democratic National Committee chair Howard Dean and third-party candidates like Libertarian Bob Barr, the Green Party's Cynthia McKinney and Ralph Nader.

And instant runoff voting has begun to catch on with the public. IRV has won thirteen of the last fourteen times it appeared on a ballot, winning landslides in cities like Oakland (69 percent), Minneapolis (65 percent), Sarasota (78 percent) and Santa Fe (65 percent). San Francisco just held its fourth IRV election, and exit polls have found it popular there with every measurable demographic. This fall, Pierce County, Washington, with a population of nearly 800,000, will use it for the first time for a hotly contested county executive election. And new cities voting to adopt it will include Glendale, California; St. Paul, Minnesota; and Memphis, Tennessee. A bill instituting IRV for Congressional elections in Vermont was vetoed by that state's Republican governor but will be back next year.

Finally, fusion voting has the weight of long experience behind it. Before the twentieth century, it was a frequent tool of emerging parties, until major parties started banning it. Fusion allows two or more parties to nominate the same candidate on separate ballot lines. That simple change permits people to vote their values without "wasting" their vote or supporting "spoilers." The positive experience of New York's Working Families Party in the past decade shows you can build a viable minority party this way. And fusion has also helped progressives focus on the challenge of building majorities in a winner-take-all system. These options would dramatically open our electoral system to more choices, ensuring the representation of diverse views instead of seeing them co-opted or suppressed by the "least worst" options presented by the duopoly.

Money, Money, Money

Our representatives should represent all of us, not just big-money donors who can afford to buy access. Restoring accountability and responsiveness depends on cleansing politics of the influence of money. Full public financing for campaigns would free the best of our elected officials from that influence and increase the power of people over our representatives—or even let them *become* representatives; full public financing is almost the only way for citizens of average means to run for office.

The good news is that signs of discontent are clear. Americans of diverse backgrounds are fed up with politicians who don't listen to them, who don't care about them and who don't respond to their concerns. Clear majorities favor reforms such as public financing of campaigns. A survey conducted on behalf of pro-democracy groups like Public Campaign and Common Cause found that a full 74 percent of voters favor a voluntary system of public funding for elections (with only 16 percent opposed). This support stretches across party lines, netting 80 percent of Democrats, 78 percent of Independents and 65 percent of Republicans.

The not-so-good news: public financing in the form of matching funds has been available to presidential candidates since the mid-1970s, but as the primary season drags on ever longer and the cost of television airtime has skyrocketed, the need for campaign cash has become ever more desperate, causing candidates increasingly to opt out of the system. As Nick Nyhart, executive director of Public Campaign, put it, "The system is broken and badly needs an overhaul."

And we need to update the system: various modernizing reforms, among other provisions, are included in the Presidential Funding Act (S 436), introduced in the Senate by Russ Feingold and, ironically, Barack Obama. Because Obama is the first presidential candidate to opt out of public financing for a general election, it is incumbent on him to commit to making passage of comprehensive and updated public financing of all federal elections a top priority.

Short of introducing a system of full public financing, one modest proposal to reduce fundraising pressures would be to increase dramatically the amount a candidate receives for donations of $100 or less, by matching such donations on a 1:4 basis (this could be reinforced by eliminating matching funds for donations of more than $100). This simple formula could serve as the basis for a system of public financing of Congressional elections as well. Candidates would then have a greater incentive to cultivate small donors, restoring some degree of sanity to the fundraising process. Another way to decrease the pressure for campaign cash: guarantee free airtime to qualified candidates and make that airtime a condition for FCC renewal of lucrative TV and radio licenses.

For too long, the fundraising arms race has deterred Congress from taking meaningful steps to overhaul this dysfunctional system. Fortunately the convergence of democratic ideals and pragmatic considerations wrought by fundraising fatigue—key senators lament that they spend almost a third of their time raising money—has led to two excellent bills with impressive sponsorship. Senators Dick Durbin and Arlen Specter's Fair Elections

Now Act has garnered eight co-sponsors, including Obama (the first co-sponsor). In the House the Clean Money, Clean Elections Act of 2007 has fifty-five co-sponsors. Under both these bills, candidates who show a qualifying level of support and opt out of further private contributions would be supported by public funding.

Until now, however, the most promising and smartest experiments with voluntary systems of public financing have come from the states. In Arizona, where qualified candidates have been able to take advantage of public financing since the 2000 election, 42 percent of the State Legislature has been elected using public funds. In Maine, which inaugurated its public funding system four years earlier, 84 percent of the State Legislature has been elected using matching funds. Connecticut, New Jersey and New Mexico all have Clean Elections statutes.

Maine's experience with Clean Elections also suggests that these reforms successfully promote diversity. Eighteen percent more women have run for office since the reforms were enacted than in the decade before. In Arizona's 2006 primary, 69 percent of female candidates (as opposed to 52 percent of male candidates) took advantage of the state's public funding, and the percentage of minority candidates went from 6 percent in 2000 to 14 percent in 2006.

Meanwhile, analysis suggests that Latino communities and people with low incomes are much more actively involved as donors in Arizona's Clean Elections than they are in the privately financed campaigns in the state. The success of bringing more diverse, less affluent candidates into politics has led reform groups to downplay the fight against corruption and focus more on why change is necessary to give ordinary people more representation, voice and, yes, power in the electoral process.

The Way Forward

The Congressional Progressive Caucus could take the first step, calling on Democratic leaders to support the agenda detailed here. It could then be introduced in Congress as a package of bills, with the CPC demanding a roll-call vote on each. There should be a balance between paving the way for far-reaching change and reforms we can win now. Already Senator Bill Nelson's One Person, One Vote Initiative shows how a compelling package of reforms can enhance the case for each of its elements.

Meanwhile, campaigns should push this agenda in the states and at the grassroots, enlisting a broad coalition—beginning with voting, civil rights and media groups, along with the new secretaries of state—to organize in every district. (*AlterNet* is publishing a book, *Count My Vote*, that will be an invaluable resource for grassroots activists. It compiles the voting regulations of every state and offers sections exploring the unique situations of everyone from students to seniors to new voters.) Those politicians who vote against democracy should be targeted and made examples of, with the coalition fielding and supporting challengers to go after their seats. The muscle is there; it just has to be flexed.

Before the Voting Rights Act was passed, President Lyndon Johnson is said to have urged Dr. Martin Luther King Jr. to go out there and make it possible for him to do the right thing. Our elected representatives need pressure from a broad-based movement—reaching from the grassroots to the halls of Congress—if they're going to champion Just Democracy. Enlisting the netroots and the blogosphere, along with the progressive media, will be vital in getting the word out. The new democracy will come only when the defenders of the citadels of privilege find they are threatened on the terms of the old system. We're calling for radical democracy, birthed by bare-knuckled politics.

Admittedly, defining an agenda and building a movement is just a beginning; the fight will be long and hard. Few politicians have been willing to take the lead in calling for the measures proposed here. Trapped in the rapidly escalating race of campaign finance, who will set aside the weapons of dollars and incumbency to rebuild a truly representative democracy? If they won't do it, we will.

A Just Democracy movement will require idealism and diligent organizing; it will demand a broad coalition committed to making these reforms a high priority. Working together, we can repair the broken system we've been handed and confront the crisis of disenfranchisement that has overtaken our democracy. We want 100 percent registration. We want increased participation. We want full representation with majority rule. We want the right to vote. We want to vote without fear—that our votes will not count, or be counted by hacked machines.

It is long past time to place democracy at the center of our politics, where it belongs. We don't exist just to curse the political darkness but to craft solutions to make America a more perfect union.

Discussion Questions

1. Explain the main contours of the crisis in the American electoral system, as discussed by vanden Heuvel. Delineate between deep-rooted historical issues and more recent ones. At one point she observes: "The machinery of American democracy is broken." Are you surprised by any of these problems? Have you encountered any of them?

2. According to vanden Heuvel, the "opportunity" we now have is to mobilize people to demand and support a broad agenda of electoral reform. Discuss her proposed reforms. Which seem most likely to succeed? Are any of these reforms more difficult to envision than others?

Interest Groups

10   The Logic of Collective Action

Mancur Olson

It's just common sense. If I am a Democrat, and the Democratic Party actually promotes my interests, then I will contribute to my party's efforts. Right? Wrong. This negative reply is the conclusion of University of Maryland economist Mancur Olson, who says that people do not act in groups in the manner in which they have traditionally been thought to act. Much of what is written in economics and political science is based upon the rational actor theory, which states that under normal conditions people will act in their own interests. Much of what is called organizational theory also accepts the idea that at least some "group think" occurs in organizations. Group think means that people tend to take on the attitudes of other members of the groups they join. If both rationality and group think operate most of the time, then most members of most organizations should actively work to help their organizations succeed without either personal reward or coercion. Olson concludes, however, that this automatic support for organizations occurs much less frequently than we should expect. Olson then proceeds to tell us why this is so.

*I*t is often taken for granted, at least where economic objectives are involved, that groups of individuals with common interests usually attempt to further those common interests. Groups of individuals with common interests are expected to act on behalf of their personal interests. This opinion . . . has, in addition, occupied a prominent place in political science, at least in the United States, where the study of pressure groups has been dominated by a celebrated "group theory" based on the idea that groups will act when necessary to further their common or group goals. . . .

. . . The view that groups act to serve their interests, presumably, is based upon the assumption that the individuals in groups act out of self-interest. If the individuals in a group altruistically disregarded their personal welfare, it would not be very likely that collectively they would seek some selfish common or group objective. Such altruism, is, however, considered exceptional, and self interested behavior is usually thought to be the rule, at least when economic issues are at stake; no one is surprised when individual businessmen seek higher profits, when individual workers seek higher wages, or when individual consumers seek lower prices. The idea that groups tend to act in support of their group interests is supposed to follow logically from this widely accepted premise of rational, self-interested behavior. In other words, if the members of some group have a

Reprinted from *The Logic of Collective Action: Public Goods and the Theory of Groups*, 1965, Harvard University Press.

common interest or objective, and if they would all be better off if that objective were achieved, it has been thought to follow logically that the individuals in that group would, if they were rational and self-interested, act to achieve that objective.

But it is *not* in fact true that the idea that groups will act in their self-interest follows logically from the premise of rational and self-interested behavior. It does *not* follow, because all of the individuals in a group would gain if they achieved their group objectives, that they would act to achieve that objective, even if they were all rational and self-interested. Indeed, unless the number of individuals in a group is quite small, or unless there is coercion or some other special device to make individuals act in their common interest, *rational, self-interested individuals will not act to achieve their common or group interests*. In other words, even if all of the individuals in a large group are rational and self-interested, and they would gain if, as a group, they acted to achieve their common interest or objective, they still will not voluntarily act to achieve their common or group interest. The notion that groups of individuals will act to achieve their common or groups interests, far from being a logical implication of the assumption that the individuals in a group will rationally further their individual interests, is in fact inconsistent with that assumption.

. . . If the members of a large group rationally seek to maximize their personal welfare, they will not act to advance their common or group objectives unless there is coercion to force them to do so, or unless some separate incentive, distinct from the achievement of the common or group interest, is offered to the members of the group individually on the condition that they help bear the costs or burdens involved in the achievement of the group objectives. Nor will such large groups form organizations to further their common goals in the absence of coercion or the separate incentives just mentioned. These points hold true even when there is unanimous agreement in a group about the common good and the methods of achieving it.

The widespread view, common throughout the social science, that groups tend to further their interests, is accordingly unjustified, at least when it is based, as it usually is, on the (sometimes implicit) assumption that groups act in their self-interest because individuals do. There is paradoxically the logical possibility that groups composed of either altruistic individuals or irrational individuals may sometimes act in their common or group interests. . . . Thus the customary view that groups of individuals with common interests tend to further those common interests appears to have little if any merit.

★ **Mancur Olson,** *distinguished professor of economics at the University of Maryland until his death in 1998, is recognized as one of a handful of scholars responsible for changing the field of economics to ensure that politics became an integral part of economic thinking and policy formation. The founder of and principal investigator for the Center for Institutional Reform and the Informal Sector (IRIS), Olson worked closely with governmental leaders and other decision-makers to help them understand that a country's economic policies and institutions principally determine its economic performance. His works include* The Logic of Collective Action *and* The Rise and Decline of Nations, *both considered seminal works in economics and political science.*

Questions

1. What is Olson's explanation for the failure of rational self-interest to adequately explain group behavior?

2. What are the factors that, according to Olson, actually influence the behavior of individuals in most organizations?

3. Under what conditions does nationalism have its greatest effect upon national political organizations?

Voting and Elections

11 *The Responsible Electorate*

V. O. Key, Jr.

In his reflective moments even the most experienced politician senses a nagging curiosity about why people vote as they do. His power and his position depend upon the outcome of the mysterious rites we perform as opposing candidates harangue the multitudes who finally march to the polls to prolong the rule of their champion, to thrust him, ungratefully, back into the void of private life, or to raise to eminence a new tribune of the people. What kinds of appeals enable a candidate to win the favor of the great god, The People? What circumstances move voters to shift their preferences in this direction or that? What clever propaganda tactic or slogan led to this result? What mannerism of oratory or style of rhetoric produced another outcome? What band of electors rallied to this candidate to save the day for him? What policy of state attracted the devotion of another bloc of voters? What action repelled a third sector of the electorate?

The victorious candidate may claim with assurance that he has the answers to all such questions. He may regard his success as vindication of his beliefs about why voters vote as they do. And he may regard the swing of the vote to him as indubitably a response to the campaign positions he took, as an indication of the acuteness of his intuitive estimates of the mood of the people, and as a ringing manifestation of the esteem in which he is held by a discriminating public. This narcissism assumes its most repulsive form among election winners who have championed intolerance, who have stirred the passions and hatreds of people, or who have advocated causes known by decent men to be outrageous or dangerous in their long-run consequences. No functionary is more repugnant or more arrogant than the unjust man who asserts, with a color of truth, that he speaks from a pedestal of popular approbation.

It thus can be a mischievous error to assume, because a candidate wins, that a majority of the electorate shares his views on public questions, approves his past actions, or has specific expectations about his future conduct. Nor does victory establish that the candidate's campaign strategy, his image, his television style, or his fearless stand against cancer and polio turned the trick. The election returns establish only that a winner attracted a majority of votes—assuming the existence of a modicum of rectitude in election administration. They tell us precious little about why the plurality was his.

Reprinted from *The Responsible Electorate: Rationality in Presidential Voting, 1936-1960* (1966), Harvard University Press.

For a glaringly obvious reason, electoral victory cannot be regarded as necessarily a popular ratification of a candidate's outlook. The voice of the people is but an echo. The output of an echo chamber bears an inevitable and invariable relation to the input. As candidates and parties clamor for attention and vie for popular support, the people's verdict can be no more than a selective reflection from among the alternatives and outlooks presented to them. Even the most discriminating popular judgment can reflect only ambiguity, uncertainty, or even foolishness if those are the qualities of the input into the echo chamber. A candidate may win despite his tactics and appeals rather than because of them. If the people can choose only from among rascals, they are certain to choose a rascal.

Scholars, though they have less at stake than do politicians, also have an abiding curiosity about why voters act as they do. In the past quarter of a century they have vastly enlarged their capacity to check the hunches born of their curiosities. The invention of the sample survey—the most widely known example of which is the Gallup poll—enabled them to make fairly trustworthy estimates of the characteristics and behaviors of large human populations. This method of mass observation revolutionized the study of politics—as well as the management of political campaigns. The new technique permitted large-scale tests to check the validity of old psychological and sociological theories of human behavior. These tests led to new hunches and new theories about voting behavior, which could in turn, be checked and which thereby contributed to the extraordinary ferment in the social sciences during recent decades.

The studies of electoral behavior by survey methods cumulate into an imposing body of knowledge which conveys a vivid impression of the variety and subtlety of factors that enter into individual voting decisions. In their first stages in the 1930s the new electoral studies chiefly lent precision and verification to the working maxims of practicing politicians and to some of the crude theories of political speculators. Thus, sample surveys established that people did, indeed, appear to vote their pocketbooks. Yet the demonstration created its embarrassments because it also established that exceptions to the rule were numerous. Not all factory workers, for example, voted alike. How was the behavior of the deviants from "group interest" to be explained? Refinement after refinement of theory and analysis added complexity to the original simple explanation. By introducing a bit of psychological theory it could be demonstrated that factory workers with optimistic expectations tended less to be governed by pocketbook considerations than did those whose outlook was gloomy. When a little social psychology was stirred into the analysis, it could be established that identifications formed early in life, such as attachments to political parties, also reinforced or resisted the pull of the interest of the moment. A sociologist, bringing to play the conceptual tools of his trade, then could show that those factory workers who associate intimately with like-minded persons on the average vote with greater solidarity than do social isolates. Inquiries conducted with great ingenuity along many such lines have enormously broadened our knowledge of the factors associated with the responses of people to the stimuli presented to them by political campaigns.

Yet, by and large, the picture of the voter that emerges from a combination of the folklore of practical politics and the findings of the new electoral studies is not a pretty one. It is not a portrait of citizens moving to considered decision as they play their solemn role of making and unmaking governments. The older tradition from practical politics may regard the voter as an erratic and irrational fellow susceptible to manipulation by skilled humbugs. One need not live through many campaigns to observe politicians, even successful politicians, who act as though they regarded the people as manageable fools. Nor does a heroic conception of the voter emerge from the new analyses of electoral behavior. They can be added up to a conception of voting not as a civic decision but as an almost purely deterministic act. Given knowledge of certain characteristics of a voter—his occupation, his residence, his religion, his national origin, and perhaps certain of his attributes—one can predict with a high probability the direction of his vote. The actions of persons are made to appear to be only predictable and automatic responses to campaign stimuli.

Most findings of the analysts of voting never travel beyond the circle of the technicians; the popularizers, though, give wide currency to the most bizarre—and most dubious—theories of electoral behavior. Public-relations experts share in the process of dissemination as they sell their services to politicians (and succeed in establishing that politicians are sometimes as gullible as businessmen). Reporters pick up the latest psychological secret from campaign managers and spread it through a larger public. Thus, at one time a goodly proportion of the literate population must have placed some store in the theory that the electorate was a pushover for a candidate who projected an appropriate "father image." At another stage, the "sincere" candidate supposedly had an overwhelming advantage. And even so kindly a gentleman as General Eisenhower was said to have an especial attractiveness to those of authoritarian personality within the electorate.

Conceptions and theories of the way voters behave do not raise solely arcane problems to be disputed among the democratic and antidemocratic theorists or questions to be settled by the elegant techniques of the analysts of electoral behavior. Rather, they touch upon profound issues at the heart of the problem of the nature and workability of systems of popular government. Obviously the perceptions of the behavior of the electorate held by political leaders, agitators, and activists condition if they do not fix, the types of appeals politicians employ as they seek popular support. These perceptions—or theories—affect the nature of the input to the echo chamber, if we may revert to our earlier figure, and thereby control its output. They may govern, too, the kinds of actions that governments take as they look forward to the next election. If politicians perceive the electorate as responsive to father images, they will give it father images. If they see voters as most certainly responsive to nonsense, they will give them nonsense. If they see voters as susceptible to delusion, they will delude them. If they see an electorate receptive to the cold, hard realities, they will give it the cold, hard realities.

In short, theories of how voters behave acquire importance not because of their effects on voters, who may proceed blithely unaware of them. They gain significance because of their effects, both potentially and in reality, on candidates and other political leaders. If leaders believe the route to victory is by projection of images and cultivation of styles rather than by advocacy of policies to cope with the problems of the country, they will project images and cultivate styles to the neglect of the substance of politics. They will abdicate their prime function in a democratic system, which amounts, in essence, to the assumption of the risk of trying to persuade us to lift ourselves by our bootstraps.

Among the literary experts on politics there are those who contend that, because of the development of tricks of the manipulation of the masses, practices of political leadership in the management of voters have moved far toward the conversion of election campaigns into obscene parodies of the models set up by democratic idealists. They point to the good old days when politicians were deep thinkers, eloquent orators, and farsighted statesmen. Such estimates of the course of change in social institutions must be regarded with reserve. They may be only manifestations of the inverted optimism of aged and melancholy men who, estopped from hope for the future, see in the past a satisfaction of their yearning for greatness in our political life.

Whatever the trends may have been, the perceptions that leadership elements of democracies hold of the modes of response of the electorate must always be a matter of fundamental significance. Those perceptions determine the nature of the voice of the people, for they determine the character of the input into the echo chamber. While the output may be governed by the nature of the input, over the longer run the properties of the echo chamber may themselves be altered. Fed a steady diet of buncombe, the people may come to expect and to respond with highest predictability to buncombe. And those leaders most skilled in the propagation of buncombe may gain lasting advantage in the recurring struggles for popular favor.

[My] perverse and unorthodox argument . . . is that voters are not fools. To be sure, many individual voters act in odd ways indeed; yet in the large the electorate behaves about as rationally and responsibly as we should expect, given the clarity of the alternatives presented to it and the character of the information available to it. In American presidential campaigns of recent decades the portrait of the American electorate that develops from the data is not one of an electorate straitjacketed by social determinants or moved by subconscious urges triggered by devilishly skillful propagandists. It is rather one of an electorate moved by concern about central and relevant questions of public policy, of governmental performance, and of executive personality. Propositions so uncompromisingly stated inevitably represent overstatements. Yet to the extent that they can be shown to resemble the reality, they are propositions of basic importance for both the theory and the practice of democracy. . . .

Congress

12   *Federalist No. 62*

Publius

To the People of the State of New York:

HAVING examined the constitution of the House of Representatives, and answered such of the objections against it as seemed to merit notice, I enter next on the examination of the Senate.

The heads into which this member of the government may be considered are: I. The qualification of senators; II. The appointment of them by the State legislatures; III. The equality of representation in the Senate; IV. The number of senators, and the term for which they are to be elected; V. The powers vested in the Senate.

I. The qualifications proposed for senators, as distinguished from those of representatives, consist in a more advanced age and a longer period of citizenship. A senator must be thirty years of age at least; as a representative must be twenty-five. And the former must have been a citizen nine years; as seven years are required for the latter. The propriety of these distinctions is explained by the nature of the senatorial trust, which, requiring greater extent of information and stability of character, requires at the same time that the senator should have reached a period of life most likely to supply these advantages; and which, participating immediately in transactions with foreign nations, ought to be exercised by none who are not thoroughly weaned from the prepossessions and habits incident to foreign birth and education. The term of nine years appears to be a prudent mediocrity between a total exclusion of adopted citizens, whose merits and talents may claim a share in the public confidence, and an indiscriminate and hasty admission of them, which might create a channel for foreign influence on the national councils.

II. It is equally unnecessary to dilate on the appointment of senators by the State legislatures. Among the various modes which might have been devised for constituting this branch of the government, that which has been proposed by the convention is probably the most congenial with the public opinion. It is recommended by the double advantage of favoring a select appointment, and of giving to the State governments such an agency in the formation of the federal government as must secure the authority of the former, and may form a convenient link between the two systems.

III. The equality of representation in the Senate is another point, which, being evidently the result of compromise between the opposite pretensions of the large and the small States, does not call for much discussion. If indeed it be right, that among a people thoroughly incorporated into one nation, every district ought to have a PROPORTIONAL share in the government, and that among independent and sovereign States, bound together by a simple league, the parties, however unequal in size, ought to have an EQUAL share in the common councils, it does not appear to be without some reason that in a compound republic, partaking both of the national and federal character, the government ought to be founded on a mixture of the principles of proportional and equal representation. But it is superfluous to try, by the standard of theory, a part of the Constitution which is allowed on all hands to be the result, not of theory, but "of a spirit of amity, and that mutual deference and concession which the peculiarity of our political situation rendered indispensable." A common government, with powers equal to its objects, is called for by the voice, and still more loudly by the political situation, of America. A government founded on principles more consonant to the wishes of the larger States, is not likely to be obtained from the smaller States. The only option, then, for the former, lies between the proposed government and a government still more objectionable. Under this alternative, the advice of prudence must be to embrace the lesser evil; and, instead of indulging a fruitless anticipation of the possible mischiefs which may ensue, to contemplate rather the advantageous consequences which may qualify the sacrifice.

In this spirit it may be remarked, that the equal vote allowed to each State is at once a constitutional recognition of the portion of sovereignty remaining in the individual States, and an instrument for preserving that residuary sovereignty. So far the equality ought to be no less acceptable to the large than to the small States; since they are not less solicitous to guard, by every possible expedient, against an improper consolidation of the States into one simple republic.

Another advantage accruing from this ingredient in the constitution of the Senate is, the additional impediment it must prove against improper acts of legislation. No law or resolution can now be passed without the concurrence, first, of a majority of the people, and then, of a majority of the States. It must be acknowledged that this complicated check on legislation may in some instances be injurious as well as beneficial; and that the peculiar defense which it involves in favor of the smaller States, would be more rational, if any interests common to them, and distinct from those of the other States, would otherwise be exposed to peculiar danger. But as the larger States will always be able, by their power over the supplies, to defeat unreasonable exertions of this prerogative of the lesser States, and as the faculty and excess of law-making seem to be the diseases to which our governments are most liable, it is not impossible that this part of the Constitution may be more convenient in practice than it appears to many in contemplation.

IV. The number of senators, and the duration of their appointment, come next to be considered. In order to form an accurate judgment on both of these points, it will be proper to inquire into the purposes which are to be answered by a senate; and in order to ascertain these, it will be necessary to review the inconveniences which a republic must suffer from the want of such an institution.

First. It is a misfortune incident to republican government, though in a less degree than to other governments, that those who administer it may forget their obligations to their constituents, and prove unfaithful to their important trust. In this point of view, a senate, as a second branch of the legislative assembly, distinct from, and dividing the power with, a first, must be in all cases a salutary check on the government. It doubles the security to the people, by requiring the concurrence of two distinct bodies in schemes of usurpation or perfidy, where the ambition or corruption of one would otherwise be sufficient. This is a precaution founded on such clear principles, and now so well understood in the United States, that it would be more than superfluous to enlarge on it. I will barely remark, that as the improbability of sinister combinations will be in proportion to the dissimilarity in the genius of the two bodies, it must be politic to distinguish them from each other by every circumstance which will consist with a due harmony in all proper measures, and with the genuine principles of republican government.

Secondly. The necessity of a senate is not less indicated by the propensity of all single and numerous assemblies to yield to the impulse of sudden and violent passions, and to be seduced by factious leaders into intemperate and pernicious resolutions. Examples on this subject might be cited without number; and from proceedings within the United States, as well as from the history of other nations. But a position that will not be contradicted, need not be proved. All that need be remarked is, that a body which is to correct this infirmity ought itself to be free from it, and consequently ought to be less numerous. It ought, moreover, to possess great firmness, and consequently ought to hold its authority by a tenure of considerable duration.

Thirdly. Another defect to be supplied by a senate lies in a want of due acquaintance with the objects and principles of legislation. It is not possible that an assembly of men called for the most part from pursuits of a private nature, continued in appointment for a short time, and led by no permanent motive to devote the intervals of public occupation to a study of the laws, the affairs, and the comprehensive interests of their country, should, if left wholly to themselves, escape a variety of important errors in the exercise of their legislative trust. It may be affirmed, on the best grounds, that no small share of the present embarrassments of America is to be charged on the blunders of our governments; and that these have proceeded from the heads rather than the hearts of most of the authors of them. What indeed are all the repealing, explaining, and amending laws, which fill and disgrace our voluminous codes, but so many monuments of deficient wisdom; so many impeachments exhibited by each succeeding against each preceding session; so many admonitions to the people, of the value of those aids which may be expected from a well-constituted senate?

A good government implies two things: first, fidelity to the object of government, which is the happiness of the people; secondly, a knowledge of the means by which that object can be best attained. Some governments are deficient in both these qualities; most governments are deficient in the first. I scruple not to assert, that in American governments too little attention has been paid to the last. The federal Constitution avoids this error; and what merits particular notice, it provides for the last in a mode which increases the security for the first.

Fourthly. The mutability in the public councils arising from a rapid succession of new members, however qualified they may be, points out, in the strongest manner, the necessity of some stable institution in the government. Every new election in the States is found to change one half of the representatives. From this change of men must proceed a change of opinions; and from a change of opinions, a change of measures. But a continual change even of good measures is inconsistent with every rule of prudence and every prospect of success. The remark is verified in private life, and becomes more just, as well as more important, in national transactions.

To trace the mischievous effects of a mutable government would fill a volume. I will hint a few only, each of which will be perceived to be a source of innumerable others.

In the first place, it forfeits the respect and confidence of other nations, and all the advantages connected with national character. An individual who is observed to be inconstant to his plans, or perhaps to carry on his affairs without any plan at all, is marked at once, by all prudent people, as a speedy victim to his own unsteadiness and folly. His more friendly neighbors may pity him, but all will decline to connect their fortunes with his; and not a few will seize the opportunity of making their fortunes out of his. One nation is to another what one individual is to another; with this melancholy distinction perhaps, that the former, with fewer of the benevolent emotions than the latter, are under fewer restraints also from taking undue advantage from the indiscretions of each other. Every nation, consequently, whose affairs betray a want of wisdom and stability, may calculate on every loss which can be sustained from the more systematic policy of their wiser neighbors. But the best instruction on this subject is unhappily conveyed to America by the example of her own situation. She finds that she is held in no respect by her friends; that she is the derision of her enemies; and that she is a prey to every nation which has an interest in speculating on her fluctuating councils and embarrassed affairs.

The internal effects of a mutable policy are still more calamitous. It poisons the blessing of liberty itself. It will be of little avail to the people, that the laws are made by men of their own choice, if the laws be so voluminous that they cannot be read, or so incoherent that they cannot be understood; if they be repealed or revised before they are promulgated, or undergo such incessant changes that no man, who knows what the law is to-day, can guess what it will be to-morrow. Law is defined to be a rule of action; but how can that be a rule, which is little known, and less fixed?

Another effect of public instability is the unreasonable advantage it gives to the sagacious, the enterprising, and the moneyed few over the industrious and uniformed mass of the people. Every new regulation concerning commerce or revenue, or in any way affecting the value of the different species of property, presents a new harvest to those who watch the change, and can trace its consequences; a harvest, reared not by themselves, but by the toils and cares of the great body of their fellow-citizens. This is a state of things in which it may be said with some truth that laws are made for the FEW, not for the MANY.

In another point of view, great injury results from an unstable government. The want of confidence in the public councils damps every useful undertaking, the success and profit of which may depend on a continuance of existing arrangements. What prudent merchant will hazard his fortunes in any new branch of commerce when he knows not but that his plans may be rendered unlawful before they can be executed What farmer or manufacturer will lay himself out for the encouragement given to any particular cultivation or establishment, when he can have no assurance that his preparatory labors and advances will not render him a victim to an inconstant government In a word, no great improvement or laudable enterprise can go forward which requires the auspices of a steady system of national policy.

But the most deplorable effect of all is that diminution of attachment and reverence which steals into the hearts of the people, towards a political system which betrays so many marks of infirmity, and disappoints so many of their flattering hopes. No government, any more than an individual, will long be respected without being truly respectable; nor be truly respectable, without possessing a certain portion of order and stability.

13   *Federalist No. 52*

The House of Representatives
From the New York Packet.
Friday, February 8, 1788.
Alexander Hamilton or **James Madison**

To the People of the State of New York:

FROM the more general inquiries pursued in the four last papers, I pass on to a more particular examination of the several parts of the government. I shall begin with the House of Representatives.

The first view to be taken of this part of the government relates to the qualifications of the electors and the elected. Those of the former are to be the same with those of the electors of the most numerous branch of the State legislatures. The definition of the right of suffrage is very justly regarded as a fundamental article of republican government. It was incumbent on the convention, therefore, to define and establish this right in the Constitution. To have left it open for the occasional regulation of the Congress, would have been improper for the reason just mentioned. To have submitted it to the legislative discretion of the States, would have been improper for the same reason; and for the additional reason that it would have rendered too dependent on the State governments that branch of the federal government which ought to be dependent on the people alone. To have reduced the different qualifications in the different States to one uniform rule, would probably have been as dissatisfactory to some of the States as it would have been difficult to the convention. The provision made by the convention appears, therefore, to be the best that lay within their option. It must be satisfactory to every State, because it is conformable to the standard already established, or which may be established, by the State itself. It will be safe to the United States, because, being fixed by the State constitutions, it is not alterable by the State governments, and it cannot be feared that the people of the States will alter this part of their constitutions in such a manner as to abridge the rights secured to them by the federal Constitution.

The qualifications of the elected, being less carefully and properly defined by the State constitutions, and being at the same time more susceptible of uniformity, have been very properly considered and regulated by the convention. A representative of the United States must be of the age of twenty-five years; must have been seven years a citizen of the United States; must, at the time of his election, be an inhabitant of the State he is to represent; and, during the time of his service, must be in no office under the United States. Under these reasonable limitations, the door of this part of the federal government is open to merit of every description, whether native or adoptive, whether young or old, and without regard to poverty or wealth, or to any particular profession of religious faith.

The term for which the representatives are to be elected falls under a second view which may be taken of this branch. In order to decide on the propriety of this article, two questions must be considered: first, whether biennial elections will, in this case, be safe; secondly, whether they be necessary or useful.

First. As it is essential to liberty that the government in general should have a common interest with the people, so it is particularly essential that the branch of it under consideration should have an immediate dependence on, and an intimate sympathy with, the people. Frequent elections are unquestionably the only policy by which this dependence and sympathy can be effectually secured. But what particular degree of frequency may be absolutely necessary for the purpose, does not appear to be susceptible of any precise calculation, and must depend on a variety of circumstances with which it may be connected. Let us consult experience, the guide that ought always to be followed whenever it can be found.

The scheme of representation, as a substitute for a meeting of the citizens in person, being at most but very imperfectly known to ancient polity, it is in more modern times only that we are to expect instructive examples. And even here, in order to avoid a research too vague and diffusive, it will be proper to confine ourselves to the few examples which are best known, and which bear the greatest analogy to our particular case. The first to which this character ought to be applied, is the House of Commons in Great Britain. The history of this branch of the English Constitution, anterior to the date of Magna Charta, is too obscure to yield instruction. The very existence of it has been made a question among political antiquaries. The earliest records of subsequent date prove that parliaments were to SIT only every year; not that they were to be ELECTED every year. And even these annual sessions were left so much at the discretion of the monarch, that, under various pretexts, very long and dangerous intermissions were often contrived by royal ambition. To remedy this grievance, it was provided by a statute in the reign of Charles II. , that the intermissions should not be protracted beyond a period of three years. On the accession of William III. , when a revolution took place in the government, the subject was still more seriously resumed, and it was declared to be among the fundamental rights of the people that parliaments ought to be held FREQUENTLY. By another statute, which passed a few years later in the same reign, the term "frequently," which had alluded to the triennial period settled in the time of Charles II. , is reduced to a precise meaning, it being expressly enacted that a new parliament shall be called within three years after the termination of the former. The last change, from three to seven years, is well known to have been introduced pretty early in the present century, under on alarm for the Hanoverian succession. From these facts it appears that the greatest frequency of elections which has been deemed necessary in that kingdom, for binding the representatives to their constituents, does not exceed a triennial return of them. And if we may argue from the degree of liberty retained even under septennial elections, and all the other vicious ingredients in the parliamentary constitution, we cannot doubt that a reduction of the period from seven to three years, with the other necessary reforms, would so far extend the influence of the people over their representatives as to satisfy us that biennial elections, under the federal system, cannot possibly be dangerous to the requisite dependence of the House of Representatives on their constituents.

Elections in Ireland, till of late, were regulated entirely by the discretion of the crown, and were seldom repeated, except on the accession of a new prince, or some other contingent event. The parliament which commenced with George II. was continued throughout his whole reign, a period of about thirty-five years. The only dependence of the representatives on the people consisted in the right of the latter to supply occasional vacancies by the election of new members, and in the chance of some event which might produce a general new election. The ability also of the Irish parliament to maintain the rights of their constituents, so far as the disposition might exist, was extremely shackled by the control of the crown over the subjects of their deliberation. Of late these shackles, if I mistake not, have been broken; and octennial parliaments have besides been established. What effect may be produced by this partial reform, must be left to further experience. The example of Ireland, from this view of it, can throw but little light on the subject. As far as we can draw any conclusion from it, it must be that if the people of that country have been able under all these disadvantages to retain any liberty whatever, the advantage of biennial elections would secure to them every degree of liberty, which might depend on a due connection between their representatives and themselves.

Let us bring our inquiries nearer home. The example of these States, when British colonies, claims particular attention, at the same time that it is so well known as to require little to be said on it. The principle of representation, in one branch of the legislature at least, was established in all of them. But the periods of election were different. They varied from one to seven years. Have we any reason to infer, from the spirit and conduct of the representatives of the people, prior to the Revolution, that biennial elections would have been dangerous to the public liberties? The spirit which everywhere displayed itself at the commencement of the struggle, and which vanquished the obstacles to independence, is the best of proofs that a sufficient portion of liberty had been everywhere enjoyed to inspire both a sense of its worth and a zeal for its proper enlargement This remark holds good, as well with regard to the then colonies whose elections were least frequent, as to those whose elections were most frequent Virginia was the colony which stood first in resisting the parliamentary usurpations of Great Britain; it was the first also in espousing, by public act, the resolution of independence. In Virginia, nevertheless, if I have not been misinformed, elections under the former government were septennial. This particular example is brought into view, not as a proof of any peculiar merit, for the priority in those instances was probably accidental; and still less of any advantage in SEPTENNIAL elections, for when compared with a greater frequency they are inadmissible; but merely as a proof, and I conceive it to be a very substantial proof, that the liberties of the people can be in no danger from BIENNIAL elections.

The conclusion resulting from these examples will be not a little strengthened by recollecting three circumstances. The first is, that the federal legislature will possess a part only of that supreme legislative authority which is vested completely in the British Parliament; and which, with a few exceptions, was exercised by the colonial assemblies and the Irish legislature. It is a received and well-founded maxim, that where no other circumstances affect the case, the greater the power is, the shorter ought to be its duration; and, conversely, the smaller the power, the more safely may its duration be protracted. In the second place, it has, on another occasion, been shown that the federal legislature will not only be restrained by its dependence on its people, as other legislative bodies are, but that it will be, moreover, watched and controlled by the several collateral legislatures, which other legislative bodies are not. And in the third place, no comparison can be made between the means that will be possessed by the more permanent branches of the federal government for seducing, if they should be disposed to seduce, the House of Representatives from their duty to the people, and the means of influence over the popular branch possessed by the other branches of the government above cited. With less power, therefore, to abuse, the federal representatives can be less tempted on one side, and will be doubly watched on the other.

PUBLIUS.

14   *The Rise of the Washington Establishment*

Morris P. Fiorina
Dramatis Personae

In this [selection] I will set out a theory of the Washington establishment(s). The theory is quite plausible from a common-sense standpoint, and it is consistent with the specialized literature of academic political science. Nevertheless, it is still a theory, not proven fact. Before plunging in let me bring out in the open the basic axiom on which the theory rests: the self-interest axiom.

I assume that most people most of the time act in their own self-interest. This is not to say that human beings seek only to amass tangible wealth but rather to say that human beings seek to achieve their own ends—tangible and intangible—rather than the ends of their fellow men. I do not condemn such behavior nor do I condone it (although I rather sympathize with Thoreau's comment that "if I knew for a certainty that a man was coming to my house with the conscious design of doing me good, I should run for my life."). I only claim that political and economic theories which presume self-interested behavior will prove to be more widely applicable than those which build on more altruistic assumptions.

What does the axiom imply when used in the specific context of this [selection], a context peopled by congressmen, bureaucrats, and voters? I assume that the primary goal of the typical congressman is reelection. Over and above the [six-figure] salary plus "perks" and outside money, the office of congressman carries with it prestige, excitement, and power. It is a seat in the cockpit of government. But in order to retain the status, excitement, and power (not to mention more tangible things) of office, the congressman must win reelection every two years. Even those congressmen genuinely concerned with good public policy must achieve reelection in order to continue their work. Whether narrowly self-serving or more publicly oriented, the individual congressman finds reelection to be at least a necessary condition for the achievement of his goals.

Moreover, there is a kind of natural selection process at work in the electoral arena. On average, those congressmen who are not primarily interested in re-election will not achieve reelection as often as those who are interested. We, the people, help to weed out congressmen whose primary motivation is not re-election. We admire politicians

Reprinted from *Congress: Keystone of the Washington Establishment* (1977), Yale University Press.

who courageously adopt the aloof role of the disinterested statesman, but we vote for those politicians who follow our wishes and do us favors.

What about the bureaucrats? A specification of their goals is somewhat more controversial—those who speak of appointed officials as public servants obviously take a more benign view than those who speak of them as bureaucrats. The literature provides ample justification for asserting that most bureaucrats wish to protect and nurture their agencies. The typical bureaucrat can be expected to seek to expand his agency in terms of personnel, budget, and mission. One's status in Washington (again, not to mention more tangible things) is roughly proportional to the importance of the operation one oversees. And the sheer size of the operation is taken to be a measure of importance. As with congressmen, the specified goals apply even to those bureaucrats who genuinely believe in their agency's mission. If they believe in the efficacy of their programs, they naturally wish to expand them and add new ones. All of this requires more money and more people. The genuinely committed bureaucrat is just as likely to seek to expand his agency as the proverbial empire-builder.

And what of the third element in the equation, us? What do we, the voters who support the Washington system, strive for? Each of us wishes to receive a maximum of benefits from government for the minimum cost. This goal suggests maximum government efficiency, on the one hand, but it also suggests mutual exploitation on the other. Each of us favors an arrangement in which our fellow citizens pay for our benefits.

With these brief descriptions of the cast of characters in hand, let us proceed.

Tammany Hall Goes to Washington

What should we expect from a legislative body composed of individuals whose first priority is their continued tenure in office? We should expect, first, that the normal activities of its members are those calculated to enhance their chances of reelection. And we should expect, second, that the members would devise and maintain institutional arrangements which facilitate their electoral activities. . . .

For most of the twentieth century, congressmen have engaged in a mix of three kinds of activities: lawmaking, pork barreling, and casework. Congress is first and foremost a lawmaking body, at least according to constitutional theory. In every postwar session Congress "considers" thousands of bills and resolutions, many hundreds of which are brought to a record vote. . . . Naturally the critical consideration in taking a position for the record is the maximization of approval in the home district. If the district is unaffected by and unconcerned with the matter at hand, the congressman may then take into account the general welfare of the country. (This sounds cynical, but remember that "profiles in courage" are sufficiently rare that their occurrence inspires books and articles.) Abetted by political scientists of the pluralist school, politicians have propounded an ideology which maintains that the good of the country on any given issue is simply what is best for a majority of congressional districts. This ideology provides a philosophical justification for what congressmen do while acting in their own self-interest.

A second activity favored by congressmen consists of efforts to bring home the bacon to their districts. Many popular articles have been written about the pork barrel, a term originally applied to rivers and harbors legislation but now generalized to cover all manner of federal largesse. Congressmen consider new dams, federal buildings, sewage treatment plants, urban renewal projects, etc. as sweet plums to be plucked. Federal projects are highly visible, their economic impact is easily detected by constituents, and sometimes they even produce something of value to the district. The average constituent may have some trouble translating his congressman's vote on some civil rights issue into a change in his personal welfare. But the workers hired and supplies purchased in connection with a big federal project provide benefits that are widely appreciated. The historical importance congressmen attach to the pork barrel is reflected in the rules of the House. That body accords certain classes of legislation "privileged" status: they may come directly to the floor without passing through the Rules Committee, a traditional graveyard for legislation. What kinds of legislation are privileged? Taxing and spending bills, for one: the government's power to raise and spend money must be kept relatively unfettered. But in addition, the omnibus rivers and harbors bills of the Public Works Committee and public lands bills from the Interior Committee share privileged status. The House will allow a civil rights or defense procurement or environmental bill to languish in the Rules Committee, but it takes special precautions to insure that nothing slows down the approval of dams and irrigation projects.

A third major activity takes up perhaps as much time as the other two combined. Traditionally, constituents appeal to their congressman for myriad favors and services. Sometimes only information is needed, but often constituents request that their congressman intervene in the internal workings of federal agencies to affect a decision in a favorable way, to reverse an adverse decision, or simply to speed up the glacial bureaucratic process. On the basis of extensive personal interviews with congressmen, Charles Clapp writes:

> Denied a favorable ruling by the bureaucracy on a matter of direct concern to him, puzzled or irked by delays in obtaining a decision, confused by the administrative maze through which he is directed to proceed, or ignorant of whom to write, a constituent may turn to his congressman for help. These letters offer great potential for political benefit to the congressman since they affect the constituent personally. If the legislator can be of assistance, he may gain a firm ally; if he is indifferent, he may even lose votes.

Actually congressmen are in an almost unique position in our system, a position shared only with high-level members of the executive branch. Congressmen possess the power to expedite and influence bureaucratic decisions. This capability flows directly from congressional control over what bureaucrats value most: higher budgets and new program authorizations. In a very real sense each congressman is a monopoly supplier of bureaucratic unsticking services for his district.

Every year the federal budget passes through the appropriations committees of Congress. Generally these committees make perfunctory cuts. But on occasion they vent displeasure on an agency and leave it bleeding all over the Capitol. The most extreme case of which I am aware came when the House committee took away the entire budget of the Division of Labor Standards in 1947 (some of the budget was restored elsewhere in the appropriations process). Deep and serious cuts are made occasionally, and the threat of such cuts keeps most agencies attentive to congressional wishes. Professors Richard Fenno and Aaron Wildavsky have provided extensive documentary and interview evidence of the great respect (and even terror) federal bureaucrats show for the House Appropriations Committee. Moreover, the bureaucracy must keep coming back to Congress to have its old programs reauthorized and new ones added. Again, most such decisions are perfunctory, but exceptions are sufficiently frequent that bureaucrats do not forget the basis of their agencies' existence. . . . The bureaucracy needs congressional approval in order to survive, let alone expand. Thus, when a congressman calls about some minor bureaucratic decision or regulation, the bureaucracy considers his accommodation a small price to pay for the goodwill its cooperation will produce, particularly if he has any connection to the substantive committee or the appropriations subcommittee to which it reports.

From the standpoint of capturing voters, the congressman's lawmaking activities differ in two important respects from his pork-barrel and casework activities. First, programmatic actions are inherently controversial. Unless his district is homogeneous, a congressman will find his district divided on many major issues. Thus when he casts a vote, introduces a piece of nontrivial legislation, or makes a speech with policy content he will displease some elements of his district. Some constituents may applaud the congressman's civil rights record, but others believe integration is going too fast. Some support foreign aid, while others believe its money poured down a rat hole. Some advocate economic equality, others stew over welfare cheaters. On such policy matters the congressman can expect to make friends as well as enemies. Presumably he will behave so as to maximize the excess of the former over the latter, but nevertheless a policy stand will generally make some enemies.

In contrast, the pork barrel and casework are relatively less controversial. New federal projects bring jobs, shiny new facilities, and general economic prosperity, or so people believe. Snipping ribbons at the dedication of a new post office or dam is a much more pleasant pursuit than disposing of a constitutional amendment on abortion. Republicans and Democrats, conservatives and liberals, all generally prefer a richer district to a poorer one. Of course, in recent years the river damming and stream-bed straightening activities of the Army Corps of Engineers have aroused some opposition among environmentalists. Congressmen happily reacted by absorbing the opposition and adding environmentalism to the pork barrel: water treatment plants are currently a hot congressional item.

Casework is even less controversial. Some poor, aggrieved constituent becomes enmeshed in the tentacles of an evil bureaucracy and calls upon Congressman St. George to do battle with the dragon. Again Clapp writes:

> A person who has a reasonable complaint or query is regarded as providing an opportunity rather than as adding an extra burden to an already busy office. The party affiliation of the individual even when known to be different from that of the congressman does not normally act as a deterrent to action. Some legislators have built

their reputations and their majorities on a program of service to all constituents irrespective of party. Regularly, voters affiliated with the opposition in other contests lend strong support to the lawmaker whose intervention has helped them in their struggle with the bureaucracy.

Even following the revelation of sexual improprieties, Wayne Hays won his Ohio Democratic primary by a two-to-one margin. According to a *Los Angeles Times* feature story, Hay's constituency base was built on a foundation of personal service to constituents:

> They receive help in speeding up bureaucratic action on various kinds of federal assistance—black lung benefits to disabled miners and their families, Social Security payments, veterans' benefits and passports.
>
> Some constituents still tell with pleasure of how Hays stormed clear to the seventh floor of the State Department and into Secretary of State Dean Rusk's office to demand, successfully, the quick issuance of a passport to an Ohioan.

Practicing politicians will tell you that word of mouth is still the most effective mode of communication. News of favors to constituents gets around and no doubt is embellished in the process.

In sum, when considering the benefits of his programmatic activities, the congressman must tote up gains and losses to arrive at a net profit. Pork barreling and casework, however, are basically pure profit.

A second way in which programmatic activities differ from casework and the pork barrel is the difficulty of assigning responsibility to the former as compared with the latter. No congressman can seriously claim that he is responsible for the 1964 Civil Rights Act, the ABM, or the 1972 Revenue Sharing Act. Most constituents do have some vague notion that their congressman is only one of hundreds and their senator one of an even hundred. Even committee chairmen may have a difficult time claiming credit for a piece of major legislation, let alone a rank-and-file congressman. Ah, but casework, and the pork barrel. In dealing with the bureaucracy, the congressman is not merely one vote of 435. Rather, he is a nonpartisan power, someone whose phone calls snap an office to attention. He is not kept on hold. The constituent who receives aid believes that his congressman and his congressman alone got results. Similarly, congressmen find it easy to claim credit for federal projects awarded their districts. The congressman may have instigated the proposal for the project in the first place, issued regular progress reports, and ultimately announced the award through his office. Maybe he can't claim credit for the 1965 Voting Rights Act, but he can take credit for Littletown's spanking new sewage treatment plant.

Overall then, programmatic activities are dangerous (controversial), on the one hand, and programmatic accomplishments are difficult to claim credit for, on the other. While less exciting, casework and pork barreling are both safe and profitable. For a reelection-oriented congressman the choice is obvious.

The key to the rise of the Washington establishment (and the vanishing marginals) is the following observation: the growth of an activist federal government has stimulated a change in the mix of congressional activities. Specifically, a lesser proportion of congressional effort is now going into programmatic activities and a greater proportion into pork-barrel and casework activities. As a result, today's congressmen make relatively fewer enemies and relatively more friends among the people of their districts.

To elaborate, a basic fact of life in twentieth-century America is the growth of the federal role and its attendant bureaucracy. Bureaucracy is the characteristic mode of delivering public goods and services. *Ceteris paribus,* the more government attempts to do for people, the more extensive a bureaucracy it creates. As the scope of government expands, more and more citizens find themselves in direct contact with the federal government. Consider the rise in such contacts upon passage of the Social Security Act, work relief projects and other New Deal programs. Consider the millions of additional citizens touched by the veterans' programs of the postwar period. Consider the untold numbers whom the Great Society and its aftermath brought face to face with the federal government. In 1930 the federal bureaucracy was small and rather distant from the everyday concerns of Americans. By 1975 it was neither small nor distant.

As the years have passed, more and more citizens and groups have found themselves dealing with the federal bureaucracy. They may be seeking positive actions—eligibility for various benefits and awards of government grants. Or they may be seeking relief from the costs imposed by bureaucratic regulations—on working conditions, racial and sexual quotas, market restrictions, and numerous other subjects. While not malevolent, bureaucracies make mistakes, both of commission and omission, and normal attempts at redress often meet with unresponsiveness and inflexibility and sometimes seeming incorrigibility. Whatever the problem, the citizen's congressman is a source of succor. The greater the scope of government activity, the greater the demand for his services.

Private monopolists can regulate the demand for their product by raising or lowering the price. Congressmen have no such (legal) option. When the demand for their services rises, they have no real choice except to meet that demand—to supply more bureaucratic unsticking services—so long as they would rather be elected than unelected. This vulnerability to escalating constituency demands is largely academic, though. I seriously doubt that congressmen resist their gradual transformation from national legislators to errand boy-ombudsmen. As we have noted, casework is all profit. Congressmen have buried proposals to relieve the casework burden by establishing a national ombudsman or Congressman Reuss's proposed Administrative Counsel of the Congress. One of the congressmen interviewed by Clapp stated:

> Before I came to Washington I used to think that it might be nice if the individual states had administrative arms here that would take care of necessary liaison between citizens and the national government. But a congressman running for reelection is interested in building fences by providing personal services. The system is set to reelect incumbents regardless of party, and incumbents wouldn't dream of giving any of this service function away to any subagency. As an elected member I feel the same way.

In fact, it is probable that at least some congressmen deliberately stimulate the demand for their bureaucratic fixit services. Recall that the new Republican in district A travels about his district saying:

I'm your man in Washington. What are your problems? How can I help you?

And in district B, did the demand for the congressman's services rise so much between 1962 and 1964 that a "regiment" of constituency staff became necessary? Or, having access to the regiment, did the new Democrat stimulate the demand to which he would apply his regiment?

In addition to greatly increased casework, let us not forget that the growth of the federal role has also greatly expanded the federal pork barrel. The creative pork barreler need not limit himself to dams and post offices—rather old-fashioned interests. Today, creative congressmen can cadge LEAA money for the local police, urban renewal and housing money for local politicians, educational program grants for the local education bureaucracy. And there are sewage treatment plants, worker training and retraining programs, health services, and programs for the elderly. The pork barrel is full to overflowing. The conscientious congressman can stimulate applications for federal assistance (the sheer number of programs makes it difficult for local officials to stay current with the possibilities), put in a good word during consideration, and announce favorable decisions amid great fanfare.

In sum, everyday decisions by a large and growing federal bureaucracy bestow significant tangible benefits and impose significant tangible costs. Congressmen can affect these decisions. Ergo, the more decisions the bureaucracy has the opportunity to make, the more opportunities there are for the congressman to build up credits.

The nature of the Washington system is . . . quite clear. Congressmen (typically the majority Democrats) earn electoral credits by establishing various federal programs (the minority Republicans typically earn credits by fighting the good fight). The legislation is drafted in very general terms, so some agency, existing or newly established, must translate a vague policy mandate into a functioning program, a process that necessitates the promulgation of numerous rules and regulations and, incidentally, the trampling of numerous toes. At the next stage, aggrieved and/or hopeful constituents petition their congressman to intervene in the complex (or at least obscure) decision processes of the bureaucracy. The cycle closes when the congressman lends a sympathetic ear, piously denounces the evils of bureaucracy, intervenes in the latter's decisions, and rides a grateful electorate to ever more impressive electoral showings. Congressmen take credit coming and going. They are the alpha and the omega.

The popular frustration with the permanent government in Washington is partly justified, but to a considerable degree it is misplaced resentment. Congress is the linchpin of the Washington establishment. The bureaucracy serves as a convenient lightning rod for public frustration and a convenient whipping boy for congressmen. But so long as the bureaucracy accommodates congressmen, the latter will oblige with ever larger budgets and grants of authority. Congress does not just react to big government—it creates it. All of Washington prospers. More and more bureaucrats promulgate more and more regulations and dispense more and more money. Fewer and fewer congressmen suffer electoral defeat. Elements of the electorate benefit from government programs, and all of the electorate is eligible for ombudsman services. But the general, long-term welfare of the United States is no more than an incidental by-product of the system.

15   *Congress: The Electoral Connection*

David R. Mayhew

Whether they are safe or marginal, cautious or audacious, congressmen must constantly engage in activities related to reelection. There will be differences in emphasis, but all members share the root need to do things—indeed, to do things day in and day out during their terms. The next step here is to present a typology, a short list of the kinds of activities congressmen find it electorally useful to engage in. The case will be that there are three basic kinds of activities. It will be important to lay them out with some care. . . .

One activity is *advertising,* defined here as any effort to disseminate one's name among constituents in such a fashion as to create a favorable image but in messages having little or no issue content. A successful congressman builds what amounts to a brand name, which may have a generalized electoral value for other politicians in the same family. The personal qualities to emphasize are experience, knowledge, responsiveness, concern, sincerity, independence, and the like. Just getting one's name across is difficult enough; only about half the electorate, if asked, can supply their House members' names. It helps a congressman to be known. "In the main, recognition carries a positive valence; to be perceived at all is to be perceived favorably." A vital advantage enjoyed by House incumbents is that they are much better known among voters than their November challengers. They are better known because they spend a great deal of time, energy, and money trying to make themselves better known. There are standard routines—frequent visits to the constituency, nonpolitical speeches to home audiences, the sending out of infant care booklets and letters of condolence and congratulations. Of 158 House members questioned . . . 121 said that they regularly sent newsletters to their constituents; 48 wrote separate news or opinion columns for newspapers; 82 regularly reported to their constituencies by radio or television; 89 regularly sent out mail questionnaires. Some routines are less standard. Congressman George E. Shipley (D., Ill.) claims to have met personally about half his constituents (i.e., some 200,000 people). For over twenty years Congressman Charles C. Diggs, Jr. (D., Mich.) has run a radio program featuring himself as a "combination disc jockey-commentator and minister." Congressman Daniel J. Flood (D., Pa.) is

Reprinted from *Congress: The Electoral Connection* (1974), Yale University Press.

"famous for appearing unannounced and often uninvited at wedding anniversaries and other events." Anniversaries and other events aside, congressional advertising is done largely at public expense. Use of the franking privilege has mushroomed in recent years; in early 1973 one estimate predicted that House and Senate members would send out about 476 million pieces of mail in the year 1974, at a public cost of $38.1 million—or about 900,000 pieces per member with a subsidy of $70,000 per member. By far the heaviest mailroom traffic comes in Octobers of even-numbered years. There are some differences between House and Senate members in the ways they go about getting their names across. House members are free to blanket their constituencies with mailings for all boxholders; senators are not. But senators find it easier to appear on national television—for example, in short reaction statements on the nightly news shows. Advertising is a staple congressional activity, and there is no end to it. For each member there are always new voters to be apprised of his worthiness and old voters to be reminded of it.

A second activity may be called *credit claiming,* defined here as acting so as to generate a belief in a relevant political actor (or actors) that one is personally responsible for causing the government, or some unit thereof, to do something that the actor (or actors) considers desirable. The political logic of this, from the congressman's point of view, is that an actor who believes that a member can make pleasing things happen will no doubt wish to keep him in office so that he can make pleasing things happen in the future. The emphasis here is on individual accomplishment (rather than, say, party or governmental accomplishment) and on the congressman as doer (rather than as, say, expounder of constituency views). Credit claiming is highly important to congressmen, with the consequence that much of congressional life is a relentless search for opportunities to engage in it.

Where can credit be found? If there were only one congressman rather than 535, the answer would in principle be simple enough. Credit (or blame) would attach in Downsian fashion to the doing of the government as a whole. But there are 535. Hence it becomes necessary for each congressman to try to peel off pieces of governmental accomplishment for which he can believably generate a sense of responsibility. For the average congressman the staple way of doing this is to traffic in what may be called "particularized benefits." Particularized governmental benefits, as the term will be used here, have two properties: (1) Each benefit is given out to a specific individual, group, or geographical constituency, the recipient unit being of a scale that allows a single congressman to be recognized (by relevant political actors and other congressmen) as the claimant for the benefit (other congressmen being perceived as indifferent or hostile). (2) Each benefit is given out in apparently ad hoc fashion (unlike, say, social security checks) with a congressman apparently having a hand in the allocation. A particularized benefit can normally be regarded as a member of a class. That is, a benefit given out to an individual, group, or constituency can normally be looked upon by congressmen as one of a class of similar benefits given out to sizable numbers of individuals, groups, or constituencies. Hence the impression can arise that a congressman is getting "his share" of whatever it is the government is offering. (The classes may be vaguely defined. Some state legislatures deal in what their members call "local legislation.")

In sheer volume the bulk of particularized benefits come under the heading of "case-work"—the thousands of favors congressional offices perform for supplicants in ways that normally do not require legislative action. High school students ask for essay materials, soldiers for emergency leaves, pensioners for location of missing checks, local governments for grant information, and on and on. Each office has skilled professionals who can play the bureaucracy like an organ—pushing the right pedals to produce the desired effects. But many benefits require new legislation, or at least they require important allocative decisions on matters covered by existent legislation. Here the congressman fills the traditional role of supplier of goods to the home district. It is a believable role; when a member claims credit for a benefit on the order of a dam, he may well receive it. Shiny construction projects seem especially useful. . . .

The third activity congressmen engage in may be called *position taking,* defined here as the public enunciation of a judgmental statement on anything likely to be of interest to political actors. The statement may take the form of a roll call vote. The most important classes of judgmental statements are those prescribing American governmental ends (a vote cast against the war; a statement that "the war should be ended immediately") or governmental means (a statement that "the way to end the war is to take it to the United Nations"). The judgments may be implicit rather than explicit, as in: "I will support the president on this matter." But judgments may range far beyond these classes to take in implicit or explicit statements on what almost anybody should do or how he should do it: "The great Polish scientist Copernicus has been unjustly neglected"; "The way for Israel to achieve peace is to give up the Sinai." The congressman as position taker is a speaker rather than a doer. The electoral requirement is not that he make pleasing things happen but that he make pleasing judgmental statements. The position itself is the political commodity. Especially on matters where governmental responsibility is widely diffused it is not surprising that political actors should fall back on positions as tests of incumbent virtue. For voters ignorant of congressional processes the recourse is an easy one. The following comment [by a Congressman] is highly revealing: "Recently, I went home and began to talk about the—act. I was pleased to have sponsored that bill, but it soon dawned on me that the point wasn't getting through at all. What was getting through was that the act might be a help to people. I changed the emphasis: I didn't mention my role particularly, but stressed my support of the legislation."

The ways in which positions can be registered are numerous and often imaginative. There are floor addresses ranging from weighty orations to mass-produced "nationality day statements." There are speeches before home groups, television appearances, letters, newsletters, press releases, ghostwritten books, *Playboy* articles, even interviews with political scientists. On occasion congressmen generate what amount to petitions; whether or not to sign the 1956 Southern Manifesto defying school desegregation rulings was an important decision for southern members. Outside the roll call process the congressman is usually able to tailor his positions to suit his audiences. A solid consensus in the constituency calls for ringing declarations. . . .

Probably the best position-taking strategy for most congressmen at most times is to be conservative—to cling to their own positions of the past where possible and to reach for new ones with great caution where necessary. Yet in an earlier discussion of strategy the suggestion was made that it might be rational for members in electoral danger to resort to innovation. The form of innovation available is entrepreneurial position taking, its logic being that for a member facing defeat with his old array of positions it makes good sense to gamble on some new ones. It may be that congressional marginals fulfill an important function here as issue pioneers—experimenters who test out new issues and thereby show other politicians which ones are usable. An example of such a pioneer is Senator Warren Magnuson (D., Wash.), who responded to a surprisingly narrow victory in 1962 by reaching for a reputation in the area of consumer affairs. Another example is Senator Ernest Hollings (D., S.C.), a servant of a shaky and racially heterogeneous southern constituency who launched "hunger" as an issue in 1969—at once pointing to a problem and giving it a useful nonracial definition. One of the most successful issue entrepreneurs of recent decades was the late Senator Joseph McCarthy (R., Wis.); it was all there—the close primary in 1946, the fear of defeat in 1952, the desperate casting about for an issue, the famous 1950 dinner at the Colony Restaurant where suggestions were tendered, the decision that "Communism" might just do the trick.

The effect of position taking on electoral behavior is about as hard to measure as the effect of credit claiming. Once again there is a variance problem; congressmen do not differ very much among themselves in the methods they use or the skills they display in attuning themselves to their diverse constituencies. All of them, after all, are professional politicians. . . .

There can be no doubt that congressmen believe positions make a difference. An important consequence of this belief is their custom of watching each other's elections to try to figure out what positions are salable. Nothing is more important in Capitol Hill politics than the shared conviction that election returns have proven a point. . . .

These, then, are the three kinds of electorally oriented activities congressmen engage in—advertising, credit claiming, and position taking. . . .

16   *Four Amendments and a Funeral: Inside The House of Horrors That is Congress*

Matt Taibbi

In the summer of 2005, Rolling Stone reporter Matt Taibbi spent a month shadowing Vermont's lone congressman, Rep. Bernie Sanders, around the corridors of the House of Representatives. Sanders is the longest-serving Independent in the history of the U.S. Congress. He served eight terms in the House of Representatives before winning election to the Senate in 2006. As Taibbi's "tour guide," Sanders afforded him the opportunity to watch the legislative process from the trenches. What Taibbi witnessed actually was a series of victories for Sanders—some called it "the best winning streak of his career"—as four of his roll call amendments fared well in the House, in the process challenging several powerful business interests as well as the Bush administration. Two of the amendments attempted to curb the scope of the Patriot Act, one sought to block a $5 billion loan to Westinghouse to build a nuclear power plant in China, and a fourth would have cancelled a $1.9 billion contract to corporate giant Lockheed Martin. In the end, though, the power wielded by Republican congressional leaders trumped Sanders's carefully crafted legislative coalitions, and he ultimately came away empty-handed. None of the insider details Taibbi reveals are particularly unusual. Indeed, they were business as usual, as private power overcame public purpose. But the public seldom has this clear a glimpse into the inner workings of congressional battles. When paired with the battle over Medicare prescription drug program in Article 22, the picture that emerges raises serious questions about the nature of our representative democracy.

It was a fairy-tale political season for George W. Bush, and it seemed like no one in the world noticed. Amid bombs in London, bloodshed in Iraq, a missing blonde in Aruba and a scandal curling up on the doorstep of Karl Rove, Bush's Republican Party quietly celebrated a massacre on Capitol Hill. Two of the most long-awaited legislative wet dreams of the Washington Insiders Club—an energy bill and a much-delayed highway bill—breezed into law. One mildly nervous evening was all it took to pass through the House the Central American Free Trade Agreement (CAFTA), for years

---

Reprinted from *Rolling Stone*, August 25, 2005.

now a primary strategic focus of the battle-in-Seattle activist scene. And accompanied by scarcely a whimper from the Democratic opposition, a second version of the notorious USA Patriot Act passed triumphantly through both houses of Congress, with most of the law being made permanent this time.

Bush's summer bills [in 2005] were extraordinary pieces of legislation, broad in scope, transparently brazen and audaciously indulgent. They gave an energy industry drowning in the most obscene profits in its history billions of dollars in subsidies and tax breaks, including $2.9 billion for the coal industry. The highway bill set new standards for monstrous and indefensibly wasteful spending, with Congress allocating $100,000 for a single traffic light in Canoga Park, California, and $223 million for the construction of a bridge linking the mainland and an Alaskan island with a population of just fifty.

It was a veritable bonfire of public money, and it raged with all the brilliance of an Alabama book-burning. And what fueled it all were the little details you never heard about. The energy bill alone was 1,724 pages long. By the time the newspapers reduced this Tolstoyan monster to the size of a single headline announcing its passage, only a very few Americans understood that it was an ambitious giveaway to energy interests. But the drama of the legislative process is never in the broad strokes but in the bloody skirmishes and power plays that happen behind the scenes.

To understand the breadth of Bush's summer sweep, you had to watch the hand-fighting at close range. You had to watch opposition gambits die slow deaths in afternoon committee hearings, listen as members fell on their swords in exchange for favors and be there to see hordes of lobbyists rush in to reverse key votes at the last minute. All of these things I did—with the help of a tour guide.

"Nobody knows how this place is run," says Rep. Bernie Sanders. "If they did, they'd go nuts."

Sanders is a tall, angular man with a messy head of gull-white hair and a circa-1977 set of big-framed eyeglasses. Minus the austere congressional office, you might mistake him for a physics professor or a journalist of the Jimmy Breslin school.

Vermont's sole representative in the House, Sanders is expected to become the first Independent ever elected to the U.S. Senate next year. He is something of a cause célèbre on both the left and right these days, with each side overreacting to varying degrees to the idea of a self-described "democratic socialist" coming so near to a seat in the upper house.

Some months before, a Sanders aide had tried to sell me on a story about his boss, but over lunch we ended up talking about Congress itself. Like a lot of people who have worked on the Hill a little too long, the aide had a strange look in his eyes—the desperate look of a man who's been marooned on a remote island, subsisting on bugs and abalone for years on end. You worry that he might grab your lapel in frustration at any moment. "It's unbelievable," he said. "Worse than you can possibly imagine. The things that go on . . ."

Some time later I came back to the aide and told him that a standard campaign-season political profile was something I probably couldn't do, but if Sanders would be willing to give me an insider's guided tour of the horrors of Congress, I'd be interested.

"Like an evil, adult version of *Schoolhouse Rock*," I said.

The aide laughed and explained that the best time for me to go would be just before the summer recess, a period when Congress rushes to pass a number of appropriations bills. "It's like orgy season," he said. "You won't want to miss that."

I thought Sanders would be an ideal subject for a variety of reasons, but mainly for his Independent status. For all the fuss over his "socialist" tag, Sanders is really a classic populist outsider. The mere fact that Sanders signed off on the idea of serving as my guide says a lot about his attitude toward government in general: He wants people to see exactly what he's up against.

I had no way of knowing that Sanders would be a perfect subject for another, more compelling reason. In the first few weeks of my stay in Washington, Sanders introduced and passed, against very long odds, three important amendments. A fourth very nearly made it and would have passed had it gone to a vote. During this time, Sanders took on powerful adversaries, including Lockheed Martin, Westinghouse, the Export-Import Bank and the Bush administration. And by using the basic tools of democracy—floor votes on clearly posed questions, with the aid of painstakingly built coalitions of allies from both sides of the aisle—he, a lone Independent, beat them all.

It was an impressive run, with some in his office calling it the best winning streak of his career. Except for one thing.

By my last week in Washington, all of his victories had been rolled back, each carefully nurtured amendment perishing in the grossly corrupt and absurd vortex of political dysfunction that is today's U.S. Congress. What began as a tale of political valor ended as a grotesque object lesson in the ugly realities of American politics—the pitfalls of digging for hope in a shit mountain.

Sanders, to his credit, was still glad that I had come. "It's good that you saw this," he said. "People need to know."

Amendment 1

At 2 P.M. on Wednesday, July 20th, Sanders leaves his office in the Rayburn Building and heads down a tunnel passageway to the Capitol, en route to a Rules Committee hearing. "People have this impression that you can raise any amendment you want," he says. "They say, 'Why aren't you doing something about this?' That's not the way the system works."

Amendments occupy a great deal of most legislators' time, particularly those lawmakers in the minority. Members of Congress do author major bills, but more commonly they make minor adjustments to the bigger bills. Rather than write their own anti-terrorism bill, for instance, lawmakers will try to amend the Patriot Act, either by creating a new clause in the law or expanding or limiting some existing provision. The bill that ultimately becomes law is an aggregate of the original legislation and all the amendments offered and passed by all the different congresspersons along the way.

Sanders is the amendment king of the current House of Representatives. Since the Republicans took over Congress in 1995, no other lawmaker—not Tom DeLay, not Nancy Pelosi—has passed more roll-call amendments (amendments that actually went to a vote on the floor) than Bernie Sanders. He accomplishes this on the one hand by being relentlessly active, and on the other by using his status as an Independent to form left-right coalitions.

On this particular day, Sanders carries with him an amendment to Section 215 of the second version of the Patriot Act, which is due to go to the House floor for a reauthorization vote the next day. Unlike many such measures, which are often arcane and shrouded in minutiae, the Sanders amendment is simple, a proposed rollback of one of the Patriot Act's most egregious powers: Section 215 allows law enforcement to conduct broad searches of ordinary citizens—even those not suspected of ties to terrorism—without any judicial oversight at all. To a civil libertarian like Sanders, it is probably a gross insult that at as late a date as the year 2005 he still has to spend his time defending a concept like probable cause before an ostensibly enlightened legislature. But the legislation itself will prove not half as insulting as the roadblocks he must overcome to force a vote on the issue.

The House Rules Committee is perhaps the free world's outstanding bureaucratic abomination—a tiny, airless closet deep in the labyrinth of the Capitol where some of the very meanest people on earth spend their days cleaning democracy like a fish. The official function of the committee is to decide which bills and amendments will be voted on by Congress and also to schedule the parameters of debate. If Rules votes against your amendment, your amendment dies. If you control the Rules Committee, you control Congress.

The committee has nine majority members and four minority members. But in fact, only one of those thirteen people matters. Unlike on most committees, whose chairmen are usually chosen on the basis of seniority, the Rules chairman is the appointee of the Speaker of the House.

The current chairman, David Dreier, is a pencil-necked Christian Scientist from Southern California, with exquisite hygiene and a passion for brightly colored ties. While a dependable enough yes man to have remained Rules chairman for six years now, he is basically a human appendage, a prosthetic attachment on the person of the House majority leader, Tom DeLay. "David carries out the wishes of the Republican leadership right down the line," said former Texas Congressman Martin Frost, until last year the committee's ranking Democrat.

There is no proven method of influencing the Rules Committee. In fact, in taking on the committee, Democrats and Independents like Sanders normally have only one weapon at their disposal.

"Shame," says James McGovern, a Massachusetts Democrat and one of the minority members on the committee. "Once in a great while we can shame them into allowing a vote on something or other."

The Rules Committee meets in a squalid little space the size of a high school classroom, with poor lighting and nothing on the walls but lifeless landscapes and portraits of stern-looking congressmen of yore. The grim setting is an important part of the committee's character. In the vast, majestic complex that is the U.S. Capitol—an awesome structure where every chance turn leads to architectural wonderment—the room where perhaps the most crucial decisions of all are made is a dark, seldom-visited hole in the shadow of the press gallery.

The committee is the last stop on the legislative express, a kind of border outpost where bills are held up before they are allowed to pass into law. It meets sporadically, convening when a bill is ready to be sent to the floor for a vote.

Around 3 P.M., Sanders emerges from this hole into the hallway. For the last hour or so, he has been sitting with his hands folded on his lap in a corner of the cramped committee room, listening as a parade of witnesses and committee members babbled on in stream-of-consciousness fashion about the vagaries of the Patriot Act. He heard, for instance, Texas Republican Pete Sessions explain his "philosophy" of how to deal with terrorists, which includes, he said, "killing them or removing them from the country."

Tom Cole of Oklahoma, another Republican committee member, breathlessly congratulated witnesses who had helped prepare the act. "This is a very important piece of legislation," he drawled. "Y'all have done a really good job."

Nodding bashfully in agreement with Cole's words was Wisconsin Republican James Sensenbrenner Jr. As chairman of the Judiciary Committee, Sensenbrenner is the majority lawmaker in whose scaly womb the Patriot Act gestated until its recent delivery to Rules. Though he was here as a witness, his obvious purpose was to bare his fangs in the direction of anyone or anything who would threaten his offspring.

Sensenbrenner is your basic Fat Evil Prick, perfectly cast as a dictatorial committee chairman: He has the requisite moist-with-sweat pink neck, the dour expression, the penchant for pointless bile and vengefulness. Only a month before, on June 10th, Sensenbrenner suddenly decided he'd heard enough during a Judiciary Committee hearing on the Patriot Act and went completely Tasmanian devil on a group of Democratic witnesses who had come to share stories of abuses at places like Guantanamo Bay. Apparently not wanting to hear any of that stuff, Sensenbrenner got up midmeeting and killed the lights, turned off the microphones and shut down the C-SPAN feed, before marching his fellow Republicans out of the room—leaving the Democrats and their witnesses in the dark.

This lights-out technique was actually pioneered by another Republican, former Commerce Committee chairman Thomas Bliley, who in 1995 hit the lights on a roomful of senior citizens who had come to protest Newt Gingrich's Medicare plan. Bliley, however, went one step further than Sensenbrenner, ordering Capitol police to arrest the old folks when they refused to move. Sensenbrenner might have tried the same thing in his outburst, except that his party had just voted to underfund the Capitol police.

Thus it is strange now, in the Rules Committee hearing, to see the legendarily impatient Sensenbrenner lounging happily in his witness chair like a giant toad sunning on nature's perfect rock. He speaks at length about the efficacy of the Patriot Act in combating the certain evils of the free-library system ("I don't think we want to turn libraries into sanctuaries") and responds to questions about the removal of an expiration date on the new bill ("We don't have sunsets on Amtrak or Social Security, either").

Such pronouncements provoke strident responses from the four Democratic members of the committee—Doris Matsui of California, Alcee Hastings of Florida,

Louise Slaughter of upstate New York and McGovern of Massachusetts—who until now have scarcely stirred throughout the hearing. The Democrats generally occupy a four-seat row on the far left end of the panel table, and during hearings they tend to sit there in mute, impotent rage, looking like the unhappiest four heads of lettuce to ever come out of the ground. The one thing they are allowed to do is argue. Sensenbrenner gives them just such an opportunity, and soon he and McGovern fall into a row about gag orders.

In the middle of the exchange, Sanders gets up and, looking like a film lover leaving in the middle of a bad movie, motions for me to join him in the hallway. He gestures at the committee room. "It's cramped, it's uncomfortable, there isn't enough room for the public or press," he says. "That's intentional. If they wanted people to see this, they'd pick a better hall."

Sanders then asks me if I noticed anything unusual about the squabbling between Sensenbrenner and McGovern. "Think about it," he says, checking his watch. "How hard is it to say, 'Mr. Sanders, be here at 4:30 p.m.'? Answer: not hard at all. You see, a lot of the things we do around here are structured. On the floor, in other committees, it's like that. But in the Rules Committee, they just go on forever. You see what I'm getting at?"

I shrug.

"It has the effect of discouraging people from offering amendments," he says. "Members know that they're going to have to sit for a long time. Eventually they have to choose between coming here and conducting other business. And a lot of them choose other business . . . That's what that show in there was about."

Amendment 2

As he waits for his chance to address the Rules Committee, Sanders is actually armed with not one but two amendments. The measures are essentially the same, both using identical language to prohibit warrantless searches of libraries and bookstores. The only difference is, the amendment Sanders is trying to get past the committee would permanently outlaw such searches under the Patriot Act. The second amendment takes a more temporary approach, denying the Justice Department funding in next year's budget to conduct those types of searches.

This kind of creative measure—so-called limitation amendments—are often the best chance for a minority member like Sanders to influence legislation. For one thing, it's easier to offer such amendments to appropriations bills than it is to amend bills like the Patriot Act. Therefore, Sanders often brings issues to a vote by attempting to limit the funds for certain government programs—targeting a federal loan here, a bloated contract there. "It's just another way of getting at an issue," says Sanders.

In this case, the tactic worked. A month earlier, on June 15th, the House passed Sanders' amendment to limit funding for library and bookstore searches by a vote of 238-187, with thirty-eight Republicans joining 199 Democrats.

The move wasn't a cure-all; it was just a short-term fix. But it enabled Sanders to approach the Rules Committee holding more than his hat in his hand. With the June vote, he had concrete evidence to show the committee that if his amendment to permanently alter the Patriot Act were allowed to reach the floor, it would pass. Now, if Tom DeLay & Co. were going to disallow Sanders' amendment, they were going to have to openly defy a majority vote of the U.S. Congress to do so.

Which, it turns out, isn't much of a stumbling block.

While Sanders was facing the Rules Committee, House leaders were openly threatening their fellow members about the upcoming vote on CAFTA. "We will twist their arms until they break" was the Stalin-esque announcement of Arizona Republican Jim Kolbe. The hard-ass, horse-head-in-the-bed threat is a defining characteristic of this current set of House leaders, whose willingness to go to extreme lengths to get their way has become legend. In 2003, Nick Smith, a Michigan legislator nearing retirement, was told by Republican leadership that if he didn't vote for the GOP's Medicare bill, the party would put forward a primary challenger against his son Brad, who was planning to run for his seat.

Members who cross DeLay & Co. invariably find themselves stripped of influence and/or important committee positions. When Rep. Chris Smith complained about Bush's policy toward veterans, he was relieved of his seat as the Veterans' Committee chairman. When Joel Hefley locked horns with Dennis Hastert during the Tom DeLay ethics flap, Hefley lost his spot as the House Ethics Committee chairman.

In other words, these leaders don't mind screwing even their friends any chance they get. Take the kneecapping of Arizona Republican Jeff Flake, whose surrender on the Patriot Act issue paved the way for the trashing of the Sanders amendment.

Flake, who sits on Sensenbrenner's Judiciary Committee, had been one of the leading Republican critics of the Patriot Act. He was particularly explicit in his support for sunset provisions in the law, which would prevent it from being made permanent. In April, for instance, a Flake spokesman told the *Los Angeles Times*, "Law enforcement officials would be more circumspect if they were faced with the prospect of having to come to Congress every couple of years and justify the provisions."

When Sanders offered his amendment to deny funding for warrantless searches, Flake was right there by his side. But now, only a few weeks later, Flake suddenly offers his own amendment, aimed at the same provision of the Patriot Act as Sanders', but with one big difference: It surrenders on the issue of probable cause. The Flake amendment would require only that the FBI director approve any library and bookstore searches.

It is hard to imagine a more toothless, pantywaist piece of legislation than Flake's measure. In essence, it is a decree from the legislative branch righteously demanding that the executive branch authorize its own behavior—exactly the kind of comical "compromise" measure one would expect the leadership to propose as a replacement for the Sanders plan.

Flake clearly had made a deal with the House leadership. It is not known what he got in return, but it appears that his overlords made him pay for it. Before the final vote on any bill, the opposition party has a chance to offer what is called a "motion to recommit," which gives Congress a last chance to re-examine a bill before voting on it. When the Democrats introduced this motion before the final vote, the House Republican leadership had to ask someone to stand up against it. They, naturally, turned to Flake, the chastened dissenter, to run the errand.

Flake is a sunny-looking sort of guy with a slim build and blow-dried blond hair. He looks like a surfer or maybe the manager of a Guitar Center in Ventura or El Segundo: outwardly cheerful, happy and ill-suited, facially anyway, for the real nut-cutting politics of this sort. When it comes time for him to give his speech, Flake meanders to the podium like a man who has just had his head clanged between a pair of cymbals. The lump in his throat is the size of a casaba melon. He begins, "Mr. Speaker, I am probably the last person expected to speak on behalf of the committee or the leadership in genera . . ."

When Flake mentions his own amendments, his voice drops as he tries to sound proud of them—but the most he can say is, "They are good." Then he becomes down-right philosophical: "Sometimes as my hero in politics said once . . . Barry Goldwater said, 'Politics is nothing more than public business . . . You don't always get everything you want.' "

It is a painful performance. Later, commenting on the Flake speech, Sanders shakes his head. "They made him walk the plank there," he says.

Flake denies he cut a deal to sell out on the Patriot Act. But his cave-in effectively spelled the end of the Sanders amendment. The Republicans point to the Flake amendment to show that they addressed concerns about library and bookstore searches. Essentially, the House leaders have taken the Sanders measure, cut all the guts out of it, bullied one of their own into offering it in the form of a separate amendment and sent it sailing through the House, leaving Sanders—and probable cause—to suck eggs.

Amendment 1 Redux

Late in the afternoon, after waiting several hours for his turn, Sanders finally gets a chance to address the Rules Committee. His remarks are short but violent. He angrily demands that the committee let Congress vote on his amendment, noting that the appropriations version of it had already passed the House by fifty-one votes. "I would regard it as an outrageous abuse of power to deny this amendment the opportunity to be part of this bill," he shouts. "We had this debate already—and our side won."

In response, Republicans on the committee cast a collective "whatever, dude" gaze. "Sometimes, you can engage them a little," Sanders says later. But most of the time it works out like this.

Shortly after Sanders finishes his remarks, the Rules Committee members scurry to begin what will be a very long night of work. To most everyone outside those nine majority members, what transpires in the committee the night before a floor vote is a mystery on the order of the identity of Jack the Ripper or the nature of human after-life. Even the Democrats who sit on the committee have only a vague awareness of what goes on. "They can completely rewrite bills," says McGovern. "Then they take it to the floor an hour later. Nobody knows what's in those bills."

One singular example of this came four years ago, when the Judiciary Committee delivered the first Patriot Act to the Rules Committee for its consideration. Dreier trashed that version of the act, which had been put together by the bipartisan committee, and replaced it with a completely different bill that had been written by John Ashcroft's Justice Department.

The bill went to the floor a few hours later, where it passed into law. The Rules Committee is supposed to wait out a three-day period before sending the bill to the House, ostensibly in order to give the members a chance to read the bill. The three-day period is only supposed to be waived in case of emergency. However, the Rules Committee of DeLay and Dreier waives the three-day period as a matter of routine. This forces members of Congress to essentially cast blind yes-or-no votes to bills whose contents are likely to be an absolute mystery to them.

There is therefore an element of Christmas morning in each decision of the committee. On the day of a floor vote, you look under the tree (i.e., the Rules Committee Web site) and check to see if your amendment survived. And so, on the morning of July 21st, Sanders' staff goes online and clicks on a link H.R. 3199—USA PATRIOT AND TERRORISM PREVENTION REAUTHORIZATION ACT OF 2005. Twenty of sixty-three amendments have survived, most of them inconsequential. The Sanders amendment isn't one of them.

On a sweltering Tuesday morning in the Rayburn Building, a bookend location in the multibuilding home of the House of Representatives, a very long line has formed in the first-floor corridor, outside the Financial Services Committee. In the ongoing orgy of greed that is the U.S. Congress, the Financial Services Committee is the hottest spot. Joel Barkin, a former press aide to Sanders, calls Financial Services the "job committee," because staffers who work for members on that committee move into high-paying jobs on Wall Street or in the credit-card industry with ridiculous ease.

"It seems like once a week, I'd get an e-mail from some staffer involved with that committee," he says, shaking his head. "They'd be announcing their new jobs with MBNA or MasterCard or whatever. I mean, to send that over an e-mail all over Congress—at least try to hide it, you know?"

On this particular morning, about half of the people in the line to get into the committee appear to be congressional staffers, mostly young men in ties and dress shirts. The rest are disheveled, beaten-down-looking men, most of them black, leaning against the walls.

These conspicuous characters are called "line-standers." A lot of them are homeless. This is their job: They wait in line all morning so some lobbyist for Akin, Gump or any one of a thousand other firms doesn't have to. "Three days a week," says William McCall (who has a home), holding up three fingers. "Come in Tuesday, Wednesday and Thursday. Get between twelve and forty dollars."

When a photographer approaches to take a picture of the line, all the line-standers but McCall refuse to be photographed and cover their faces with newspapers. I smile at this: Only the homeless have enough sense to be ashamed of being seen in Congress.

In reality, everybody in Congress is a stand-in for some kind of lobbyist. In many cases it's difficult to tell whether it's the companies that are lobbying the legislators or whether it's the other way around.

Amendment 3

Across the Rayburn building on the second floor, a two-page memo rolls over the fax machine in Sanders' office. Warren Gunnels, the congressman's legislative director, has been working the phones all day long, monitoring the Capitol Hill gossip around a vote that is to take place in the Senate later that afternoon. Now a contact of his has sent him a fax copy of an item making its way around the senatorial offices that day. Gunnels looks at the paper and laughs.

The memo appears to be printed on the official stationery of the Export-Import Bank, a federally subsidized institution whose official purpose is to lend money to overseas business ventures as a means of creating a market for U.S. exports. That's the official mission. A less full-of-shit description of Ex-Im might describe it as a federal slush fund that gives away massive low-interest loans to companies that a) don't need the money and b) have recently made gigantic contributions to the right people.

The afternoon Senate vote is the next act in a genuinely thrilling drama that Sanders himself started in the House a few weeks before. On June 28th, Sanders scored a stunning victory when the House voted 313-114 to approve his amendment to block a $5 billion loan by the Ex-Im Bank to Westinghouse to build four nuclear power plants in China.

The Ex-Im loan was a policy so dumb and violently opposed to American interests that lawmakers who voted for it had serious trouble coming up with a plausible excuse for approving it. In essence, the U.S. was giving $5 billion to a state-subsidized British utility (Westinghouse is a subsidiary of British Nuclear Fuels) to build up the infrastructure of our biggest trade competitor, along the way sharing advanced nuclear technology with a Chinese conglomerate that had, in the past, shared nuclear know-how with Iran and Pakistan.

John Hart, a spokesman for Oklahoma Republican Sen. Tom Coburn (who would later sponsor the Senate version of the Sanders amendment), laughs when asked what his opponents were using as an excuse for the bill. "One reason I got," Hart says, "was that if we build nuclear power plants in China, then China would be less dependent on foreign oil, and they would consume less foreign oil, and so as a result our oil prices would go down." He laughs again. "You'd think there would be more direct ways of lowering gas prices," he says.

Oddly enough, Coburn, a hard-line pro-war, pro-life conservative who once advocated the death penalty for abortion doctors, is a natural ally for the "socialist" Sanders on an issue like this one. Sanders frequently looks for co-sponsors among what he and his staff call "honest conservatives," people like California's Dana Rohrabacher and Texas libertarian Ron Paul, with whom Sanders frequently works on trade issues. "A lot of times, guys like my boss will have a lot in common with someone like Sanders," says Jeff Deist, an aide to Rep. Paul. "We're frustrated by the same obstacles in the system."

In the case of Westinghouse, the bill's real interest for the Senate had little to do with gas prices and a lot to do with protecting a party member in trouble. Many of the 5,000 jobs the loan was supposed to create were in Pennsylvania, where Rick Santorum, the GOP incumbent, was struggling to hold off a challenger. "Five billion for 5,000 jobs," Sanders says, shaking his head in disbelief. "That's $1 million per job. And they say I'm crazy."

This morning, with the Senate vote only a few hours away, the lobbying has kicked into very high gear. That lobbyists for Westinghouse are phone-blitzing senatorial offices is no surprise. Somewhat more surprising are reports that the Ex-Im Bank itself is hustling the senatorial staff.

"Technically speaking, government agencies aren't allowed to lobby," says Gunnels. "But they sure do a lot of informing just before big votes."

The document that has just spilled over the Sanders fax line is printed with a cover sheet from the Ex-Im Bank. It looks like an internal memo, sent by Ex-Im's "Senior Legislative Analyst," Beverley Thompson.

The document contains a series of cheery talking points about the Ex-Im loan to China, which taken together seem to indicate that the loan is a darn good idea. Nowhere does the document simply come out and say, "We recommend that the Sanders amendment against this loan be defeated." But the meaning is fairly clear.

One odd feature of the document is a notation at the top of the page that reads, "FYI—this info has not been cleared." In government offices, documents must be cleared for public consumption before they can be distributed outside the agency. What this memo seems to suggest, then, is that the recipient was being given choice inside info from the Ex-Im Bank, a strange thing for the bank to be doing out in the open.

The Sanders office has seen this kind of thing before. In the summer of 2003, it received a very similar kind of document purportedly from the Treasury. Printed on Treasury stationery, the document contained, like the Ex-Im memo, a list of talking points that seemed to argue against a Sanders amendment. The issue in that case involved a set of new Treasury regulations that would have made it easier for companies to convert their employees' traditional pension plans into a new type of plan called a cash-balance pension plan.

Among the companies that would have been affected by the regulations was IBM, which stood to save billions by converting to this new system. And guess who turned out to have written the "Treasury Department Memo" that was circulated to members of Congress, on the eve of the vote?

That's right: IBM.

"It was hilarious," recalls Gunnels. "The Treasury Department logo was even kind of tilted, like it had been pasted on. It looked like a third-grader had done it."

Persistent questioning by Sanders' staff led to an admission by the Treasury Department that the document had indeed been doctored by IBM. The company, in turn, issued a utterly nonsensical mea culpa ("We believed that we were redistributing a public document that we had understood was widely distributed by the Treasury") that has to rank as one of the lamer corporate non-apologies in recent years.

It seemed obvious that the company had acted in conjunction with one or more Treasury employees to create the phony document. But no Treasury employee has ever been exposed, nor has IBM ever been sanctioned. "They turned the case over to the Inspector General's Office," says Gunnels. Jeff Weaver, Sanders' chief of staff, adds, "And they've done absolutely nothing."

So long as the investigation is still open, Gunnels explains, there is no way to request documents pertaining to the case through the Freedom of Information Act. "That investigation will probably stay open a long time," he says.

Every time Congress is ordered to clean up its lobbyist culture, its responses come off like leprechaun tricks. For instance, when the Lobby Disclosure Act of 1995 ordered the House and the Senate to create an electronic lobbyist registry system, so that the public could use the latest technology to keep track of Washington's 34,000-plus lobbyists and whom they work for, the two houses only half-complied.

The secretary of the Senate created an electronic database, all right, but what a database: The system was little more than a giant computerized pile of downloadable scanned images of all the individual registration forms and semiannual reports. The Senate system, however, was a significant improvement over the House system. The House responded to the 1995 law by entirely ignoring it.

All of Washington seems to be in on the lobbyist leprechaun game. News even leaked that corporations had managed to convince the local sports teams, the Wizards and the Capitals, to create special courtside and/or rinkside tickets. The tickets would not be available to the general public but would have an official list price of $49.50 and could be purchased by corporate customers. Why the low list price? Because congressional rules prohibit gifts to congressmen with a cost above fifty dollars.

Amendment 4

The Ex-Im amendment was not the only victory Sanders had scored on the government-waste front that month. In fact, just two days after he passed the Ex-Im amendment, Sanders secured another apparent major victory against a formidable corporate opponent. By a vote of 238–177, the House passed a Sanders amendment to cancel a $1.9 billion contract that the Federal Aviation Administration had awarded to Lockheed Martin to privatize a series of regional Flight Service Stations.

Several factors went into the drafting of this amendment. For one thing, the FAA-Lockheed deal would have resulted in the loss of about 1,000 jobs around the country from the closure of thirty-eight Flight Service Stations, which are basically small regional centers that give out weather information and provide some basic air-traffic assistance. Thirty-five of those projected job losses would have come from a station in Burlington, Vermont, so in opposing the deal, Sanders was behaving like a traditional congressman, protecting his home turf.

But there were other concerns. The FAA deal was an early test run for a Bush policy idea called "competitive sourcing," which is just a clunky euphemism for the privatization of traditionally governmental services. Sanders is generally opposed to competitive sourcing, mainly on cost and quality grounds.

Beyond that, Sanders sees in issues like the Westinghouse deal and the Lockheed Martin deal a consistent pattern of surrender to business interests by Congress. Too often, he says, Congress fails to tie government assistance to the company's record in preserving American jobs.

"I have no problem with the argument that we should help businesses out," Sanders says. "But if you go to these hearings, no one ever asks the question 'How many jobs have you exported over the years? If we give you money, will you promise not to export any more jobs?' "

He laughs. "It's funny. Some of these companies, they'll be straight with you. General Electric, for instance. They come right out and say, 'We're moving to China.' And if you ask them why, in that case, you should subsidize them, they say, 'If you don't help us, we'll move to China faster.' "

Given how powerful Lockheed Martin is on Capitol Hill—the company even has the contract to maintain the server for the computers in Congress—the Lockheed vote was surprisingly easy. Maybe too easy. On the surface, it looked like traditional politics all the way, with Sanders applying his usual formula of securing as many Democratic votes as possible, then working to pry loose enough Republicans to get the vote through. In this case, the latter task proved not all that difficult, as Sanders had natural allies in each of those Republican representatives with targeted flight stations in their districts.

But when the vote sailed through by a comfortable margin, Sanders didn't celebrate. Sometimes, he says, a vote like this one will pass easily in the House precisely because the leadership knows it will be able to kill it down the line.

"I don't want to accuse my fellow members of cynicism," he says, "but sometimes they'll vote for an amendment just so they can go back home and say they fought for this or that. In reality, they've been assured by the leadership that the measure will never make it through."

And if an offending bill somehow makes it through the House and the Senate, there's always the next and last step: the conference committee. Comprising bipartisan groups of "conferees" from the relevant House and Senate authorizing committees, these committees negotiate the final version of a bill. Like the Rules Committee, it has absolute power to make wholesale changes—which it usually does, safely out of the public's view.

With a measure like Sanders' Lockheed amendment, the chances were always going to be very slim that it would survive the whole process. Among other things, President Bush responded to the passage of the anti-Lockheed amendment by immediately threatening to veto the entire Transportation budget to which it was attached. (Bush made the same threat, incidentally, in response to the Ex–Im amendment, which was attached to the Foreign Operations budget.)

"Now the conference committee has political cover," Sanders says. "It's either take them out and restore that loan and that contract or the president vetoes an entire appropriations bill—and there's no funding for Foreign Operations or Transportation. There's really no choice."

In the case of the Lockheed amendment, however, things never get that far. Despite the amendment's comfortable victory in the House, weeks pass, and the Sanders staff cannot find a senator to sponsor the measure in the upper house. Though the staff still has hopes that a sponsor will be found, it's not always that easy to arrange. Especially when the president threatens a veto over the matter.

As for the Ex-Im amendment, the Sanders gambit against it perishes on that Tuesday afternoon, July 19th, as the Senate wallops the Coburn version of the amendment, 62–37. According to Gunnels, the key vote ends up being cast by Democrat Harry Reid of Nevada.

"It was still close, around 24–23 or so, before Reid voted," he says. "It looked like a lot of Democrats were waiting to see which way he would go, him being the minority leader and all. As soon as he voted no, a whole slew of Democrats followed him, and the amendment was dead."

Reid's predecessor as minority leader, Tom Daschle, was a marionette of the banking and credit-card industries whose public persona recalled a hopped-up suburban vacuum-cleaner salesman. In the wake of the Daschle experiment, Reid is the perfect inheritor of the Democratic leadership mantle: a dour, pro-life Mormon with a campaign chest full of casino money. Trying to figure out his motives on this vote proved no less difficult than figuring out what the Democratic Party stands for in general.

When I call Reid's office, spokesman Jim Manley initially refuses to offer an explanation for the senator's vote. He seems weirdly defensive about the issue, and we go back and forth on the matter for a while before he finally reads a statement explaining—or purporting to, anyway—his boss's vote on the China loan.

"As with questions raised about other transactions involving China, legitimate concerns are at issue," he reads. "But rather than Congress intervening in one transaction after another, what we really need is a coherent and comprehensive policy to address the emergence of China as an economic threat. This administration has failed to develop a China policy . . . and this utter failure has fueled congressional and public unease . . . Got that?"

"Um," I say, copying it down. "Sure. Wait—if the problem is that there's no comprehensive policy for China, why give them $5 billion to build nuclear plants? Why not give them, say, nothing at all?"

Silence on the other end of the line. Finally, Manley speaks.

"This administration has failed to develop a China policy," he repeats coldly. "And this utter failure has fueled congressional and public unease . . ."

In the end, after just a few weeks, every one of Sanders' victories was transformed into a defeat. He had won three major amendments and would likely have won a fourth, if the Rules Committee had permitted a vote on his Patriot Act measure. In each case, Sanders proved that his positions held wide support—even among a population as timid and corrupt as the U.S. Congress. Yet even after passing his amendments by wide margins, he never really came close to converting popular will into law.

Sanders seem to take it strangely in stride. After a month of watching him and other members, I get the strong impression that even the idealists in Congress have learned to accept the body on its own terms. Congress isn't the steady assembly line of consensus policy ideas it's sold as, but a kind of permanent emergency in which a majority of members work day and night to burgle the national treasure and burn the Constitution. A largely castrated minority tries, Alamo-style, to slow them down—but in the end spends most of its time beating calculated retreats and making loose plans to fight another day.

Taken all together, the whole thing is an ingenious system for inhibiting progress and the popular will. The deck is stacked just enough to make sure that nothing ever changes. But just enough is left to chance to make sure that hope never completely dies out. And who knows, maybe it evolved that way for a reason.

"It's funny," Sanders says. "When I first came to Congress, I'd been mayor of Burlington, Vermont—a professional politician. And I didn't know any of this. I assumed that if you get majorities in both houses, you win. I figured, it's democracy, right?"

Well, that's what they call it, anyway.

Discussion Questions

1. Reflecting on life on Capitol Hill, Rep. Sanders tells Taibbi: "Nobody knows how this place is run. If they did, they'd go nuts." Why do you think the legislative process is so unknown to the American people? Do you agree that people would "go nuts" if they were aware of what happens within Congress?

2. With each of Sanders's legislative initiatives, a victory seemingly was won, only to be reversed and turned into a defeat at the last minute. What were the obstacles he encountered with his amendments? Comment on the quality of representative democracy in light of Taibbi's account of his time as an observer of the public policy process.

17   Congressional Inertia: Iron Triangles Old and New

Patricia Siplon and William F. Grover

American citizens often complain about the performance of Congress. They are generally unhappy with the lack of cooperation between the two political parties in Congress and how little actually gets done in Washington. And when Congress does act, citizens seldom view that action as benefiting the average middle-class and working-class American. In this article, political scientists Patricia Siplon and William Grover draw upon the time-tested concept of the "iron triangle" to explain the causes of congressional inertia. They trace the history of iron triangles to the earlier notion of the "military–industrial complex," which was articulated most notably by President Dwight Eisenhower in his 1961 Farewell Address, and later expanded into a full-blown analysis of defense contracting by political scientist Gordon Adams. Adams defined the iron triangle as a symbiotic relationship among three sets of political actors: congressional committees and subcommittees, executive branch agencies, and private interest groups, particularly corporations. He was troubled by ever-rising defense budgets and how in the process of forming U.S. defense policy, private corporate interests regularly came to be equated with the public interest. Congress too willingly abandoned its oversight function in favor of promoting, seemingly at any cost, the smooth advancement of Pentagon plans and defense contractor profits. Moving beyond the classic example of military budgets, Siplon and Grover turn their attention to the role of iron triangles in human immunodeficiency virus (HIV)/acquired immunodeficiency syndrome (AIDS) policy. Since the early 1980s, the pharmaceutical industry has vigorously lobbied Congress, and worked closely with the Food and Drug Administration, to shape the nation's approach to the development, regulation, and pricing of drugs to fight the AIDS pandemic. The resulting pharmaceutical iron triangle dramatically impacted the development, pricing, and availability of the drugs azidothymidine (AZT) and Norvir. In the face of the deaths of millions suffering from AIDS worldwide over more than two decades, the fight to provide widespread access to cheap generic AIDS drugs continues, with occasional victories for social groups challenging this particular iron triangle. As with the classic example of defense contracting, when it comes to the life and death circumstances with HIV/AIDS policy, Congress far too often plays the role of a lapdog for corporate and executive branch policymakers, instead of acting as a watchdog for the interests of American citizens.

Reprinted from *Voices of Dissent* (2009).

What Congress does matters. As the new 110th Congress convened in January of 2007, it began the process of constructing the fiscal year 2008 budget, authorizing spending in the vicinity of $2.8 trillion when the new fiscal year begins October 1. This is an incomprehensibly large amount of money—a sum that represents many things.[1] Most notably, it is a numerical statement about priorities; what we value as a society is indicated in how we allocate our budgetary resources. What do U.S. citizens think of those who allocate our budgetary resources? If we follow poll data, the answer clearly is: "not much." It has long been noted that while citizens routinely rate their own Senators and Representatives favorably, Congress as an institution gets very low marks. A *New York Times*/CBS news poll released in late September 2006 showed the approval rating for Congress at barely 25 percent, a dozen points below President George W. Bush's own anemic approval rating. The accompanying story observed that public "disdain for Congress is as intense as it has been since 1994," when Republicans captured both the House and Senate for the first time in decades. A full 77 percent of respondents in the *Times*/CBS poll said the 109th Congress had not done a good enough job to merit being reelected. Accordingly, voters expressed their displeasure with Republican control of Congress in November 2006, returning Democrats to power in the House and, more narrowly, in the Senate. Clearly something is afoot here. Opposition to the Bush administration's debacle in Iraq surely soured voters, as did corruption scandals involving some leading officials. But beneath those immediate issues lies a deeper sense that Congress does not deliver the goods— at least for ordinary Americans. As an institution, Congress is widely perceived to suffer from entrenched inertia that leaves it unable to change course. Why is it so difficult for our legislative branch to change direction to respond to shifting priorities?

A Brief History of a Metaphor

Political science is awash in metaphors. The intent of a well-constructed metaphor is to capture some complex aspect of politics with an easily understood example. The opening paragraph above involves the most important and complicated function performed by Congress—readily conceptualized as controlling the national "purse strings." A multitude of metaphors winds its way through our political landscape: "horse races," "landslides," "pork," "log rolling," "hawks and doves," "quagmires"—these barely scratch the surface. Indeed, sociologist Max Weber once famously argued that a combination of passion and perspective is needed to succeed in politics, characterizing politics itself as, metaphorically, "a strong and slow boring of hard boards." Understanding the difficulty in getting Congress to change course, to address policy issues in a fresh way with the public interest at heart, involves one of the most apt metaphors used in congressional studies: the "iron triangle."

The origins of the iron triangle metaphor are rooted in the development of a closely related concept known as the "military–industrial complex." Although references to the military–industrial complex go back at least to the early part of the twentieth century, the most well-known usage came in President Dwight Eisenhower's Farewell Address on January 17, 1961. Eisenhower was a moderate Republican with vast military experience, having served as Supreme Commander of allied forces in World War II. He used his Farewell Address to issue a prescient warning about the combined power of the military bureaucracy of the executive branch (particularly the Defense Department) and the arms industry:

> This conjunction of an immense military establishment and a large arms industry is new in the American experience. The total influence—economic, political, even spiritual—is felt in every city, every statehouse, every office of the federal government. We recognize the imperative need for this development. Yet we must not fail to comprehend its grave implications. Our toil, resources and livelihood are all involved; so is the very structure of our society. In the councils of government, we must guard against the acquisition of unwarranted influence, whether sought or unsought, by the *military–industrial complex*. The potential for the disastrous rise of misplaced power exists and will persist.

From President Eisenhower's perspective, the stakes involved could not have been higher. He went on to characterize the "huge industrial and military machinery of defense" as a potential threat to our liberties and to democracy itself. In a draft of his address, Eisenhower had referred to the "military–industrial–congressional complex," dropping the word "congressional" in deference to the sensitivities of members of Congress. But it was clear that he was concerned about the role Congress played in perpetuating the power of this alliance of the Pentagon and private corporate defense contractors.

It fell to Gordon Adams, a defense analyst and professor of international affairs, to more fully flesh out the political and economic implications of the iron triangle in his 1981 book *The Politics of Defense Contracting: The Iron Triangle*. Adams defined the iron triangle as a political relationship among three sets of participants in a specific policy area. This symbiotic relationship involves congressional committees and subcommittees, agencies within the executive branch bureaucracy, and private interest groups. In the case of defense policy, the relevant policy actors are the House and Senate Armed Services Committees, as well as the House and Senate Defense Appropriations Subcommittees; for the executive branch the chief player is the Defense Department, although the Department of Energy and National Aeronautics and Space Administration (NASA) also might be involved; and the key interest groups are corporate defense contractors, their trade associations, and policy research institutions. In his study, Adams focused particularly on defense contractors such as Boeing, General Dynamics, Grumman, Lockheed, McDonnell Douglas, Northrop, several of which have long since merged. Working together to pursue a common set of interests, these three points of the triangle form a policy "subgovernment" whose political and economic power is exceptionally hard to challenge. Through lobbying and entertainment, campaign contributions, congressional hearings, shared personnel, and public policy articulation, these three sets of institutional actors develop a high level of expertise in the area of defense policy and a shared outlook on what constitutes "acceptable" debate on defense spending. From the perspective of those participating in the triangle, it looks as though the vital area of national defense policy is capably handled by this alliance of Congress, bureaucratic agencies, and interest groups. What could be wrong with a system that promotes shared knowledge and broadened expertise?

From Watchdog to Capdog

As these triangular interactions grow, a set of mutually beneficial "sweetheart" relationships develop. Members of congressional committees and subcommittees constantly need campaign contributions and continually seek the perspective of Pentagon and corporate players for the latest information. Representatives and Senators from the defense-related committees protect their expertise and specialization, becoming insulated from views outside the triangle that might question their priorities and their definitions of national security. The Pentagon always seeks new weapons systems and more funding for troops to support the administration's defense strategy and fosters a particular outlook on foreign and military policy through research institutions that share a pro-military perspective. For their part, defense contractors want to market new and improved weapons systems, which are central to their pursuit of profit and the provision of millions of jobs. So all three sets of participants have a vested interest in the perpetuation of the triangle.

As Adams pointed out, the normal operation of the iron triangle has troubling implications for democracy, blurring if not eliminating the distinction between the public interest and private interests. Corporate views of "national security" merge with governmental views, as Congress and the Defense Department come to equate the private interests of contractors with the public interest. With the growing role of high-tech weapons systems in the U.S. economy, what emerges is, something critics of the military have long called a "permanent war economy," wherein the nation's economic health requires actual war and the continual threat of future wars—a situation that raises grave moral concerns and confirms one of President Eisenhower's worst fears. It is in the area of congressional politics, though, where we find perhaps the most unsettling impact, involving the interconnected role of *money*, *people*, and *oversight*.

The House and Senate are the governing institutions most closely aligned with the people. It is here that citizens have their most direct contact with national policy. The strength of the iron triangle can erode that contact. Earlier we mentioned that the most important function Congress performs is control of the nation's "purse strings." Each year Congress raises (through taxation) and spends (through appropriations) our hard-earned money. Money is the conduit for much of our politics. Campaign contributions from individuals and political action committees are the lifeblood of incumbent reelection campaigns. The Pentagon wants a larger portion of the budget each year from committees that authorize and spend money on national defense. Defense contractors spend millions of dollars lobbying Congress for contracts that can run into the billions. By one estimate, there are some 35,000 registered lobbyists in Washington, DC, and collectively all types of interest groups spend upwards of $200 million per month to sway the opinions of federal policymakers. And who does the swaying? In addition to money, this is where personnel come in to play.

The iron triangle fosters close personal relations among people who sit at all three points of the triangle. It is common for, say, a Senator who serves on the Armed Services Committee to retire and go to work as a lobbyist for a defense contractor with whom he has worked on military policy for years. Thus he will be paid handsomely to lobby his former colleagues on the relevant Senate committee. Likewise, senior Pentagon officials are often drawn from the ranks of defense corporations, or from corporately funded policy research institutes with a shared, friendly view of military strategy. The degree to which personnel are interlocked is quite high. This revolving-door situation leads to the phenomenon of "recycled elites," people who move around to various points of the triangle, further insulating policymakers from outsider influences. The examples are many.

One especially clear current illustration of recycled elites within the iron triangle is Vice President Dick Cheney. Cheney worked in the administrations of both Presidents Nixon and Ford. In 1978, he was elected to Congress where he served as Wyoming's lone Representative for six terms, developing a reputation as an extremely pro-defense Congressman. He served as Secretary of Defense for President George H. W. Bush from 1989 to 1993 and joined a conservative think tank, the American Enterprise Institute, in 1993. From 1995 to 2000, he was Chair and CEO of Halliburton Energy Services. Halliburton is an oil services corporation that has been lavished with military contracts worth tens of millions of dollars to help rebuild Iraq during the war and is now charged with defrauding the federal government for its work on many of those contracts. During his Halliburton days, he also was a member of the conservative "Project for a New American Century," along with Donald Rumsfeld and several other future architects of President George W. Bush's foreign and defense policy. And of course, he has been vice president in President Bush's administration since 2001. Cheney thus has held positions on all three points of the iron triangle. He is a prime example of how a community of interests, a way of looking at the world, is forged within the triangle. Such a worldview insulates the players from dissenting perspectives. While expertise surely is gathered over time, discussion of military policy is confined to a stiflingly narrow range of debate over the means of achieving a shared set of perspectives. Those perspectives themselves—the ends of policy—are not on the table. As a result, while policymakers may come and go, weapons systems are built, soldiers fight and die, and roots of U.S. foreign and military policy—the basic political and economic interests that underlie them—remain essentially unchanged.

In addition to money and personnel, a third factor to consider in exploring the impact of the iron triangle on congressional relations is oversight. If the most fundamental role of Congress is to control the nation's "purse strings," oversight is its second most pressing job. Oversight means that the House and Senate are charged with looking out for the public interest by overseeing the conduct of executive branch agencies that implement the policies Congress passes into law. Congress performs this role in many ways, for example, by holding congressional committee hearings and by conducting studies (armed with subpoena power) to investigate various agencies of the executive branch. The average citizen would have difficulty finding the time to single-handedly monitor the details of policy making and policy implementation. Congress is supposed to do that for us. In a sense, our elected representatives serve as our eyes and ears in Washington. It is this oversight role—the role of a "watchdog"—that is so valuable to a healthy democracy. But if Congress has been captured by the industry it is supposed to oversee and regulate—in the classic iron triangle case, the defense industry—then the watchdog becomes a mere lapdog of industry, tethered to a set of interests from which it is ideally supposed to maintain some critical distance. When that critical distance has been lost, and the watchdog is tamed and transformed into a lapdog, the foundation of representative democracy is weakened.

The iron triangle began as a way to understand the intractability of an insulated way of approaching military budgets and national security policy. Yet the concept can be applied to virtually any policy area, as this case study demonstrates with regard to human immunodeficiency virus (HIV)/acquired immunodeficiency syndrome (AIDS)—another public policy issue where life and death literally hang in the balance.

New Policy, New Triangles

In 1981, scientists at the government agency in charge of monitoring the nation's health, the Centers for Disease Control and Prevention (CDC), realized that they were tracking a new and deadly disease. No one knew what caused it or how to treat it. They only knew that it seemed to be attacking people in the prime of their lives, whose condition then quickly deteriorated and who died of diseases such as rare types of pneumonia seldom seen among healthy populations. From people experiencing the new illness in themselves or a loved one, there was an urgent call for new drugs to fight the causative agent—which we now know as HIV—or at least the diseases and infections that HIV was facilitating. For ill and at-risk populations, new treatments were literally a matter of life and death. For drug companies, they were an opportunity to market an array of new products at the high prices that desperate people are willing to pay.

As a corporate interest group, it is hard to imagine one more well situated to achieve its aims in Washington than the pharmaceutical lobby. Although iron triangles work by making sure that members of key congressional committees and subcommittees are deeply beholden to the industry at hand, the pharmaceutical industry has hedged its bets by spreading its largess more widely. A 2005 report for the Center for Public Integrity found that it has spent more than $800 million in state and federal lobbying and campaign donations in the preceding seven years, making it second only to the insurance industry in combined expenditures (and first, when looking at lobbying only). The report also noted that most of this lobbying money was spent on the salaries of the three-thousand-strong lobbying force it has assembled, more than a third of which comes from the ranks of Congress and federal bureaucracies.

During the early 1980s, private and public laboratories raced to identify the new disease agent and find and mass-produce both treatments for infections caused by HIV and medicines designed to combat the virus itself. The pharmaceutical industry was already well placed to take advantage of the output of these laboratories. As the outlines of the AIDS pandemic began to take shape, a preexisting iron triangle, or more accurately, several iron triangles, anchored by the pharmaceutical industry absorbed this new policy area. The iron triangle most directly involved with the drug-related aspects of

AIDS policy is the same iron triangle that operates around the development, regulation, and pricing of drugs generally. Like other iron triangles, it consists of a congressional committee or subcommittee, executive branch agencies, and private interests. On the House side, the congressional committee that most directly oversees the pharmaceutical industry is the House Energy and Commerce Committee, which is divided into six subcommittees, of which the Subcommittee on Health has most direct oversight of both public health and food and drugs. Of the executive branch agencies, the Food and Drug Administration (FDA), the organization charged with making sure that medicines are both safe and effective, has direct regulatory power over the pharmaceutical industry, although others, including the National Institutes of Health (NIH), also work very closely with the industry. The FDA also oversees the approval process of new drugs, a task that would prove extremely important as new drugs emerged in the early years after the discovery of HIV. Finally, the pharmaceutical industry is well represented by a host of lobbyists and industry representatives: the two largest are Pharmaceutical Research and Manufacturers of America (PhRMA) and the Biotechnology Industry Organization. To say that these triangle elements are closely connected is a gross understatement: one telling indication of just how close is the fact that PhRMA's president is the former Chair of the Energy and Commerce Committee, twenty-four-year House veteran Billy Tauzin. This fact is all the more remarkable when one considers that Tauzin began negotiating the terms of his new employment with PhRMA (reported to include an annual salary in excess of $2 million) only weeks after he had achieved the passage of a Medicare reform bill he had helped to write (see Article 22). That bill had many provisions straight out of the PhRMA playbook, including prohibitions of government negotiations with pharmaceutical companies for lower prices and refusal to allow lower-cost imports from Canada. The cozy relationship was reinforced when Tauzin's successor as chair of the committee, fellow Republican James Greenwood, was snapped up for a similar position (and a high six-figure salary) by the pharmaceutical industry's other main lobbying group, the Biotechnology Industry Organization.

Government Giveaways and the First Aids Drug

The first drug approved to combat HIV—azidothymidine (AZT), otherwise known as Retrovir—was licensed to the drug company Burroughs Wellcome (now two mergers later the international giant GlaxoSmithKline) in 1987. Although Burroughs Wellcome claimed the right to price the new drug—at the hefty price tag of $10,000 for a year's supply—the company had not actually discovered it. That distinction belonged to a researcher, Jerome Horwitz, who developed the compound as an anticancer drug in 1964, with funding from the National Cancer Institute (NCI). Nor did they conduct the original laboratory research that determined that AZT worked in a test tube against HIV. That was done by government-funded laboratories at Duke University and the NCI.

After Burroughs Wellcome got the good news from Duke and the NCI, the company quickly found a way to put its close relationship with the FDA to its advantage. David Barry, a virologist at Wellcome and a former researcher at the FDA, called Ellen Cooper, head of the Division of Antiviral Drug Products at the FDA, to see about expediting AZT's classification as an Investigational New Drug, the next stage in its approval process. Cooper suggested that preliminary data be sent as they were completed; when the final full application was sent, Cooper took less than a week to approve it. Burroughs Wellcome then put the drug through two of the three phases that the FDA traditionally requires for drug approval. Phase I ran for six weeks with nineteen subjects at the NCI and Duke University. Phase II followed, also at Duke and NCI, with 282 subjects, although only 27 participated in the full twenty-four weeks of the trial. Phase III trials were then waived, and the drug was approved on a 10–1 vote by an FDA advisory committee on January 16, 1987. By drug research standards, this one had been a relatively straightforward undertaking. It was formulated in a laboratory supported by a government grant and researched by two other publicly funded entities in small trials with few subjects, with steps explicitly expedited or waived along the way.

So why the $10,000 price tag? That question was asked, but not answered, during hearings of the House Subcommittee on Health and Environment (predecessor to the current Health Subcommittee) in March 1987. After pointing vaguely to the expenses that generally go into the development of any new drug, T. E. Haigler, the then CEO of Burroughs Wellcome, refused to divulge numbers to the more pointed questions of Democratic Congressman Ron Wyden, who asked for actual research and development costs. Though Wyden showed his exasperation (asking "why didn't you just set the price at $100,000 per patient?"), the direction of the power in this relationship was clearly displayed. The government might finance the discovery of the drug and the research that went into it, but to question the price set for this publicly financed medication by a private company was clearly not within its power.

Eventually the price of AZT came down, though not through pressure from either the FDA or Congress. Rather, it was the work of enraged activists, banding together in a new group, the AIDS Coalition to Unleash Power (ACT UP), that forced the drop. Two weeks after Congress' ill-fated hearing, ACT UP staged the first protest of its existence on Wall Street, garnering headlines in major newspapers, and forcing Burroughs Wellcome to drop their prices by 20 percent to stem the tide of negative publicity. Two years later, with AZT still the only approved antiretroviral on the market and in the face of findings that AZT was helpful for those not yet suffering from full-blown AIDS, Burroughs Wellcome saw a ten-fold increase in its potential market, but once again resisted demands to lower its price. AIDS activists fought back, this time with an imaginative action within and outside the New York Stock Exchange that noisily shut down transactions for five minutes. Four days later, Burroughs Wellcome announced a second 20 percent price cut.

The More Things Change, the More They Stay the Same

Two decades and millions of AIDS deaths later, the power of the pharmaceutical iron triangle appears to have remained intact. One thing that has changed is that, at least in wealthy countries, AIDS has moved from being a fatal disease to a chronic condition, manageable through a combination of drug therapies, often referred to as the "cocktail." Protease inhibitors are one type of drugs within the cocktail, and one of these is the drug ritonavir, more commonly known by its trade name, Norvir. The patent for Norvir is held by Abbott Laboratories, which now markets the drug not as a protease inhibitor but as a booster to be taken with the cocktail to heighten the effects of other protease inhibitors. But Abbott never actually developed Norvir. That was done with federal money in the form of a multimillion-dollar government grant from the NIH. The public interest group Consumer Project on Technology has estimated that, in all, Abbott's investment in clinical trials to test the drug it did not pay to develop was under $15 million, yet during its first five years on the market (1996–2001), Abbott's sales of Norvir totaled $1 billion. Yet despite these very healthy sales, none of which need to go to recoup costs of research and development (a common drug company justification for high prices), Abbott chose to raise its price again in 2003 by a whopping 400 percent. The price of the most common booster dose went from $1,600 to $7,800 per year. This price increase was particularly galling to AIDS activists in light of the fact that even before the increase, Norvir was selling in other wealthy countries for less than half the price, and the price increase meant that U.S. citizens were paying five to ten times more for a drug developed with their tax dollars than people in other wealthy countries.

Early attempts to sway Abbott were of the less confrontational variety: AIDS doctors around the country signed petitions asking Abbott to reexamine its pricing policies, and advocacy organizations organized similar petition drives on the same topic. When these failed, HIV-infected people and activists decided to use Norvir as a worst-case example for calling in a never-used power referred to as "march in" authority. This authority came from a piece of legislation passed in 1980 known as the Bayh–Dole Act, which gives the Secretary of Health and Human Services the power to open competition on a patent that was developed with federal funding (as Norvir was with an NIH grant) but is not available at a reasonable price to the public. Jamie Love, president of the nonprofit group Essential Inventions, made the formal petition to the government in January 2004. The NIH responded in May by holding a hearing, for which there is no official written record. Among those invited to testify was Birch Bayh, who had been one of the Senators who had drafted the original law. As the national press noted, he testified *against* the march-in provision he had drafted, arguing that march-in could only be used if it were proven that the drug was not reaching the people who needed it. In his early August ruling, NIH Director Elias Zerhouni concurred, finding that Norvir was being made available to patients "on reasonable terms."

In the same year that the NIH was doing the bidding of the pharmaceutical industry at home, a newer government bureaucracy, the Office of the Global AIDS Coordinator, was serving it abroad. In 2003, President Bush had shocked many by announcing in his State of the Union a new global AIDS initiative, the President's Emergency Plan for AIDS Relief (PEPFAR), as a new five-year multibillion-dollar program to address the AIDS pandemic in some of the worst-affected countries on the planet. Equally surprising was his mention in the speech of the possibility of treating people for under $300 a year—a possibility that could only happen through the purchase of generic drugs adamantly opposed by the pharmaceutical lobby in the United States. Activists were cautiously optimistic, thinking the speech signaled that the Administration might be coming around to accept the use of these generic medicines being used by private humanitarian pilot programs in Africa. But these hopes were dashed when the Administration announced that it was opposed to using these products and called for a meeting in the African country of Botswana. At the meeting, the Office of the Global AIDS Coordinator argued that these generic drugs, some of which were four times cheaper than the most deeply discounted drugs offered by the U.S.-based companies, should not be given to sub-Saharan Africans because, though they had been through the World Health Organization's approval process, they had not been approved by the FDA. In the face of pressure from activist and humanitarian groups, the government eventually allowed some of the drugs to go through the FDA process, but in the months between the meeting and approval, they were not made available to the tens of thousands under treatment. During the interim, the shadow cast by the American iron triangle controlled by the pharmaceutical industry extended all the way to remote villages in Africa.

Prospects and Conclusions: Even Iron Melts

Although iron triangles are incredibly strong, there is evidence to suggest that they are not indestructible. Secrecy, citizen ignorance and indifference, and the absence of countervailing forces all foster their development and maintenance. But conversely, public education, citizen monitoring, and mass mobilization are valuable tools in weakening these structures. President Eisenhower acknowledged as much in his aforementioned Farewell Address, noting that "an alert and knowledgeable citizenry" was needed to serve as a check on military-industrial ambitions. More specifically, two aspects of politics can weaken the solidity of iron triangles. First, budgetary restrictions can diminish the financial resources available to fund projects favored by corporate interests. In conditions of huge budget deficits or economic crisis, even privileged business groups can come up empty-handed. But this potential impediment to iron triangles tends to be transitory. When the financial cloud lifts, the priorities of private interests are quickly reasserted. And as we have learned in the aftermath of 9/11, even in situations of massive budgetary red ink, with deficits as far as the eye can see, certain corporate interests still can get what they want if their specific interest in profits comes to be tied directly to the general "national interest," as with private defense contractors like Halliburton and it subsidiaries, who continue to flourish while most competing domestic interests languish in Congress.

Beyond such budgetary considerations, though, lies a second, more long-term avenue for weakening iron triangles. Pressure from social movements can serve to challenge our legislators and the private interest groups whose priorities Congress too often serves. As the drug company Burroughs Wellcome discovered in our AIDS case study, it was easier to flout the authority of nominal holders of power—members of the Congressional subcommittee tasked to oversee their pricing policies—than it was to maintain their pricing in the face of an implacable social movement willing to take to the streets and colorfully demonstrate in front of television cameras that profits were taking precedence over access to life-saving medicines. If pressure such as this from democratic grassroots movements can be sustained over time by committed activists, it can have a lasting impact on our national priorities. In sum, at high enough temperatures (1,535°C, to be exact) even iron melts. And when it comes to iron triangles, "street heat" can be the catalyst.

Discussion Questions

1. Identify the three components of the "iron triangle." Siplon and Grover list budgeting and oversight as two important powers that Congress could use to provide for the public interest. Why is it so difficult to use them to weaken iron triangles?

2. To what extent do you believe that the AIDS activist movement that has challenged the iron triangles related to pharmaceutical policy can be a model for others seeking to weaken iron triangles? Do you believe there were factors specific to AIDS that might not be replicable to other social movements, and if so, what are they?

3. If President Eisenhower was right in viewing an "alert and knowledgeable citizenry" as an effective check on the military–industrial complex (and by extension, other iron triangles), how might public education of the citizenry occur?

The Presidency and
the Bureaucracy

18   *Federalist No. 67*

The Executive Department
From the New York Packet.
Tuesday, March 11, 1788.
Alexander Hamilton

To the People of the State of New York:

THE constitution of the executive department of the proposed government, claims next our attention.

There is hardly any part of the system which could have been attended with greater difficulty in the arrangement of it than this; and there is, perhaps, none which has been inveighed against with less candor or criticised with less judgment.

Here the writers against the Constitution seem to have taken pains to signalize their talent of misrepresentation. Calculating upon the aversion of the people to monarchy, they have endeavored to enlist all their jealousies and apprehensions in opposition to the intended President of the United States; not merely as the embryo, but as the full-grown progeny, of that detested parent. To establish the pretended affinity, they have not scrupled to draw resources even from the regions of fiction. The authorities of a magistrate, in few instances greater, in some instances less, than those of a governor of New York, have been magnified into more than royal prerogatives. He has been decorated with attributes superior in dignity and splendor to those of a king of Great Britain. He has been shown to us with the diadem sparkling on his brow and the imperial purple flowing in his train. He has been seated on a throne surrounded with minions and mistresses, giving audience to the envoys of foreign potentates, in all the supercilious pomp of majesty. The images of Asiatic despotism and voluptuousness have scarcely been wanting to crown the exaggerated scene. We have been taught to tremble at the terrific visages of murdering janizaries, and to blush at the unveiled mysteries of a future seraglio.

Attempts so extravagant as these to disfigure or, it might rather be said, to metamorphose the object, render it necessary to take an accurate view of its real nature and form: in order as well to ascertain its true aspect and genuine appearance, as to unmask the disingenuity and expose the fallacy of the counterfeit resemblances which have been so insidiously, as well as industriously, propagated.

In the execution of this task, there is no man who would not find it an arduous effort either to behold with moderation, or to treat with seriousness, the devices, not less weak than wicked, which have been contrived to pervert the public opinion in relation to the subject. They so far exceed the usual though unjustifiable licenses of party artifice, that even in a disposition the most candid and tolerant, they must force the sentiments which favor an indulgent construction of the conduct of political adversaries to give place to a voluntary and unreserved indignation. It is impossible not to bestow the imputation of deliberate imposture and deception upon the gross pretense of a similitude between a king of Great Britain and a magistrate of the character marked out for that of the President of the United States. It is still more impossible to withhold that imputation from the rash and barefaced expedients which have been employed to give success to the attempted imposition.

In one instance, which I cite as a sample of the general spirit, the temerity has proceeded so far as to ascribe to the President of the United States a power which by the instrument reported is EXPRESSLY allotted to the Executives of the individual States. I mean the power of filling casual vacancies in the Senate.

This bold experiment upon the discernment of his countrymen has been hazarded by a writer who (whatever may be his real merit) has had no inconsiderable share in the applauses of his party[1]; and who, upon this false and unfounded suggestion, has built a series of observations equally false and unfounded. Let him now be confronted with the evidence of the fact, and let him, if he be able, justify or extenuate the shameful outrage he has offered to the dictates of truth and to the rules of fair dealing.

The second clause of the second section of the second article empowers the President of the United States "to nominate, and by and with the advice and consent of the Senate, to appoint ambassadors, other public ministers and consuls, judges of the Supreme Court, and all other OFFICERS of United States whose appointments are NOT in the Constitution OTHERWISE PROVIDED FOR, and WHICH SHALL BE ESTABLISHED BY LAW." Immediately after this clause follows another in these words: "The President shall have power to fill up? VACANCIES that may happen DURING THE RECESS OF THE SENATE, by granting commissions which shall EXPIRE AT THE END OF THEIR NEXT SESSION." It is from this last provision that the pretended power of the President to fill vacancies in the Senate has been deduced. A slight attention to the connection of the clauses, and to the obvious meaning of the terms, will satisfy us that the deduction is not even colorable.

The first of these two clauses, it is clear, only provides a mode for appointing such officers, "whose appointments are NOT OTHERWISE PROVIDED FOR in the Constitution, and which SHALL BE ESTABLISHED BY LAW"; of course it cannot extend to the appointments of senators, whose appointments are OTHERWISE PROVIDED FOR in the Constitution[2], and who are ESTABLISHED BY THE CONSTITUTION, and will not require a future establishment by law. This position will hardly be contested.

The last of these two clauses, it is equally clear, cannot be understood to comprehend the power of filling vacancies in the Senate, for the following reasons: First. The relation in which that clause stands to the other, which declares the general mode of appointing officers of the United States, denotes it to be nothing more than a supplement to the other, for the purpose of establishing an auxiliary method of appointment, in cases to which the general method was inadequate. The ordinary power of appointment is confined to the President and Senate JOINTLY, and can therefore only be exercised during the session of the Senate; but as it would have been improper to oblige this body to be continually in session for the appointment of officers and as vacancies might happen IN THEIR RECESS, which it might be necessary for the public service to fill without delay, the succeeding clause is evidently intended to authorize the President, SINGLY, to make temporary appointments "during the recess of the Senate, by granting commissions which shall expire at the end of their next session." Secondly. If this clause is to be considered as supplementary to the one which precedes, the VACANCIES of which it speaks must be construed to relate to the "officers" described in the preceding one; and this, we have seen, excludes from its description the members of the Senate. Thirdly. The time within which the power is to operate, "during the recess of the Senate," and the duration of the appointments, "to the end of the next session" of that body, conspire to elucidate the sense of the provision, which, if it had been intended to comprehend senators, would naturally have referred the temporary power of filling vacancies to the recess of the State legislatures, who are to make the permanent appointments, and not to the recess of the national Senate, who are to have no concern in those appointments; and would have extended the duration in office of the temporary senators to the next session of the legislature of the State, in whose representation the vacancies had happened, instead of making it to expire at the end of the ensuing session of the national Senate. The circumstances of the body authorized to make the permanent appointments would, of course, have governed the modification of a power which related to the temporary appointments; and as the national Senate is the body, whose situation is alone contemplated in the clause upon which the suggestion under examination has been founded, the vacancies to which it alludes can only be deemed to respect those officers in whose appointment that body has a concurrent agency with the President. But lastly, the first and second clauses of the third section of the first article, not only obviate all possibility of doubt, but destroy the pretext of misconception. The former provides, that "the Senate of the United States shall be composed of two Senators from each State, chosen BY THE LEGISLATURE THEREOF for six years"; and the latter directs, that, "if vacancies in that body should happen by resignation or otherwise, DURING THE RECESS OF THE LEGISLATURE OF ANY STATE, the Executive THEREOF may make temporary appointments until the NEXT MEETING OF THE LEGISLATURE, which shall then fill such vacancies." Here is an express power given, in clear and unambiguous terms, to the State Executives, to fill casual vacancies in the Senate, by temporary appointments; which not only invalidates the supposition, that the clause before considered could have been intended to confer that power upon the President of the United States, but proves that this supposition, destitute as it is even of the merit of plausibility, must have originated in an intention to deceive the people, too palpable to be obscured by sophistry, too atrocious to be palliated by hypocrisy.

I have taken the pains to select this instance of misrepresentation, and to place it in a clear and strong light, as an unequivocal proof of the unwarrantable arts which are practiced to prevent a fair and impartial judgment of the real merits of the Constitution submitted to the consideration of the people. Nor have I scrupled, in so flagrant a case, to allow myself a severity of animadversion little congenial with the general spirit of these papers. I hesitate not to submit it to the decision of any candid and honest adversary of the proposed government, whether language can furnish epithets of too much asperity, for so shameless and so prostitute an attempt to impose on the citizens of America.

PUBLIUS.

1. See CATO, No. V.
2. Article I, section 3, clause I.

19 *Federalist No. 68*

The Mode of Electing the President
From the New York Packet.
Friday, March 14, 1788.
Alexander Hamilton

To the People of the State of New York:

THE mode of appointment of the Chief Magistrate of the United States is almost the only part of the system, of any consequence, which has escaped without severe censure, or which has received the slightest mark of approbation from its opponents. The most plausible of these, who has appeared in print, has even deigned to admit that the election of the President is pretty well guarded.[1] I venture somewhat further, and hesitate not to affirm, that if the manner of it be not perfect, it is at least excellent. It unites in an eminent degree all the advantages, the union of which was to be wished for.

It was desirable that the sense of the people should operate in the choice of the person to whom so important a trust was to be confided. This end will be answered by committing the right of making it, not to any preestablished body, but to men chosen by the people for the special purpose, and at the particular conjuncture.

It was equally desirable, that the immediate election should be made by men most capable of analyzing the qualities adapted to the station, and acting under circumstances favorable to deliberation, and to a judicious combination of all the reasons and inducements which were proper to govern their choice. A small number of persons, selected by their fellow-citizens from the general mass, will be most likely to possess the information and discernment requisite to such complicated investigations.

It was also peculiarly desirable to afford as little opportunity as possible to tumult and disorder. This evil was not least to be dreaded in the election of a magistrate, who was to have so important an agency in the administration of the government as the President of the United States. But the precautions which have been so happily concerted in the system under consideration, promise an effectual security against this mischief. The choice of SEVERAL, to form an intermediate body of electors, will be much less apt to convulse the community with any extraordinary or violent movements, than the choice of ONE who was himself to be the final object of the public wishes. And as the electors, chosen in each State, are to assemble and vote in the State in which they are chosen, this detached and divided situation will expose them much less to heats and ferments, which might be communicated from them to the people, than if they were all to be convened at one time, in one place.

Nothing was more to be desired than that every practicable obstacle should be opposed to cabal, intrigue, and corruption. These most deadly adversaries of republican government might naturally have been expected to make their approaches from more than one querter, but chiefly from the desire in foreign powers to gain an improper ascendant in our councils. How could they better gratify this, than by raising a creature of their own to the chief magistracy of the Union? But the convention have guarded against all danger of this sort, with the most provident and judicious attention. They have not made the appointment of the President to depend on any preexisting bodies of men, who might be tampered with beforehand to prostitute their votes; but they have referred it in the first instance to an immediate act of the people of America, to be exerted in the choice of persons for the temporary and sole purpose of making the appointment. And they have excluded from eligibility to this trust, all those who from situation might be suspected of too great devotion to the President in office. No senator, representative, or other person holding a place of trust or profit under the United States, can be of the numbers of the electors. Thus without corrupting the body of the people, the immediate agents in the election will at least enter upon the task free from any sinister bias. Their transient existence, and their detached situation, already taken notice of, afford a satisfactory prospect of their continuing so, to the conclusion of it. The business of corruption, when it is to embrace so considerable a number of men, requires time as well as means. Nor would it be found easy suddenly to embark them, dispersed as they would be over thirteen States, in any combinations founded upon motives, which though they could not properly be denominated corrupt, might yet be of a nature to mislead them from their duty.

Another and no less important desideratum was, that the Executive should be independent for his continuance in office on all but the people themselves. He might otherwise be tempted to sacrifice his duty to his complaisance for those whose favor was necessary to the duration of his official consequence. This advantage will also be secured, by making his re-election to depend on a special body of representatives, deputed by the society for the single purpose of making the important choice.

All these advantages will happily combine in the plan devised by the convention; which is, that the people of each State shall choose a number of persons as electors, equal to the number of senators and representatives of such State in the national government, who shall assemble within the State, and vote for some fit person as President. Their votes, thus given, are to be transmitted to the seat of the national government, and the person who may happen to have a majority of the whole number of votes will be the President. But as a majority of the votes might not always happen to centre in one man, and as it might be unsafe to permit less than a majority to be conclusive, it is provided that, in such a contingency, the House of Representatives shall select out of the candidates who shall have the five highest number of votes, the man who in their opinion may be best qualified for the office.

The process of election affords a moral certainty, that the office of President will never fall to the lot of any man who is not in an eminent degree endowed with the requisite qualifications. Talents for low intrigue, and the little arts of popularity, may alone suffice to elevate a man to the first honors in a single State; but it will require other talents, and a different kind of merit, to establish him in the esteem and confidence of the whole Union, or of so considerable a portion of it as would be necessary to make him a successful candidate for the distinguished office of President of the

United States. It will not be too strong to say, that there will be a constant probability of seeing the station filled by characters pre-eminent for ability and virtue. And this will be thought no inconsiderable recommendation of the Constitution, by those who are able to estimate the share which the executive in every government must necessarily have in its good or ill administration. Though we cannot acquiesce in the political heresy of the poet who says: "For forms of government let fools contest That which is best administered is best," yet we may safely pronounce, that the true test of a good government is its aptitude and tendency to produce a good administration.

The Vice-President is to be chosen in the same manner with the President; with this difference, that the Senate is to do, in respect to the former, what is to be done by the House of Representatives, in respect to the latter.

The appointment of an extraordinary person, as Vice-President, has been objected to as superfluous, if not mischievous. It has been alleged, that it would have been preferable to have authorized the Senate to elect out of their own body an officer answering that description. But two considerations seem to justify the ideas of the convention in this respect. One is, that to secure at all times the possibility of a definite resolution of the body, it is necessary that the President should have only a casting vote. And to take the senator of any State from his seat as senator, to place him in that of President of the Senate, would be to exchange, in regard to the State from which he came, a constant for a contingent vote. The other consideration is, that as the Vice-President may occasionally become a substitute for the President, in the supreme executive magistracy, all the reasons which recommend the mode of election prescribed for the one, apply with great if not with equal force to the manner of appointing the other. It is remarkable that in this, as in most other instances, the objection which is made would lie against the constitution of this State. We have a Lieutenant-Governor, chosen by the people at large, who presides in the Senate, and is the constitutional substitute for the Governor, in casualties similar to those which would authorize the Vice-President to exercise the authorities and discharge the duties of the President.

PUBLIUS.

1. Vide FEDERAL FARMER.

20   *Presidential Power*

Richard E. Neustadt

In the United States we like to "rate" a president. We measure him as "weak" or "strong" and call what we are measuring his "leadership." We do not wait until a man is dead; we rate him from the moment he takes office. We are quite right to do so. His office has become the focal point of politics and policy in our political system. Our commentators and our politicians make a specialty of taking the man's measurements. The rest of us join in when we feel "government" impinging on our private lives. In the third quarter of the twentieth century millions of us have that feeling often.

. . . Although we all make judgments about presidential leadership, we often base our judgments upon images of office that are far removed from the reality. We also use those images when we tell one another whom to choose as president. But it is risky to appraise a man in office or to choose a man for office on false premises about the nature of his job. When the job is the presidency of the United States, the risk becomes excessive. . . .

We deal here with the president himself and with his influence on governmental action. In institutional terms the presidency now includes 2,000 men and women. The president is only one of them. But *his* performance scarcely can be measured without focusing on *him*. In terms of party, or of country, or the West, so-called, his leadership involves far more than governmental action. But the sharpening of spirit and of values and of purposes is not done in a vacuum. Although governmental action may not be the whole of leadership, all else is nurtured by it and gains meaning from it. Yet if we treat the presidency as the president, we cannot measure him as though he were the government. Not action as an outcome but his impact on the outcome is the measure of the man. His strength or weakness, then, turns on his personal capacity to influence the conduct of the men who make up government. His influence becomes the mark of leadership. To rate a president according to these rules, one looks into the man's own capabilities as seeker and as wielder of effective influence upon the other men involved in governing the country . . .

"Presidential" . . . means nothing but the president. "Power" means *his* influence. It helps to have these meanings settled at the start.

There are two ways to study "presidential power." One way is to focus on the tactics, so to speak, of influencing certain men in given situations: how to get a bill through Congress, how to settle strikes, how to quiet Cabinet feuds, or how to stop a Suez. The other way is to step back from tactics on those "givens" and to deal

Reprinted from *Presidential Power* (1986), Pearson Education, Inc.

with influence in more strategic terms: what is its nature and what are its sources? What can *this* man accomplish to improve the prospect that he will have influence when he wants it? Strategically, the question is not how he masters Congress in a peculiar instance, but what he does to boost his chance for mastery in any instance, looking toward tomorrow from today. The second of these two ways has been chosen for this [selection]. . . .

In form all presidents are leaders, nowadays. In fact this guarantees no more than that they will be clerks. Everybody now expects the man inside the White House to do something about everything. Laws and customs now reflect acceptance of him as the Great Initiator, an acceptance quite as widespread at the Capitol as at his end of Pennsylvania Avenue. But such acceptance does not signify that all the rest of government is at his feet. It merely signifies that other men have found it practically impossible to do *their* jobs without assurance of initiatives from him. Service for themselves, not power for the president, has brought them to accept his leadership in form. They find his actions useful in their business. The transformation of his routine obligations testifies to their dependence on an active White House. A president, these days, is an invaluable clerk. His services are in demand all over Washington. His influence, however, is a very different matter. Laws and customs tell us little about leadership in fact.

Why have our presidents been honored with this clerkship? The answer is that no one else's services suffice. Our Constitution, our traditions, and our politics provide no better source for the initiatives a president can take. Executive officials need decisions, and political protection, and a referee for fights. Where are these to come from but the White House? Congressmen need an agenda from outside, something with high status to respond to or react against. What provides it better than the program of the president? Party politicians need a record to defend in the next national campaign. How can it be made except by "their" Administration? Private persons with a public ax to grind may need a helping hand or they may need a grinding stone. In either case who gives more satisfaction than a president? And outside the United States, in every country where our policies and postures influence home politics, there will be people needing just the "right" thing said and done or just the "wrong" thing stopped in *Washington*. What symbolizes Washington more nearly than the White House?

A modern president is bound to face demands for aid and service from five more or less distinguishable sources: the Executive officialdom, from Congress, from his partisans, from citizens at large, and from abroad. The presidency's clerkship is expressive of these pressures. In effect they are constituency pressures and each president has five sets of constituents. The five are not distinguished by their membership; membership is obviously an overlapping matter. And taken one by one they do not match the man's electorate; one of them, indeed, is outside his electorate. They are distinguished, rather, by their different claims upon him. Initiatives are what they want, for five distinctive reasons. Since government and politics have offered no alternative, our laws and customs turn those wants into his obligations.

Why, then, is the president not guaranteed an influence commensurate with services performed? Constituent relations are relations of dependence. Everyone with any share in governing this country will belong to one (or two, or three) of his "constituencies." Since everyone depends on him why is he not assured of everyone's support? The answer is that no one else sits where he sits, or sees quite as he sees; no one else feels the full weight of his obligations. Those obligations are a tribute to his unique place in our political system. But just because it is unique they fall on him alone. *The same conditions that promote his leadership in form preclude a guarantee of leadership in fact.* No man or group at either end of Pennsylvania Avenue shares his peculiar status in our government and politics. That is why his services are in demand. By the same token, though, the obligations of all other men are different from his own. His Cabinet officers have departmental duties and constituents. His legislative leaders head *Congressional* parties, one in either House. His national party organization stands apart from his official family. His political allies in the states need not face Washington, or one another. The private groups that seek him out are not compelled to govern. And friends abroad are not compelled to run in our elections. Lacking his position and prerogatives, these men cannot regard his obligations as his own. They have their jobs to do; none is the same as his. As they perceive their duty they may find it right to follow him, in fact, or they may not. Whether they will feel obliged *on their responsibility* to do what he wants done remains an open question. . . .

There is reason to suppose that in the years immediately ahead the power problems of a president will remain what they have been in the decades just behind us. If so there will be equal need for presidential expertise of the peculiar sort . . . that has [been] stressed [i.e., political skill]. Indeed, the need is likely to be greater. The president himself and with him the whole government are likely to be more than ever at the mercy of his personal approach.

What may the sixties do to politics and policy and to the place of presidents in our political system? The sixties may destroy them as we know them; that goes without saying. But barring deep depression or unlimited war, a total transformation is the least of likelihoods. Without catastrophes of those dimensions nothing in our past experience suggests that we shall see either consensus of the sort available to FDR in 1933 and 1942, or popular demand for institutional adjustments likely to assist a president. Lacking popular demand, the natural conservatism of established institutions will keep Congress and the party organizations quite resistant to reforms that could give him a clear advantage over them. Four-year terms for congressmen and senators might do it, if the new terms ran with his. What will occasion a demand for that? As for crisis consensus it is probably beyond the reach of the next president. We may have priced ourselves out of the market for "productive" crises on the pattern Roosevelt knew—productive in the sense of strengthening his chances for sustained support *within* the system. Judging from the fifties, neither limited war nor limited depression is productive in those terms. Anything unlimited will probably break the system.

In the absence of productive crises, and assuming that we manage to avoid destructive ones, nothing now foreseeable suggests that our next president will have assured support from any quarter. There is no use expecting it from the bureaucracy unless it is displayed on Capitol Hill. Assured support will not be found in Congress unless contemplation of their own electorates keeps a majority of members constantly aligned with him. In the sixties it is to be doubted . . . that pressure from electors will move the same majority of men in either House toward consistent backing for the president. Instead the chances are that he will gain majorities, when and if he does so, by ad hoc coalition-building, issue after issue. In that respect the sixties will be reminiscent of the fifties; indeed, a closer parallel may well be in the late forties. As for "party discipline" in English terms—the favorite cure-all of political scientists since Woodrow Wilson was a youth—the first preliminary is a party link between the White House and the leadership on both sides of the Capitol. But even this preliminary has been lacking in eight of the fifteen years since the Second World War. If ballot-splitting should continue through the sixties it will soon be "un-American" for president and Congress to belong to the same party.

Even if the trend were now reversed, there is no short-run prospect that behind each party label we would find assembled a sufficiently like-minded bloc of voters, similarly aligned in states and districts all across the country, to negate the massive barriers our institutions and traditions have erected against "discipline" on anything like the British scale. This does not mean that a reversal of the ballot-splitting trend would be without significance. If the White House and the legislative leadership were linked by party ties again, a real advantage would accrue to both. Their opportunities for mutually productive bargaining would be enhanced. The policy results might surprise critics of our system. Bargaining "within the family" has a rather different quality than bargaining with members of the rival clan. But we would still be a long way from "party government." Bargaining, not "discipline," would still remain the key to Congressional action on a president's behalf. The crucial distinctions between presidential party and Congressional party are not likely to be lost in the term of the next president.

21   *The "Unitary Executive" and the Threat to Democratic Government*

Jennifer Van Bergen

*After the 9/11 attacks, the Bush administration claimed sweeping new powers to pros-
ecute the "war on terror." Moving well beyond more traditional wartime assertions of
presidential power, the Bush policies are notable for their open-ended and unlimited
duration and their rejection of regulation by the legislative and judicial branches of
government. In this selection, lawyer and author Jennifer Van Bergen explores President
Bush's alarmingly frequent use of presidential signing statements to lay claim to his
power as Commander-in-Chief to interpret laws as he chooses, even if it means violat-
ing the very laws he signs. Under the invented theory of a "unitary executive,"
President Bush envisions an executive branch unbridled by the checks and balances that
mark the boundaries of constitutional government. Van Bergen then extends her analysis to the more recent case of the Military Commissions Act, enacted in the fall of 2006
before the midterm elections, as an example of the dangers inherent in logic of unilateral presidential power. In light of the executive branch's disregard for traditional notions
of due process, she asks us to consider the damage done to the very institutional balance
that underlies the American democratic system.*

When President Bush signed the new law [in late December 2005], sponsored by
Senator McCain, restricting the use of torture when interrogating detainees, he also
issued a Presidential signing statement. That statement asserted that his power as
Commander-in-Chief gives him the authority to bypass the very law he had just
signed.

This news came fast on the heels of Bush's shocking admission that, since
2002, he has repeatedly authorized the National Security Agency to conduct electronic surveillance without a warrant, in flagrant violation of applicable federal law.

Reprinted from *Findlaw.com,* January 9, 2006, FindLaw/ThomsonReuters.

And before that, Bush declared he had the unilateral authority to ignore the Geneva Conventions and to indefinitely detain without due process both immigrants and citizens as enemy combatants.

All these declarations echo the refrain Bush has been asserting from the outset of his presidency. That refrain is simple: Presidential power must be unilateral, and unchecked.

But the most recent and blatant presidential intrusions on the law and Constitution supply the verse to that refrain. They not only claim unilateral executive power, but also supply the train of the President's thinking, the texture of his motivations, and the root of his intentions.

They make clear, for instance, that the phrase "unitary executive" is a code word for a doctrine that favors nearly unlimited executive power. Bush has used the doctrine in his signing statements to quietly expand presidential authority.

In this article, I will consider the meaning of the unitary executive doctrine within a democratic government that respects the separation of powers. I will ask: Can our government remain true to its nature, yet also embrace this doctrine?

I will also consider what the President and his legal advisers mean by applying the unitary executive doctrine. And I will argue that the doctrine violates basic tenets of our system of checks and balances, quietly crossing longstanding legal and moral boundaries that are essential to a democratic society.

President Bush's Aggressive Use of Presidential Signing Statements

Bush has used presidential "signing statements"—statements issued by the President upon signing a bill into law—to expand his power. Each of his signing statements says that he will interpret the law in question "in a manner consistent with his constitutional authority to supervise the unitary executive branch."

Presidential signing statements have gotten very little media attention. They are, however, highly important documents that define how the President interprets the laws he signs. Presidents use such statements to protect the prerogative of their office and ensure control over the executive branch functions.

Presidents also—since Reagan—have used such statements to create a kind of alternative legislative history. Attorney General Ed Meese explained in 1986 that:

> To make sure that the President's own understanding of what's in a bill is the same . . . is given consideration at the time of statutory construction later on by a court, we have now arranged with West Publishing Company that the presidential statement on the signing of a bill will accompany the legislative history from Congress so that all can be available to the court for future construction of what that statute really means.

The alternative legislative history would, according to Dr. Christopher S. Kelley, professor of political science at the Miami University at Oxford, Ohio, "contain certain policy or principles that the administration had lost in its negotiations" with Congress.

The Supreme Court has paid close attention to presidential signing statements. Indeed, in two important decisions—the *Chadha* and *Bowsher* decisions—the Court relied in part on president signing statements in interpreting laws. Other federal courts, sources show, have taken note of them too.

President Bush has used presidential signing statements more than any previous president. From President Monroe's administration (1817–25) to the Carter administration (1977–81), the executive branch issued a total of 75 signing statements to protect presidential prerogatives. From Reagan's administration through Clinton's, the total number of signing statements ever issued, by all presidents, rose to a total 322.

In striking contrast to his predecessors, President Bush issued at least 435 signing statements in his first term alone. And, in these statements and in his executive orders, Bush used the term "unitary executive" 95 times. It is important, therefore, to understand what this doctrine means.

What Does the Administration Mean When It Refers to the "Unitary Executive"?

Dr. Kelley notes that the unitary executive doctrine arose as the result of the twin circumstances of Vietnam and Watergate. Kelley asserts that "the faith and trust placed into the presidency was broken as a result of the lies of Vietnam and Watergate," which resulted in a congressional assault on presidential prerogatives.

For example, consider the Foreign Intelligence Surveillance Act (FISA) which Bush evaded when authorizing the NSA to tap without warrants—even those issued by the FISA court. FISA was enacted after the fall of Nixon with the precise intention of curbing unchecked executive branch surveillance. (Indeed, Nixon's improper use of domestic surveillance was included in Article 2 paragraph (2) of the impeachment articles against him.)

According to Kelley, these congressional limits on the presidency, in turn, led "some very creative people" in the White House and the Department of Justice's Office of Legal Counsel (OLC) to fight back, in an attempt to foil or blunt these limits. In their view, these laws were legislative attempts to strip the president of his rightful powers. Prominent among those in the movement to preserve presidential power and champion the unitary executive doctrine were the founding members of the Federalist Society, nearly all of whom worked in the Nixon, Ford, and Reagan White Houses.

The unitary executive doctrine arises out of a theory called "departmentalism," or "coordinate construction." According to legal scholars Christopher Yoo, Steven Calabresi, and Anthony Colangelo, the coordinate construction approach "holds that all three branches of the federal government have the power and duty to interpret the Constitution." According to this theory, the president may (and indeed, must) interpret laws, equally as much as the courts.

The Unitary Executive Versus Judicial Supremacy

The coordinate construction theory counters the long-standing notion of "judicial supremacy," articulated by Supreme Court Chief Justice John Marshall in 1803, in the famous case of *Marbury v. Madison*, which held that the Court is the final arbiter of what is and is not the law. Marshall famously wrote there: "It is emphatically the province and duty of the judicial department to say what the law is."

Of course, the President has a duty not to undermine his own office, as University of Miami law professor A. Michael Froomkin notes. And, as Kelley points out, the President is bound by his oath of office and the "Take Care clause" to preserve, protect, and defend the Constitution and to "take care" that the laws are faithfully executed. And those duties require, in turn, that the President interpret what is, and is not constitutional, at least when overseeing the actions of executive agencies.

However, Bush's actions make it clear that he interprets the coordinate construction approach extremely aggressively. In his view, and the view of his Administration, that doctrine gives him license to overrule and bypass Congress or the courts, based on his own interpretations of the Constitution—even where that violates long-established laws and treaties, counters recent legislation that he has himself signed, or (as shown by recent developments in the Padilla case) involves offering a federal court contradictory justifications for a detention.

This is a form of presidential rebellion against Congress and the courts, and possibly a violation of President Bush's oath of office, as well.

After all, can it be possible that that oath means that the President must uphold the Constitution only as he construes it—and not as the federal courts do?

And can it be possible that the oath means that the President need not uphold laws he simply doesn't like—even though they were validly passed by Congress and signed into law by him?

Analyzing Bush's Disturbing Signing Statement for the McCain Anti-Torture Bill

Let's take a close look at Bush's signing statement on the torture bill. It says:

> The executive branch shall construe Title X in Division A of the Act, relating to detainees, in a manner consistent with the constitutional authority of the President to supervise the unitary executive branch and as Commander in Chief and consistent with the constitutional limitations on the judicial power, which will assist in achieving the shared objective of the Congress and the President, evidenced in Title X, of protecting the American people from further terrorist attacks.

In this signing statement, Bush asserts not only his authority to internally supervise the "unitary executive branch," but also his power as Commander-in-Chief, as the basis for his interpretation of the law—which observers have noted allows Bush to create a loop-hole to permit the use of torture when he wants.

Clearly, Bush believes he can ignore the intentions of Congress. Not only that but by this statement, he has evinced his intent to do so, if he so chooses.

On top of this, Bush asserts that the law must be consistent with "constitutional limitations on judicial power." But what about presidential power? Does Bush see any constitutional or statutory limitations on that? And does this mean that Bush will ignore the courts, too, if he chooses—as he attempted, recently, to do in the Padilla case?

The Unitary Executive Doctrine Violates the Separation of Powers

As *Findlaw* columnist Edward Lazarus recently showed, the President does not have unlimited executive authority, not even as Commander-in-Chief of the military. Our government was purposely created with power split between three branches, not concentrated in one.

Separation of powers, then, is not simply a talisman: It is the foundation of our system. James Madison wrote in *The Federalist Papers*, No. 47, that: "The accumulation of all powers, legislative, executive, and judiciary, in the same hands, whether of one, a few, or many, and whether hereditary, self-appointed, or elective, may justly be pronounced the very definition of tyranny."

Another early American, George Nicholas, eloquently articulated the concept of "power divided" in one of his letters:

The most effectual guard which has yet been discovered against the abuse of power, is the division of it. It is our happiness to have a constitution which contains within it a sufficient limitation to the power granted by it, and also a proper division of that power. But no constitution affords any real security to liberty unless it is considered as sacred and preserved inviolate; because that security can only arise from an actual and not from a nominal limitation and division of power.

Yet it seems a nominal limitation and division of power—with real power concentrated solely in the "unitary executive"—is exactly what President Bush seeks. His signing statements make the point quite clearly, and his overt refusal to follow the laws illustrates that point: In Bush's view, there is no actual limitation or division of power; it all resides in the executive.

Thomas Paine wrote in *Common Sense*: "In America, the law is king. For as in absolute governments the King is law, so in free countries the law ought to be king; and there ought to be no other."

The unitary executive doctrine conflicts with Paine's principle—one that is fundamental to our constitutional system. If Bush can ignore or evade laws, then the law is no longer king. Americans need to decide whether we are still a country of laws—and if we are, we need to decide whether a President who has determined to ignore or evade the law has not acted in a manner contrary to his trust as President and subversive of constitutional government.

.   .   .

Damage Control

After President George W. Bush signed the controversial Military Commissions Act [in October 2006], the Justice Department wasted no time in using its new power to deny due process to the detainees swept up in the "war on terror." Now that the bill which Sen. Patrick Leahy called "un-American" has become law, countless hours and dollars will be spent by public interest law organizations trying to undo its damage. In addition to challenges of the provisions that strip *habeas corpus* rights, we can expect constitutional challenges to the military commission procedures and amendments to the War Crimes Act.

The MCA is an unprecedented power grab by the executive branch. Among the Act's worst features, it authorizes the president to detain, without charges, anyone whom he deems an unlawful enemy combatant. This includes U.S. citizens. It eliminates *habeas corpus* review for aliens. It also makes providing "material support" to terrorists punishable by military commission. And the military commissions' procedures allow for coerced testimony, the use of "sanitized classified information"— where the source is not disclosed—and trial for offenses not historically subject to trial by military commissions. (Terrorism is not historically a military offense; it's a crime.) Finally, by amending the War Crimes Act, it allows the president to authorize interrogation techniques that may nonetheless violate the Geneva Conventions and provides future and retroactive "defenses" for those who engage in or authorize those acts.

According to former Justice Department attorney Marty Lederman, who opposed the Act, "the primary impact of the Military Commissions Act is" not to establish military commissions, but "to attempt to eliminate any judicial checks on the Executive's conduct of the conflict against al-Qaida." Conservative law professor John Yoo, a supporter of the Act, writes, "In the struggle for power between the three branches of government, it is not the presidency that 'won.' Instead, it is the judiciary that lost."

As Yoo himself admits, "The new law is, above all, a stinging rebuke to the Supreme Court." Several Supreme Court decisions in the last two years struck down Rumsfeld's previous military commissions and combatant status review tribunals, and granted Guantánamo alien detainees and citizens held in military custody in the U.S. the right to challenge their detentions via *habeas corpus* petitions in U.S. courts. The Bush administration argued against these positions (and indeed, the administration's belief that Guantánamo was not subject to U.S. court jurisdiction was the main reason it chose that as its detention site).

Reprinted from *TomPaine.com,* October 27, 2006.

Congress has now, in effect, struck down these Supreme Court decisions that struck down previous executive decisions and actions. What next?

Habeas for Some, Not All

The first challenges to the numerous provisions in the MCA will undoubtedly be about the *habeas corpus*-stripping provisions. *Habeas corpus* is the right to have a court determine the legality of one's imprisonment before trial. The U.S. Constitution states that "the privilege of the writ of *habeas corpus* shall not be suspended, unless when in cases of rebellion or invasion, the public safety may require it."

Advocates of the MCA claim that *habeas* has never applied to foreign combatants captured on the battlefield. This claim begs the question: In the "war on terror," how do you know where the battlefield is and how do you know who foreign combatants are? *Habeas* exists exactly for the purpose of challenging wrongful detentions, and in the "war on terror," it has already become abundantly clear that as many as 95 percent of the detentions may be wrongful.

The MCA contains two provisions that strip detainees of their right to *habeas corpus*. One provides that:

> *. . . no court, justice, or judge shall have jurisdiction to hear or consider any claim or cause of action whatsoever*, including any action pending on or filed after the date of the enactment of the Military Commissions Act of 2006 . . . *including challenges to the lawfulness of procedures of military commissions . . .*

The second provision, amending the *habeas* statute, adds the following:

> No court, justice, or judge shall have jurisdiction to hear or consider an application for a writ of habeas corpus filed by or on behalf of an alien detained by the United States who has been determined by the United States to have been properly detained as an enemy combatant or is awaiting such determination.

It would be surprising if these provisions were not immediately challenged. And those best situated to challenge them are, of course, those who stand to lose the most: the detainees who have already filed *habeas corpus* petitions.

The Justice Department has already asked the D.C. Circuit Court to dismiss 196 of these cases without any determination about the merits of the claims or the guilt or innocence of the petitioners. These cases involve people who have already spent several years in detention without any charges while their *habeas* petitions work their way through the courts.

In essence, the *habeas*-stripping law throws every alien detainee back to legal minus zero. In other words, such detainees cannot challenge their detentions; they must first challenge the law that disallows them from challenging the detentions. These detainees are not back to where they started; they are back to *before* where they started.

What will happen is this: after the government moves to dismiss the cases and the petitioners argue against dismissal (the D.C. Circuit Court has already ordered supplemental briefing in two packets of cases on the issue), the D.C. Circuit will either agree it no longer has jurisdiction (because the MCA stripped it) or it will rule that the MCA *habeas*-stripping provision is unconstitutional and the Constitution allows (or even requires) them to consider the petitioners' claims. If the Circuit court rules in favor of the government, the petitioners will appeal; if the court rules in favor of the petitioners, the government will appeal. Either way, these cases will undoubtedly be consolidated and appealed to the Supreme Court.

Meantime, of course, the detainees remain in detention. Remember, detention centers are not hotels. Consistent abuse, humiliation, beatings, and even torture have been documented at these places. Further, recall that there is credible evidence that a great number of these detainees are not terrorists.

Secret Evidence. Hearsay and Coercion. Oh My

Other challenges will be about military commission procedures and rules of evidence that have generated controversy because they violate traditional norms of fair trial and due process. The Act permits the admission of hearsay—a general no–no in federal courts, and for good reason, since any witness can simply make up what someone else says and the accused has no way to challenge its validity. Appeals on hearsay would likely be joined with other evidentiary, procedural, and substantive matters, although it is unlikely that hearsay appeals alone would be successful, since the D.C. Circuit Court will probably be deferential to the military commission findings.

Another MCA provision likely to be challenged will almost certainly be the section that allows the use of secret evidence where "disclosure would be detrimental to the national security." Challenges to the use of secret evidence were made in the immigration context long before 9/11. The practice of using secret evidence showed such troubling results that in 1999, Congress nearly passed the Secret Evidence Repeal Act (SERA) "to ensure that no alien is removed, denied a benefit under the Immigration and Nationality Act, or otherwise deprived of liberty, based on evidence that is kept secret from the alien."

In the context of military commissions, where detainees can be sentenced to death, the concern over the use of secret evidence is magnified, and the practice will undoubtedly be challenged at some point by detainees. However, despite these concerns, courts—including the conservative D.C. Circuit Court—have shown a reluctance to second-guess government assertions of the need for secrecy. Thus, it is unlikely that any appeals will be won on this basis alone.

Another troubling provision allows coerced testimony to be admitted into evidence where the military panel decides it is "reliable and possessing sufficient probative value" and "the interests of justice would best be served by admission of the statement into evidence." This clause appears to promote the use of coercion. What it means is that if either the detainee or a witness against him makes statements under coercion (which by some definitions might include torture)—normally inadmissible in court—his admissions can be used against the detainee. How a commission judge could determine the reliability of such testimony or what standard he would use to determine what is "in the interests of justice" are troubling uncertainties. Detainees will almost certainly argue that this provision is unconstitutional, but again challenges on this basis may fall on deaf ears.

Another traditional feature of due process in American courts that the Act removes is the accused's right to "discovery"—or to carry out his or her own investigation. Under the MCA, while the accused is permitted to present evidence in his defense, may cross-examine witnesses, and "shall receive the assistance of counsel" (or may represent himself), he has no right "to conduct his own investigation into the facts using the process of the court." This is also likely to be challenged by detainees.

It is worth remarking that all these provisions will likely be challenged as being in violation of the Supreme Court's 2006 ruling in *Hamdan v. Rumsfeld,* which overturned the administration's previous military commissions, noting that the Code of Military Justice could satisfy due process requirements.

Detainees will also likely challenge the provisions that strip them of the right to claim any protections under the Geneva Conventions. Loyola Law School professor David Glazier notes that: "For several reasons, [the Geneva Conventions] form a logical starting point for any effort to identify potential procedural constraints on the conduct of trials under the law of war."

But, again, federal courts have not widely favored application of Geneva as the basis for individual rights, despite Geneva's requirement that its protections be incorporated into the laws of countries who adopted it.

Finally, the MCA helps to shield U.S. personnel from being held responsible for abuses committed during detentions or interrogations. This is widely considered to be the Bush administration's primary motive in pushing this legislation: To keep Bush administration officials and others from being held accountable for war crimes or other grave violations of the laws of war.

While it does not grant absolute immunity, because it provides for defenses against conviction, the MCA makes it very difficult for a detainee to bring any lawsuit against U.S. personnel or officials for war and other selected crimes committed against him.

The MCA also modified the definitions of war crimes, including torture, narrowing the definitions in such a way as to permit certain forms of interrogation which may constitute torture under international law.

What's the Upshot?

Since the MCA was passed in early October, legal scholars have pointed out its weaknesses. It is a poorly drafted law, vague and overbroad to the extent that scholars cannot predict how courts will determine what some provisions mean.

But if courts are stripped from reviewing it at all, if a court may not review poorly drafted and internally contradictory laws, who will determine whether they are lawful or constitutional?

The commission procedures do not meet the requirements set forth by the Supreme Court, by the Military Code of Justice, or by due process. Given that these procedures apply only to detainees who have been designated for trial (not all detainees will necessarily be tried—many may just be held indefinitely without any legal process), one must conclude that the MCA does not give detainees an adequate mechanism—i.e., *habeas corpus*—for challenging their detentions.

What kind of law provides imprisonment without the right of *habeas* or punishment without legitimate appeal? Without those standards, the law is just "victor's justice"—which is no justice at all. The Second World War is often understood to have come about at least in part as a result of the humiliation exacted upon Germans by the victors at the end of the First World War. Victor's justice breeds resentment. It breeds more war.

Discussion Questions

1. What does Van Bergen mean by the theory of the "unitary" executive? How does it justify the expansion of presidential power? How does it relate to the Military Commissions Act and other actions of the Bush administration?

2. Supporters of President Bush might argue that his expansion of presidential power is necessary in order to confront new dangers and threats such as terrorism. How would you respond to this argument?

22   The Rise of the Bureaucratic State

James Q. Wilson

During its first 150 years, the American republic was not thought to have "bureaucracy," and thus it would have been meaningless to refer to the "problems" of a "bureaucratic state." There were, of course, appointed civilian officials: Though only about 3,000 at the end of the Federalist period, there were about 95,000 by the time Grover Cleveland assumed office in 1881, and nearly half a million by 1925. Some aspects of these numerous officials were regarded as problems—notably, the standard by which they were appointed and the political loyalties to which they were held—but these were thought to be matters of proper character and good management. The great political and constitutional struggles were not over the power of the administrative apparatus, but over the power of the President, of Congress, and of the states.

The Founding Fathers had little to say about the nature or function of the executive branch of the new government. The Constitution is virtually silent on the subject and the debates in the Constitutional Convention are almost devoid of reference to an administrative apparatus. This reflected no lack of concern about the matter, however. Indeed, it was in part because of the Founders' depressing experience with chaotic and inefficient management under the Continental Congress and the Articles of Confederation that they had assembled in Philadelphia. Management by committees composed of part-time amateurs had cost the colonies dearly in the War of Independence and few, if any, of the Founders wished to return to that system. The argument was only over how the heads of the necessary departments of government were to be selected, and whether these heads should be wholly subordinate to the President or whether instead they should form some sort of council that would advise the President and perhaps share in his authority. In the end, the Founders left it up to Congress to decide the matter.

There was no dispute in Congress that there should be executive departments, headed by single appointed officials, and, of course, the Constitution specified that these would be appointed by the President with the advice and consent of the Senate. The only issue was how such officials might be removed. After prolonged debate and by the narrowest of majorities, Congress agreed that the President should have the sole right of removal, thus confirming that the infant administrative system would be

Reprinted from *The Public Interest* 41 (fall 1975), by permission of National Affairs, Inc.

wholly subordinate—in law at least—to the President. Had not Vice-President John Adams, presiding over a Senate equally divided on the issue, cast the deciding vote in favor of presidential removal, the administrative departments might conceivably have become legal dependencies of the legislature, with incalculable consequences for the development of the embryonic government.

The "Bureaucracy Problem"

The original departments were small and had limited duties. The State Department, the first to be created, had but nine employees in addition to the Secretary. The War Department did not reach 80 civilian employees until 1801; it commanded only a few thousand soldiers. Only the Treasury Department had substantial powers—it collected taxes, managed the public debt, ran the national bank, conducted land surveys, and purchased military supplies. Because of this, Congress gave the closest scrutiny to its structure and its activities.

The number of administrative agencies and employees grew slowly but steadily during the 19th and early 20th centuries and then increased explosively on the occasion of World War I, the Depression, and World War II. It is difficult to say at what point in this process the administrative system became a distinct locus of power or an independent source of political initiatives and problems. What is clear is that the emphasis on the sheer size of the administrative establishment—conventional in many treatments of the subject—is misleading.

The government can spend vast sums of money—wisely or unwisely—without creating that set of conditions we ordinarily associate with the bureaucratic state. For example, there could be massive transfer payments made under government auspices from person to person or from state to state, all managed by a comparatively small staff of officials and a few large computers. In 1971, the federal government paid out $54 billion under various social insurance programs, yet the Social Security Administration employs only 73,000 persons, many of whom perform purely routine jobs.

And though it may be harder to believe, the government could in principle employ an army of civilian personnel without giving rise to those organizational patterns that we call bureaucratic. Suppose, for instance, that we as a nation should decide to have in the public schools at least one teacher for every two students. This would require a vast increase in the number of teachers and schoolrooms, but almost all of the persons added would be performing more or less identical tasks, and they could be organized into very small units (e.g., neighborhood schools). Though there would be significant overhead costs, most citizens would not be aware of any increase in the "bureaucratic" aspects of education—indeed, owing to the much greater time each teacher would have to devote to each pupil and his or her parents, the citizenry might well conclude that there actually had been a substantial reduction in the amount of "bureaucracy."

To the reader predisposed to believe that we have a "bureaucracy problem," these hypothetical cases may seem farfetched. Max Weber, after all, warned us that in capitalist and socialist societies alike, bureaucracy was likely to acquire an "overtowering" power position. Conservatives have always feared bureaucracy, save perhaps the police. Humane socialists have frequently been embarrassed by their inability to reconcile a desire for public control of the economy with the suspicion that a public bureaucracy may be as immune to democratic control as a private one. Liberals have equivocated, either dismissing any concern for bureaucracy as reactionary quibbling about social progress or embracing that concern when obviously nonreactionary persons (welfare recipients, for example) express a view toward the Department of Health and Human Services indistinguishable from the view businessmen take of the Internal Revenue Service.

Political Authority

There are at least three ways in which political power may be gathered undesirably into bureaucratic hands: by the growth of an administrative apparatus so large as to be immune from popular control, by placing power over a governmental bureaucracy of any size in private rather than public hands, or by vesting discretionary authority in the hands of a public agency so that the exercise of that power is not responsive to the public good. These are not the only problems that arise because of bureaucratic organization. From the point of view of their members, bureaucracies are sometimes uncaring, ponderous, or unfair; from the point of view of their political superiors, they are sometimes unimaginative or inefficient; from the point of view of their clients, they are sometimes slow or unjust. No single account can possibly treat all that is problematic in bureaucracy; even the part I discuss here—the extent to which political authority has been transferred undesirably to an unaccountable administrative realm—is itself too large for a single essay. But it is, if not the most important problem, then surely the one that would most have troubled our Revolutionary leaders, especially those that went on to produce the Constitution. It was, after all, the question of power that chiefly concerned them, both in redefining our relationship with England and in finding a new basis for political authority in the Colonies.

To some, following in the tradition of [Max] Weber, bureaucracy is the inevitable consequence and perhaps necessary concomitant of modernity. A money economy, the division of labor, and the evolution of legal-rational norms to justify organizational authority require the efficient adaptation of means to ends and a high degree of predictability in the behavior of rulers. To this, Georg Simmel added the view that organizations tend to acquire the characteristics of those institutions with which they are in conflict, so that as government becomes more bureaucratic, private organizations—political parties, trade unions, voluntary associations—will have an additional reason to become bureaucratic as well.

By viewing bureaucracy as an inevitable (or, as some would put it, "functional") aspect of society, we find ourselves attracted to theories that explain the growth of bureaucracy in terms of some inner dynamic to which all agencies respond and which makes all barely governable and scarcely tolerable. Bureaucracies grow, we are told, because of Parkinson's Law: Work and personnel expand to consume the available resources. Bureaucracies behave, we believe, in accord with various other maxims, such as the Peter Principle: In hierarchical organizations, personnel are promoted up to that point at which their incompetence becomes manifest—hence, all important positions are held by incompetents. More elegant, if not essentially different, theories have been propounded by scholars. The tendency of all bureaus to expand is explained by William A. Niskanen by the assumption, derived from the theory of the firm, that "bureaucrats maximize the total budget of their bureau during their tenure"—hence, "all bureaus are too large." What keeps them from being not merely too large but all-consuming is that fact that a bureau must deliver to some degree on its promised output, and if it consistently underdelivers, its budget will be cut by unhappy legislators. But since measuring the output of a bureau is often difficult—indeed, even *conceptualizing* the output of the State Department is mind-boggling—the bureau has a great deal of freedom within which to seek the largest possible budget.

Such theories, both the popular and the scholarly, assign little importance to the nature of the tasks an agency performs, the constitutional framework in which it is embedded, or the preferences and attitudes of citizens and legislators. Our approach will be quite different: Different agencies will be examined in historical perspective to discover the kinds of problems—if any, to which their operations give rise, and how those problems were affected—perhaps determined—by the tasks which they were assigned, the political system in which they operated, and the preferences they were required to consult. What follows will be far from a systematic treatment of such matters, and even farther from a rigorous testing of any theory of bureaucratization. Our knowledge of agency history and behavior is too sketchy to permit that.

Bureaucracy and Size

During the first half of the 19th century, the growth in the size of the federal bureaucracy can be explained, not by the assumption of new tasks by the government or by the imperialistic designs of the managers of existing tasks, but by the addition to existing bureaus of personnel performing essentially routine, repetitive tasks for which the public demand was great and unavoidable. The principal problem facing a bureaucracy thus enlarged was how best to coordinate its activities toward given and noncontroversial ends.

The increase in the size of the executive branch of the federal government at this time was almost entirely the result of the increase in the size of the Post Office. From 1816 to 1861, federal civilian employment in the executive branch increased nearly eightfold (from 4,837 to 36,672), but 86 percent of this growth was the result of additions to the postal service. The Post Office Department was expanding as population and commerce expanded. By 1869 there were 27,000 post offices scattered around the nation; by 1901, nearly 77,000. In New York alone, by 1894 there were nearly 3,000 postal employees, the same number required to run the entire federal government at the beginning of that century. . . .

The Military Establishment

Not all large bureaucracies grow in response to demands for service. The Department of Defense, since 1941 the largest employer of federal civilian officials, has become, as the governmental keystone of the "military–industrial complex," the very archetype of an administrative entity that is thought to be so vast and so well-entrenched that it can virtually ignore the political branches of government, growing and even acting on the basis of its own inner imperatives. . . .

A "Military-Industrial Complex"?

The argument for the existence of an autonomous, bureaucratically led military-industrial complex is supported primarily by events since 1950. Not only has the United States assumed during this period worldwide commitments that necessitate a larger military establishment, but the advent of new, high-technology weapons has created a vast industrial machine with an interest in sustaining a high level of military expenditures, especially on weapons research, development, and acquisition. This machine, so the argument goes, is allied with the Pentagon in ways that dominate the political officials nominally in charge of the armed forces. There is some truth in all this. We have become a world military force, though that decision was made by elected officials in 1949–1950 and not dictated by a (then nonexistent) military–industrial complex. High-cost, high-technology weapons have become important and a number of industrial concerns will prosper or perish depending on how contracts for those weapons are let. The development and purchase of weapons is sometimes made in a wasteful, even irrational, manner. And the allocation of funds among the several armed services is often dictated as much by inter-service rivalry as by strategic or political decisions. . . .

Bureaucracy and Clientelism

After 1861, the growth in the federal administrative system could no longer be explained primarily by an expansion of the postal service and other traditional bureaus. Though these continued to expand, new departments were added that reflected a new (or at least greater) emphasis on the enlargement of the scope of government. Between 1861 and 1901, over 200,000 civilian employees were added to the federal service, only 52 percent of whom were postal workers. Some of these, of course, staffed a larger military and naval establishment stimulated by the Civil War and the Spanish-American War. By 1901 there were over 44,000 civilian defense employees, mostly workers in government-owned arsenals and shipyards. But even those could account for less than one fourth of the increase in employment during the preceding 40 years.

What was striking about the period after 1861 was that the government began to give formal, bureaucratic recognition to the emergence of distinctive interest in a diversifying economy. As Richard L. Schott has written, "whereas earlier federal departments had been formed around specialized governmental functions (foreign affairs, war, finance, and the like), the new departments of this period—Agriculture, Labor, and Commerce—were devoted to the interests and aspirations of particular economic groups."

The original purpose behind these clientele-oriented departments was neither to subsidize nor to regulate, but to promote, chiefly by gathering and publishing statistics and (especially in the case of agriculture) by research. . . .

Public Power and Private Interests

. . . The New Deal was perhaps the high water mark of at least the theory of bureaucratic clientelism. Not only did various sectors of society, notably agriculture, begin receiving massive subsidies, but the government proposed, through the National Industry Recovery Act (NIRA) to cloak with public power a vast number of industrial groupings and trade associations so that they might control production and prices in ways that would end the Depression. The NIRA's Blue Eagle fell before the Supreme Court—the wholesale delegation of public power to private interests was declared unconstitutional. But the piecemeal delegation was not, as the continued growth of specialized promotional agencies attests. The Civil Aeronautics Board, for example, erroneously thought to be exclusively a regulatory agency, was formed in 1938 "to promote" as well as regulate civil aviation and it has done so by restricting entry and maintaining above-market rate fares.

Agriculture, of course, provides the leading case of clientelism. Theodore J. Lowi finds "at least 10 separate, autonomous, local self-governing systems" located in or closely associated with the Department of Agriculture that control to some significant degree the flow of billions of dollars in expenditures and loans. Local committees of farmers, private farm organizations, agency heads, and committee chairmen in Congress dominate policymaking in this area—not, perhaps, to the exclusion of the concerns of other publics, but certainly in ways not powerfully constrained by them.

"Cooperative Federalism"

The growing edge of client-oriented bureaucracy can be found, however, not in government relations with private groups, but in the relations among governmental units. In dollar volume, the chief clients of federal domestic expenditures are state and local government agencies. . . .

The degree to which such grants, and the federal agencies that administer them, constrain or even direct state and local bureaucracies is a matter of dispute. No general answer can be given—federal support of welfare programs has left considerable discretion in the hands of the states over the size of benefits and some discretion over eligibility rules, whereas federal support of highway construction carries with it specific requirements as to design, safety, and (since 1968) environmental and social impact.

A few generalizations are possible, however. The first is that the states and not the cities have been from the first, and remain today, the principal client group for grants-in-aid. It was not until the Housing Act of 1937 that money was given in any substantial amount directly to local governments and though many additional programs of this kind were later added, as late as 1970 less than 12 percent of all federal aid went directly to cities and towns. The second general observation is that the 1960s mark a major watershed in the way in which the purposes of federal aid are determined. Before that time, most grants were for purposes initially defined by states—to build highways and airports, to fund unemployment insurance programs, and the like. Beginning in the 1960s, the federal government, at the initiative of the President and his advisors, increasingly came to define the purposes of these grants—not necessarily over the objection of the states, but often without any initiative from them. Federal money was to be spent on poverty, ecology, planning, and other "national" goals for which, until the laws were passed, there were few, if any, well-organized and influential constituencies. Whereas federal money was once spent in response to the claims of distinct and organized clients, public or private, in the contemporary period federal money has increasingly been spent in ways that have created such clients.

And once rewarded or created, they are rarely penalized or abolished. . . .

Self-Perpetuating Agencies

If the Founding Fathers were to return to examine bureaucratic clientelism, they would, I suspect, be deeply discouraged. James Madison clearly foresaw that American society would be "broken into many parts, interests and classes of citizens" and that this "multiplicity of interest" would help ensure against "the tyranny of the majority," especially in a federal regime with separate branches of government. Positive action would require a "coalition of a majority"; in the process of forming this coalition, the rights of all would be protected, not merely by self-interested bargains, but because in a free society such a coalition "could seldom take place on any other principles than those of justice and the general good." To those who wrongly believed that Madison thought of men as acting only out of base motives, the phrase is instructive: Persuading men who disagree to compromise their differences can rarely be achieved solely by the parceling out of relative advantage; the belief is also required that what is being agreed to is right, proper, and defensible before public opinion.

Most of the major new social programs of the United States, whether for the good of the few or the many, were initially adopted by broad coalitions appealing to general standards of justice or to conceptions of the public weal. This is certainly the case with most of the New Deal legislation—notably such programs as Social Security—and with most Great Society legislation—notably Medicare and aid to education; it was also conspicuously the case with respect to post-Great Society legislation pertaining to consumer and environmental concerns. State occupational licensing laws were supported by majorities instead in, among other things, the contribution of these statutes to public safety and health.

But when a program supplies particular benefits to an existing or newly created interest, public or private, it creates a set of political relationships that make exceptionally difficult further alteration of that program by coalitions of the majority. What was created in the name of the common good is sustained in the name of the particular interest. Bureaucratic clientelism becomes self-perpetuating, in the absence of some crisis or scandal, because a single interest group to which the program matters greatly is highly motivated and well-situated to ward off the criticisms of other groups that have a broad but weak interest in the policy.

In short, a regime of separated powers makes it difficult to overcome objections and contrary interests sufficiently to permit the enactment of a new program or the creation of a new agency. Unless the legislation can be made to pass either with little notice or at a time of crisis or extraordinary majorities—and sometimes even then—the initiation of new programs requires public interest arguments. But the same regime works to protect agencies, once created, from unwelcome change because a major change is, in effect, new legislation that must overcome the same hurdles as the original law, but this time with one of the hurdles—the wishes of the agency and its client—raised much higher. As a result, the Madisonian system makes it relatively easy for the delegation of public power to private groups to go unchallenged and, therefore, for factional interests that have acquired a supportive public bureaucracy to rule without submitting their interests to the effective scrutiny and modification of other interests. . . .

The Courts

23 *Federalist No. 78*

The Judiciary Department
From McLEAN'S Edition, New York.
Alexander Hamilton

To the People of the State of New York:

WE PROCEED now to an examination of the judiciary department of the proposed government.

In unfolding the defects of the existing Confederation, the utility and necessity of a federal judicature have been clearly pointed out. It is the less necessary to recapitulate the considerations there urged, as the propriety of the institution in the abstract is not disputed; the only questions which have been raised being relative to the manner of constituting it, and to its extent. To these points, therefore, our observations shall be confined.

The manner of constituting it seems to embrace these several objects: 1st. The mode of appointing the judges. 2d. The tenure by which they are to hold their places. 3d. The partition of the judiciary authority between different courts, and their relations to each other.

First. As to the mode of appointing the judges; this is the same with that of appointing the officers of the Union in general, and has been so fully discussed in the two last numbers, that nothing can be said here which would not be useless repetition. Second. As to the tenure by which the judges are to hold their places; this chiefly concerns their duration in office; the provisions for their support; the precautions for their responsibility.

According to the plan of the convention, all judges who may be appointed by the United States are to hold their offices DURING GOOD BEHAVIOR; which is conformable to the most approved of the State constitutions and among the rest, to that of this State. Its propriety having been drawn into question by the adversaries of that plan, is no light symptom of the rage for objection, which disorders their imaginations and judgments. The standard of good behavior for the continuance in office of the judicial magistracy, is certainly one of the most valuable of the modern improvements in the practice of government. In a monarchy it is an excellent barrier to the despotism of the prince; in a republic it is a no less excellent barrier to the encroachments and oppressions of the representative body. And it is the best expedient which can be devised in any government, to secure a steady, upright, and impartial administration of the laws.

Whoever attentively considers the different departments of power must perceive, that, in a government in which they are separated from each other, the judiciary, from the nature of its functions, will always be the least dangerous to the political rights of the Constitution; because it will be least in a capacity to annoy or injure them. The Executive not only dispenses the honors, but holds the sword of the community. The legislature not only commands the purse, but prescribes the rules by which the duties and rights of every citizen are to be regulated. The judiciary, on the contrary, has no influence over either the sword or the purse; no direction either of the strength or of the wealth of the society; and can take no active resolution whatever. It may truly be said to have neither FORCE nor WILL, but merely judgment; and must ultimately depend upon the aid of the executive arm even for the efficacy of its judgments.

This simple view of the matter suggests several important consequences. It proves incontestably, that the judiciary is beyond comparison the weakest of the three departments of power[1]; that it can never attack with success either of the other two; and that all possible care is requisite to enable it to defend itself against their attacks. It equally proves, that though individual oppression may now and then proceed from the courts of justice, the general liberty of the people can never be endangered from that quarter; I mean so long as the judiciary remains truly distinct from both the legislature and the Executive. For I agree, that "there is no liberty, if the power of judging be not separated from the legislative and executive powers."[2] And it proves, in the last place, that as liberty can have nothing to fear from the judiciary alone, but would have every thing to fear from its union with either of the other departments; that as all the effects of such a union must ensue from a dependence of the former on the latter, notwithstanding a nominal and apparent separation; that as, from the natural feebleness of the judiciary, it is in continual jeopardy of being overpowered, awed, or influenced by its co-ordinate branches; and that as nothing can contribute so much to its firmness and independence as permanency in office, this quality may therefore be justly regarded as an indispensable ingredient in its constitution, and, in a great measure, as the citadel of the public justice and the public security.

The complete independence of the courts of justice is peculiarly essential in a limited Constitution. By a limited Constitution, I understand one which contains certain specified exceptions to the legislative authority; such, for instance, as that it shall pass no bills of attainder, no ex-post-facto laws, and the like. Limitations of this kind can be preserved in practice no other way than through the medium of courts of justice, whose duty it must be to declare all acts contrary to the manifest tenor of the Constitution void. Without this, all the reservations of particular rights or privileges would amount to nothing.

Some perplexity respecting the rights of the courts to pronounce legislative acts void, because contrary to the Constitution, has arisen from an imagination that the doctrine would imply a superiority of the judiciary to the legislative power. It is urged that the authority which can declare the acts of another void, must necessarily be superior to the one whose acts may be declared void. As this doctrine is of great importance in all the American constitutions, a brief discussion of the ground on which it rests cannot be unacceptable.

There is no position which depends on clearer principles, than that every act of a delegated authority, contrary to the tenor of the commission under which it is exercised, is void. No legislative act, therefore, contrary to the Constitution, can be valid. To deny this, would be to affirm, that the deputy is greater than his principal; that the servant is above his master; that the representatives of the people are superior to the people themselves; that men acting by virtue of powers, may do not only what their powers do not authorize, but what they forbid.

If it be said that the legislative body are themselves the constitutional judges of their own powers, and that the construction they put upon them is conclusive upon the other departments, it may be answered, that this cannot be the natural presumption, where it is not to be collected from any particular provisions in the Constitution. It is not otherwise to be supposed, that the Constitution could intend to enable the representatives of the people to substitute their WILL to that of their constituents. It is far more rational to suppose, that the courts were designed to be an intermediate body between the people and the legislature, in order, among other things, to keep the latter within the limits assigned to their authority. The interpretation of the laws is the proper and peculiar province of the courts. A constitution is, in fact, and must be regarded by the judges, as a fundamental law. It therefore belongs to them to ascertain its meaning, as well as the meaning of any particular act proceeding from the legislative body. If there should happen to be an irreconcilable variance between the two, that which has the superior obligation and validity ought, of course, to be preferred; or, in other words, the Constitution ought to be preferred to the statute, the intention of the people to the intention of their agents.

Nor does this conclusion by any means suppose a superiority of the judicial to the legislative power. It only supposes that the power of the people is superior to both; and that where the will of the legislature, declared in its statutes, stands in opposition to that of the people, declared in the Constitution, the judges ought to be governed by the latter rather than the former. They ought to regulate their decisions by the fundamental laws, rather than by those which are not fundamental.

This exercise of judicial discretion, in determining between two contradictory laws, is exemplified in a familiar instance. It not uncommonly happens, that there are two statutes existing at one time, clashing in whole or in part with each other, and neither of them containing any repealing clause or expression. In such a case, it is the province of the courts to liquidate and fix their meaning and operation. So far as they can, by any fair construction, be reconciled to each other, reason and law conspire to dictate that this should be done; where this is impracticable, it becomes a matter of necessity to give effect to one, in exclusion of the other. The rule which has obtained in the courts for determining their relative validity is, that the last in order of time shall be preferred to the first. But this is a mere rule of construction, not derived from any positive law, but from the nature and reason of the thing. It is a rule not enjoined upon the courts by legislative provision, but adopted by themselves, as consonant to truth and propriety, for the direction of their conduct as interpreters of the law. They thought it reasonable, that between the interfering acts of an EQUAL authority, that which was the last indication of its will should have the preference.

But in regard to the interfering acts of a superior and subordinate authority, of an original and derivative power, the nature and reason of the thing indicate the converse of that rule as proper to be followed. They teach us that the prior act of a superior ought to be preferred to the subsequent act of an inferior and subordinate authority; and that accordingly, whenever a particular statute contravenes the Constitution, it will be the duty of the judicial tribunals to adhere to the latter and disregard the former.

It can be of no weight to say that the courts, on the pretense of a repugnancy, may substitute their own pleasure to the constitutional intentions of the legislature. This might as well happen in the case of two contradictory statutes; or it might as well happen in every adjudication upon any single statute. The courts must declare the sense of the law; and if they should be disposed to exercise WILL instead of JUDG-MENT, the consequence would equally be the substitution of their pleasure to that of the legislative body. The observation, if it prove any thing, would prove that there ought to be no judges distinct from that body.

If, then, the courts of justice are to be considered as the bulwarks of a limited Constitution against legislative encroachments, this consideration will afford a strong argument for the permanent tenure of judicial offices, since nothing will contribute so much as this to that independent spirit in the judges which must be essential to the faithful performance of so arduous a duty.

This independence of the judges is equally requisite to guard the Constitution and the rights of individuals from the effects of those ill humors, which the arts of design-ing men, or the influence of particular conjunctures, sometimes disseminate among the people themselves, and which, though they speedily give place to better informa-tion, and more deliberate reflection, have a tendency, in the meantime, to occasion dangerous innovations in the government, and serious oppressions of the minor party in the community. Though I trust the friends of the proposed Constitution will never concur with its enemies,[3] in questioning that fundamental principle of republican government, which admits the right of the people to alter or abolish the established Constitution, whenever they find it inconsistent with their happiness, yet it is not to be inferred from this principle, that the representatives of the people, whenever a momentary inclination happens to lay hold of a majority of their constituents, incom-patible with the provisions in the existing Constitution, would, on that account, be justifiable in a violation of those provisions; or that the courts would be under a greater obligation to connive at infractions in this shape, than when they had proceeded wholly from the cabals of the representative body. Until the people have, by some solemn and authoritative act, annulled or changed the established form, it is binding upon themselves collectively, as well as individually; and no presumption, or even knowledge, of their sentiments, can warrant their representatives in a departure from it, prior to such an act. But it is easy to see, that it would require an uncommon portion of fortitude in the judges to do their duty as faithful guardians of the Constitution, where legislative invasions of it had been instigated by the major voice of the community.

But it is not with a view to infractions of the Constitution only, that the independence of the judges may be an essential safeguard against the effects of occasional ill humors in the society. These sometimes extend no farther than to the injury of the private rights of particular classes of citizens, by unjust and partial laws. Here also the firmness of the judicial magistracy is of vast importance in mitigating the severity and confining the operation of such laws. It not only serves to moderate the immediate mischiefs of those which may have been passed, but it operates as a check upon the legislative body in passing them; who, perceiving that obstacles to the success of iniquitous intention are to be expected from the scruples of the courts, are in a manner compelled, by the very motives of the injustice they meditate, to qualify their attempts. This is a circumstance calculated to have more influence upon the character of our governments, than but few may be aware of. The benefits of the integrity and moderation of the judiciary have already been felt in more States than one; and though they may have displeased those whose sinister expectations they may have disappointed, they must have commanded the esteem and applause of all the virtuous and disinterested. Considerate men, of every description, ought to prize whatever will tend to beget or fortify that temper in the courts: as no man can be sure that he may not be to-morrow the victim of a spirit of injustice, by which he may be a gainer to-day. And every man must now feel, that the inevitable tendency of such a spirit is to sap the foundations of public and private confidence, and to introduce in its stead universal distrust and distress.

That inflexible and uniform adherence to the rights of the Constitution, and of individuals, which we perceive to be indispensable in the courts of justice, can certainly not be expected from judges who hold their offices by a temporary commission. Periodical appointments, however regulated, or by whomsoever made, would, in some way or other, be fatal to their necessary independence. If the power of making them was committed either to the Executive or legislature, there would be danger of an improper complaisance to the branch which possessed it; if to both, there would be an unwillingness to hazard the displeasure of either; if to the people, or to persons chosen by them for the special purpose, there would be too great a disposition to consult popularity, to justify a reliance that nothing would be consulted but the Constitution and the laws.

There is yet a further and a weightier reason for the permanency of the judicial offices, which is deducible from the nature of the qualifications they require. It has been frequently remarked, with great propriety, that a voluminous code of laws is one of the inconveniences necessarily connected with the advantages of a free government. To avoid an arbitrary discretion in the courts, it is indispensable that they should be bound down by strict rules and precedents, which serve to define and point out their duty in every particular case that comes before them; and it will readily be conceived from the variety of controversies which grow out of the folly and wickedness of mankind, that the records of those precedents must unavoidably swell to a very considerable bulk, and must demand long and laborious study to acquire a competent knowledge of them. Hence it is, that there can be but few men in the society who will have sufficient skill in the laws to qualify them for the stations of judges. And making the proper deductions for the ordinary depravity of human nature, the number must be still smaller of those who unite the requisite integrity with the requisite knowledge. These considerations apprise us, that the government can have no great option between fit character; and that a temporary duration in office, which would naturally discourage such characters from quitting a lucrative line of practice to accept a seat on the bench, would have a tendency to throw the administration of justice into hands less able, and less well qualified, to conduct it with utility and dignity. In the present circumstances of this country, and in those in which it is likely to be for a long time to come, the disadvantages on this score would be greater than they may at first sight appear; but it must be confessed, that they are far inferior to those which present themselves under the other aspects of the subject.

Upon the whole, there can be no room to doubt that the convention acted wisely in copying from the models of those constitutions which have established GOOD BEHAVIOR as the tenure of their judicial offices, in point of duration; and that so far from being blamable on this account, their plan would have been inexcusably defective, if it had wanted this important feature of good government. The experience of Great Britain affords an illustrious comment on the excellence of the institution.

PUBLIUS.

1. The celebrated Montesquieu, speaking of them, says: "Of the three powers above mentioned, the judiciary is next to nothing." "Spirit of Laws." vol. i., page 186.

2. Idem, page 181.

3. Vide "Protest of the Minority of the Convention of Pennsylvania," Martin's Speech, etc.

24   *Supreme Court Inc.*

One of the major themes of Voices of Dissent *is the need to critically examine the relationship between American politics and the capitalist economic system. Jeffrey Rosen is a
law professor who frequently contributes analyses of legal affairs to news magazines and
journals of opinion. In this article Rosen chronicles the growing pro-business orientation of
the Supreme Court. "Hot button" cultural issues like abortion, affirmative action, and the
death penalty generate much attention when they reach the court. But as Rosen argues,
cases involving business "which include shareholder suits, antitrust challenges to corporate
mergers, patent disputes and efforts to reduce punitive-damage awards and prevent product-liability suits—are no less important. They involve billions of dollars, have huge
consequences for the economy and can have a greater effect on people's daily lives than the
often symbolic battles of the culture wars." Rosen believes that the pro-business orientation of the current Court, which includes nominal liberals as well as conservatives, reflects
an elite consensus about the virtues of private enterprise that is not necessarily shared by
the wider public. It is a product as well of a decades-long campaign by conservative and
business interests to shape the legal profession and the court system in pro-free market
ways. Whereas Ralph Nader and the public interest movement once made gains through
the courts, today economic populists in robes are virtually an endangered species.*

I.

The headquarters of the U.S. Chamber of Commerce, located across from Lafayette
Park in Washington, is a limestone structure that looks almost as majestic as the
Supreme Court. The similarity is no coincidence: both buildings were designed by the
same architect, Cass Gilbert. Lately, however, the affinities between the court and the
chamber, a lavishly financed business-advocacy organization, seem to be more than
just architectural. The Supreme Court term that ended last June was, by all measures,
exceptionally good for American business. The chamber's litigation center filed briefs
in 15 cases and its side won in 13 of them—the highest percentage of victories in the
center's 30-year history. The current term, which ends this summer, has also been
shaping up nicely for business interests.

I visited the chamber recently to talk with Robin Conrad, who heads the litigation effort, about her recent triumphs. Conrad, an appealing, soft-spoken woman, lives
with her family on a horse farm in Maryland, where she rides with a fox-chasing club
called the Howard County-Iron Bridge Hounds. Her office, playfully adorned by
action figures of women like Xena the Warrior Princess and Hillary Rodham Clinton,
has one of the most impressive views in Washington. "You can see the White House

Reprinted from *New York Times Magazine*, March 16, 2008, PARS International Corporation.

through the trees," she said as we peered through a window overlooking the park. "In the old days, you could actually see people bathing in the fountain. Homeless people."

Conrad was in an understandably cheerful mood. Though the current Supreme Court has a well-earned reputation for divisiveness, it has been surprisingly united in cases affecting business interests. Of the 30 business cases last term, 22 were decided unanimously, or with only one or two dissenting votes. Conrad said she was especially pleased that several of the most important decisions were written by liberal justices, speaking for liberal and conservative colleagues alike. In opinions last term, Ruth Bader Ginsburg, Stephen Breyer and David Souter each went out of his or her way to question the use of lawsuits to challenge corporate wrongdoing—a strategy championed by progressive groups like Public Citizen but routinely denounced by conservatives as "regulation by litigation." Conrad reeled off some of her favorite moments: "Justice Ginsburg talked about how 'private-securities fraud actions, if not adequately contained, can be employed abusively.' Justice Breyer had a wonderful quote about how Congress was trying to 'weed out unmeritorious securities lawsuits.' Justice Souter talked about how the threat of litigation 'will push cost-conscious defendants to settle.' "

Examples like these point to an ideological sea change on the Supreme Court. A generation ago, progressive and consumer groups petitioning the court could count on favorable majority opinions written by justices who viewed big business with skepticism—or even outright prejudice. An economic populist like William O. Douglas, the former New Deal crusader who served on the court from 1939 to 1975, once unapologetically announced that he was "ready to bend the law in favor of the environment and against the corporations."

Today, however, there are no economic populists on the court, even on the liberal wing. And ever since John Roberts was appointed chief justice in 2005, the court has seemed only more receptive to business concerns. Forty percent of the cases the court heard last term involved business interests, up from around 30 percent in recent years. While the Rehnquist Court heard less than one antitrust decision a year, on average, between 1988 and 2003, the Roberts Court has heard seven in its first two terms—and all of them were decided in favor of the corporate defendants.

Business cases at the Supreme Court typically receive less attention than cases concerning issues like affirmative action, abortion or the death penalty. The disputes tend to be harder to follow: the legal arguments are more technical, the underlying stories less emotional. But these cases—which include shareholder suits, antitrust challenges to corporate mergers, patent disputes and efforts to reduce punitive-damage awards and prevent product-liability suits—are no less important. They involve billions of dollars, have huge consequences for the economy and can have a greater effect on people's daily lives than the often symbolic battles of the culture wars. In the current Supreme Court term, the justices have already blocked a liability suit against Medtronic, the manufacturer of a heart catheter, and rejected a type of shareholder suit that includes a claim against Enron. In the coming months, the court will decide whether to reduce the largest punitive-damage award in American history, which resulted from the Exxon *Valdez* oil spill in 1989.

What should we make of the Supreme Court's transformation? Throughout its history, the court has tended to issue opinions, in areas from free speech to gender equality, that reflect or consolidate a social consensus. With their pro-business jurisprudence, the justices may be capturing an emerging spirit of agreement among liberal and conservative elites about the value of free markets. Among the professional classes, many Democrats and Republicans, whatever their other disagreements, have come to share a relatively laissez-faire, technocratic vision of the economy and are suspicious of excessive regulation and reflexive efforts to vilify big business. Judges, lawyers and law professors (such as myself) drilled in cost-benefit analysis over the past three decades, are no exception. It should come as little surprise that John Roberts and Stephen Breyer, both of whom studied the economic analysis of law at Harvard, have similar instincts in business cases.

This elite consensus, however, is not necessarily shared by the country as a whole. If anything, America may be entering something of a populist moment. If you combine the groups of Americans in a recent Pew survey who lean toward some strain of economic populism—from disaffected and conservative Democrats to traditional liberals to social and big-government conservatives—at least two-thirds of all voters arguably feel sympathy for government intervention in the economy. Could it be, then, that the court is reflecting an elite consensus while contravening the sentiments of most Americans? Only history will ultimately make this clear. One thing, however, is certain already: the transformation of the court was no accident. It represents the culmination of a carefully planned, behind-the-scenes campaign over several decades to change not only the courts but also the country's political culture.

II.

The origins of the business community's campaign to transform the Supreme Court can be traced back precisely to Aug. 23, 1971. That was the day when Lewis F. Powell Jr., a corporate lawyer in Richmond, Va., wrote a memo to his friend Eugene B. Sydnor, then the head of the education committee of the U.S. Chamber of Commerce. In the memo, Powell expressed his concern that the American economic system was "under broad attack." He identified several aggressors: the New Left, the liberal media, rebellious students on college campuses and, most important, Ralph Nader. Earlier that year, Nader founded Public Citizen to advocate for consumer rights, bring antitrust actions when the Justice Department did not, and sue federal agencies when they failed to adopt health and safety regulations.

Powell claimed that this attack on the economic system was "quite new in the history of America." Ever since 1937, when President Franklin D. Roosevelt threatened to pack a conservative Supreme Court with more progressive justices, the court had largely deferred to federal and state economic regulations. And by the 1960s, the Supreme Court under Chief Justice Earl Warren had embraced a form of economic populism, often favoring the interests of small business over big business, even at the expense of consumers. But what Powell saw in the work of Nader and others was altogether more extreme: a radical campaign that was "broadly based and consistently pursued."

To counter the growing influence of public-interest litigation groups like Public Citizen, Powell urged the Chamber of Commerce to begin a multifront lobbying campaign on behalf of business interests, including hiring top business lawyers to bring cases before the Supreme Court. "The judiciary," Powell predicted, "may be the most important instrument for social, economic and political change." Two months after he wrote the memo, Powell was appointed by Richard Nixon to the Supreme Court. And six years later, in 1977, after steadily expanding its lobbying efforts, the chamber established the National Chamber Litigation Center to file cases and briefs on behalf of business interests in federal and state courts.

Today, the Chamber of Commerce is an imposing lobbying force. To fulfill its mission of serving "the unified interests of American business," it collects membership dues from more than three million businesses and related organizations; last year, according to the Center for Responsive Politics, the chamber spent more than $21 million lobbying the White House, Congress and regulatory agencies on legal matters. But its battle against the forces of Naderism got off to a slow start. In 1983, when Robin Conrad arrived at the chamber, the Supreme Court was handing Nader and his allies significant victories. That year, for example, the court held that President Reagan's secretary of transportation, Andrew L. Lewis Jr., acted capriciously when he repealed a regulation, inspired by Nader's advocacy, that required automakers to install passive restraints like air bags. In 1986, the chamber supported a challenge to the Environmental Protection Agency's aerial surveillance of a Dow Chemical plant. The chamber's side lost, 5–4.

But eventually, things began to change. The chamber started winning cases in part by refining its strategy. With Conrad's help, the chamber's Supreme Court litigation program began to offer practice moot-court arguments for lawyers scheduled to argue important cases. The chamber also began hiring the most-respected Democratic and Republican Supreme Court advocates to persuade the court to hear more business cases. Although many of the businesses that belong to the Chamber of Commerce have their own in-house lawyers, they would have the chamber file "friend of the court" briefs on their behalf. The chamber would decide which of the many cases brought to its attention were in the long-term strategic interest of American business and then hire the leading business lawyers to write supporting briefs or argue the case.

Until the mid-1980s, there wasn't an organized group of law firms that specialized in arguing business cases before the Supreme Court. But in 1985, Rex Lee, the solicitor general under Reagan, left the government to start a Supreme Court appellate practice at the firm Sidley Austin. Lee's goal was to offer business clients the same level of expert representation before the Supreme Court that the solicitor general's office provides to federal agencies. Lee's success prompted other law firms to hire former Supreme Court clerks and former members of the solicitor general's office to start business practices. The Chamber of Commerce, for its part, began to coordinate the strategy of these lawyers in the most important business cases.

At times, the strategic calculations can be quite personal. Because Supreme Court clerks have tremendous influence in making recommendations about what cases the court should hear, Conrad told me, having well-known former clerks involved in submitting a brief can be especially important. "When Justice O'Connor was on the bench and we knew her vote was very important, we had a case where the opposition had her favorite clerk on the brief, so we retained her next-favorite clerk," she said with a laugh. "We won."

In our conversation, Conrad was especially enthusiastic about Maureen Mahoney, a former clerk for Chief Justice Rehnquist and one of the top Supreme Court litigators who coordinate strategy with the chamber. When Mahoney agreed in 2005 to represent an appeal by the disgraced accounting firm Arthur Andersen, which was convicted in 2002 of obstructing justice by shredding documents related to the audit of Enron, few people thought the Supreme Court would take the case. "The climate was very anti-Enron," Mahoney told me, "and it was viewed as a doomed petition."

Mahoney rehearsed her Supreme Court argument in a moot court sponsored by the chamber. ("She was absolutely dazzling," Conrad recalls.) On April 27, 2005, Mahoney stood calmly before the justices and delivered one of the best oral arguments I've ever seen at the Supreme Court. She argued that because Arthur Andersen's accountants had followed a standard document-destruction procedure before receiving the government's subpoena, they couldn't be guilty of a crime; they weren't aware what they were doing was criminal. The Supreme Court unanimously agreed and reversed the conviction, 9-0.

The Arthur Andersen case is a good example of how significantly the Supreme Court has changed its attitude about cases involving securities fraud—and business cases more generally—from the Warren to the Roberts era. In a case in 1964, the court ruled that aggrieved investors and consumers could file private lawsuits to enforce the securities laws, even in cases in which Congress hadn't explicitly created a right to sue. In the mid-1990s, however, Congress substantially cut back on these citizen suits, and the court today has shown little patience for them. Mahoney says she sees her victory in the Arthur Andersen case as significant because it applied the same principle in criminal cases involving corporate wrongdoing that the court had already been recognizing in civil cases: namely, "refusing to create greater damage remedies or criminal penalties than Congress has explicitly specified." She describes the case as "a very important win for business."

This term, the Supreme Court has continued to cut back on consumer suits. In a ruling in January, the court refused to allow a shareholder suit against the suppliers to Charter Communications, one of the country's largest cable companies. The suppliers were alleged to have "aided and abetted" Charter's efforts to inflate its earnings, but the court held that Charter's investors had to show that they had relied on the deceptive acts committed by the suppliers before the suit could proceed. A week later, the court invoked the same principle when it refused to hear an appeal in a case related to Enron, in which investors are trying to recover $40 billion from Wall Street banks that they claim aided and abetted Enron's fraud. As a result, the shareholder suit against the banks may be dead.

III.

In addition to litigating cases before the court, the Chamber of Commerce also lobbies Congress and the White House in an effort to change the composition of the court itself. (Unlike many other government officials, the justices themselves are not, of course, subject to direct corporate lobbying.) The chamber's efforts in this area were inspired by Robert Bork's thwarted nomination to the court in 1987. Business groups were enthusiastic about Bork—not because of his conservative social views but because of his skepticism of vigorous antitrust enforcement. "In reaction to the Bork nomination, it struck us that we didn't even have a process in place to be a player," Conrad said.

So the chamber set up a formal process for endorsing candidates after their nominations. The process was designed to be bipartisan; and the chamber has encouraged Democratic as well as Republican presidents to appoint justices. Nominees are evaluated solely through the prism of their views about business. "We're very surgical in our analysis," Conrad said.

After the election of Bill Clinton, for example, the chamber endorsed Ruth Bader Ginsburg, who in addition to her pioneering achievements as the head of the women's rights project at the A.C.L.U. had specialized, as a law professor, in the procedural rules in complex civil cases and was comfortable with the finer points of business litigation. The chamber was especially enthusiastic about Clinton's second nominee, Stephen Breyer, who made his name building a bipartisan consensus for airline deregulation as a special counsel on the judiciary committee; and who, as a Harvard law professor, advocated an influential and moderate view on antitrust enforcement.

During Breyer's confirmation hearings his sharpest critic was Ralph Nader, who testified that his pro-business rulings were "extraordinarily one-sided." Another critic, Senator Howard Metzenbaum of Ohio, said that the fact that the chamber was the first organization to endorse Breyer indicated that "large corporations are very pleased with this nomination" and "the fact that Ralph Nader is opposed to it indicated that the average American has a reason to have some concern." The chamber's imprimatur helped reassure Republicans about Breyer, and he was confirmed with a vote of 87 to 9. "Frankly, we didn't feel like we had anyone on the court since Justice Powell who truly understood business issues," Conrad told me. "Justice Breyer came close to that."

The Breyer and Ginsburg nominations also came at a time when liberal as well as conservative judges and academics were gravitating in increasing numbers to an economic approach to the law, originally developed at the University of Chicago. The law-and-economics movement sought to evaluate the efficiency of legal rules based on their costs and benefits for society as a whole. Although originally conservative in its orientation, the movement also attracted prominent moderate and liberal scholars and judges like Breyer, who before his nomination wrote two books on regulation, arguing that government health-and-safety spending is distorted by sensational media reports of disasters that affect relatively few citizens.

Since joining the Supreme Court, Breyer has also been an intellectual leader in antitrust and patent disputes, which often pit business against business, rather than business against consumers. In those cases, many liberal scholars sympathetic to economic analysis have applauded the court for favoring competition rather than existing competitors, innovation rather than particular innovators. "The court deserves credit for trying to rationalize a totally irrational patent system, benefiting smaller new competitors rather than existing big ones," says Lawrence Lessig, an intellectual-property scholar at Stanford.

Clinton's nominations of Ginsburg and Breyer may have been welcomed by the chamber, but with the election of George W. Bush, the chamber faced a dilemma. Ever since the Reagan administration, there had been a divide on the right wing of the court between pragmatic free-market conservatives, who tended to favor business interests, and ideological states-rights conservatives. In some business cases, these two strands of conservatism diverged, leading the most staunch states-rights conservatives on the court, Antonin Scalia and Clarence Thomas, to rule against business interests. Scalia and Thomas were reluctant to second-guess large punitive-damage verdicts by state juries, for example, or to hold that federally regulated cigarette manufacturers could not be sued in state court. As a result, under Conrad's leadership, the chamber began a vigorous campaign to urge the Bush administration to appoint pro-business conservatives.

When it came time to replace Chief Justice William Rehnquist and Justice Sandra Day O'Connor, the candidate most enthusiastically supported by states-rights conservatives, Judge Michael Luttig, had a record on the Court of Appeals for the Fourth Circuit that some corporate interests feared might make him unpredictable in business cases. ("One of my constant refrains is that being conservative doesn't necessarily mean being pro-business," Conrad told me.) The chamber and other business groups enthusiastically supported John Roberts, who had been hired by the chamber to write briefs in two Supreme Court cases in 2001 and 2002. At the time of Roberts's nomination, Thomas Goldstein, a prominent Supreme Court litigator, described him as "the go-to lawyer for the business community," adding "of all the candidates, he is the one they knew best." When Roberts was nominated, business groups lobbied senators as part of the campaign for his confirmation.

The business community was also enthusiastic about Samuel Alito, whose 15-year record as an appellate judge showed a consistent skepticism of claims against large corporations. Ted Frank of the American Enterprise Institute predicted at the time of the nomination that if Alito replaced O'Connor, he and Roberts would bring about a rise in business cases before the Supreme Court. Frank's prediction was soon vindicated.

"There wasn't a great deal of interest in classic business cases in the last few years of the Rehnquist Court," Carter Phillips, a partner at Sidley Austin and a leading Supreme Court business advocate, told me. In 2004, Judge Richard Posner, a founder of the law-and-economics movement, argued that the Rehnquist Court's emphasis on headline-grabbing constitutional cases had politicized it, and called on the court to hear more business cases. The Roberts court has unambiguously answered the call. As Phillips told me, Roberts "is more interested in those issues and understands them better than his predecessor did."

IV.

Exactly how successful has the Chamber of Commerce been at the Supreme Court? Although the court is currently accepting less than 2 percent of the 10,000 petitions it receives each year, the Chamber of Commerce's petitions between 2004 and 2007 were granted at a rate of 26 percent, according to Scotusblog. And persuading the Supreme Court to hear a case is more than half the battle: Richard Lazarus, a law professor at Georgetown who also represents environmental clients before the court, recently ran the numbers and found that the court reverses the lower court in 65 percent of the cases it agrees to hear; and when the petitioner is represented by the elite Supreme Court advocates routinely hired by the chamber, the success rate rises to 75 percent.

Faced with these daunting numbers, the progressive antagonists of big business are understandably feeling beleaguered and outgunned. "The fight before the court is generally not an even one," said David Vladeck, who once worked for the Public Citizen Litigation Group and now teaches law at Georgetown. "There's us on one side, with a brief or two, and industry on the other side, with a well-coordinated campaign of 10 or 12 briefs, with each one written by a member of the elite Supreme Court bar that address an issue in enormous depth." He added, ruefully, "You admire their handiwork, but it's frustrating as hell to deal with."

To gauge the degree of the frustration, I recently paid a visit to Ralph Nader, a few weeks before he announced his most recent campaign for president of the United States. It was a surprise to find that his office, the Center for Study of Responsive Law, shares an address in a grand building with the Carnegie Institution for Science. But the office itself, reassuringly, is buried on the ground floor, where Nader received me at a conference table surrounded by file cabinets stuffed with faded back issues of *Mother Jones* and *The Nation*.

Nader was uncontrite about his 2000 run against Al Gore—which is often credited with helping George W. Bush win the presidency—and he insisted that because Clinton appointed justices like Breyer, Gore would have done the same. "Breyer hasn't been worse than I feared, because I had real concern when he was nominated," Nader told me. He conceded that, like Breyer, Democratic justices appointed by President John Kerry would presumably have been better on civil rights and liberties than John Roberts and Samuel Alito. Nevertheless, he disparaged Breyer as a "deregulation quasi-ideologue" who was able to weave a "tapestry of illusion" in his arguments by dealing in abstractions.

The main casualty of the 2000 run, Nader said, is that he is no longer collaborating with America's trial lawyers. They would ordinarily be his natural allies in representing consumer interests, but they donated heavily to Gore's campaign. After 2000, the trial lawyers "have been vitriolic," Nader explained. He blames them for not using their money to help counteract the influence of the Chamber of Commerce and other business groups before the federal courts. In part as a result of their stinginess, he said, his colleagues at Public Citizen are underfinanced and worn down. "There were some lawyers who left Public Citizen because they got tired of losing," he said. "Everyone is desperately trying to hold on to whatever issues are left, and then they become demoralized and discouraged."

Thirty years after the Chamber of Commerce founded its litigation center to counteract his influence, Nader all but conceded defeat in the battle for the Supreme Court. With the decline of economic populism in Congress, the weakening of trade unions and the rise of globalization, the political climate, he lamented, was passing him by. "I recall a comment by Eugene Debs," Nader said, looking at me intensely. "He said: The American people live in a country where they can have almost anything they want. And my regret is that it seems that they don't want much of anything at all."

Nader chuckled quietly and shook his head. "I say ditto."

V.

If there is an anti-Nader—a crusading lawyer passionately devoted to the pro-business cause—it is Theodore Olson. One of the most influential Supreme Court advocates and a former solicitor general under President George W. Bush, Olson is best known for his winning argument before the Supreme Court in *Bush v. Gore* in 2000. But Olson has devoted most of his energies in private practice to changing the legal and political climate for American business. According to his peers in the elite Supreme Court bar, he more than anyone else is responsible for transforming the approach to one of the most important legal concerns of the American business community: punitive damages awarded to the victims of corporate negligence.

Punitive damages—money awarded by civil juries on top of any awarded for actual harm that victims have suffered—are designed to penalize especially egregious acts of corporate misconduct resulting from malice or greed, and to deter similar wrongdoing in the future. In the nineteenth century, courts generally demanded a clear assignment of fault in cases where victims sued for injuries caused by malfunctioning products. It was hard for plaintiffs to recover in personal-injury cases unless the corporation was obviously at fault. But in the twentieth century, in liability cases involving a rapidly expanding class of potentially dangerous products like cars, drugs and medical devices, courts increasingly applied a standard of "strict liability," which held that manufacturers should pay whether or not they were directly at fault.

The animating idea was that manufacturers were in the best position to prevent accidents by improving their products with better design and testing. They and their insurance companies (rather than society as a whole) would shoulder the costs of accidents, thus giving them an incentive to make their products safer. Encouraged by Ralph Nader's book, *Unsafe at Any Speed*, published in 1965, courts began to see car accidents as predictable events that better car design could have prevented. In 1968, for example, a federal court held that car manufacturers could be sued for failing to make cars safe enough for drivers to survive crashes, even if the driver was at fault for the crash.

A series of well-publicized awards in the 1980s and 1990s culminated in the largest punitive damage award in American history—the $5 billion levied against Exxon after the Exxon *Valdez* oil spill in 1989. This was hardly typical: the median punitive award actually fell to $50,000 in 2001 from $63,000 in 1992. Nevertheless, critics like Olson claimed that multimillion-dollar punitive-damage verdicts were threatening the health of the economy. They resolved to fight back on several fronts. In his first Supreme Court argument, in 1986, Olson set out the broad contours of his argument. for most of English and American history, private litigants were entitled to be compensated for whatever damages they suffered, including pain and suffering, but any public wrongs like the failure of American business to make cars safer by adopting air bags should be addressed by legislation or regulation, not by the courts.

Olson decided that his clients deserved not just a lawyer who could argue a case but a lawyer who could change the political culture. "You had to attack it in a broad-scale way in the legislatures, in the arena of public opinion and in the courts," he told me recently. "I felt the business community had to approach this in a holistic way." He set out, in lectures and op-ed pieces, to publicize especially egregious examples.

The poster child for punitive-damage abuse, widely derided in TV and radio ads paid for by the business community, was a New Mexico grandmother who, in 1994, was awarded $2.7 million in punitive damages when she scalded herself with hot McDonald's coffee. Consumer advocates countered that she had originally asked for $20,000 for medical expenses, which McDonald's refused to pay, and the award appeared to have the effect of persuading McDonald's to serve its coffee at a safer temperature. Nonetheless, the campaign to vilify plaintiffs' lawyers has been effective enough that the American Association of Trial Lawyers recently changed its name to the fuzzier American Association for Justice.

The business community made other inroads against punitive damages. Corporations financed campaigns against pro–punitive-damage state judges who had been elected with the assistance of large contributions from plaintiffs' lawyers. The business community also helped persuade more than 30 states to either impose caps on punitive-damage awards or direct substantial portions of the awards to be paid into special state funds. In 1996, it helped persuade the Republican Congress, led by Newt Gingrich, to pass legislation that would cap punitive-damage awards in product-liability cases in every state court in the country. But in 1996, President Clinton, with what must have been perverse pleasure, vetoed the bill on the grounds that it violated principles of federalism and states rights to which conservatives claimed to be devoted.

Thwarted by Clinton, and unable to persuade Congress to override the veto, opponents of punitive damages turned their attention back to the Supreme Court, looking for a victory they were unable to win in the political arena. Here, they were remarkably successful. As late as 1991, the court had refused to impose limits on a large punitive-damage award. But in a case in 1996, the court held for the first time that punitive-damage awards had to be proportional to the actual damage incurred by the plaintiff. The case involved a man who said he was deceived by BMW when it sold him a supposedly "new" car that was, in fact, used and had received a $300 touch-up job. The court, in a 5–4 opinion, overturned a $2 million punitive-damage award as "grossly excessive." In 2003, the court clarified what it meant: a single-digit ratio between punitive damages and compensatory damages was likely to be acceptable.

Last year, the business community watched with anticipation as Roberts and Alito revealed their views about punitive damages. The case involved the estate of a heavy smoker who sued Philip Morris for deceitfully distributing a "poisonous and addictive substance." A jury had awarded the estate $821,000 in compensatory damages and $79.5 million in punitive damages—a ratio of about 100 to 1. In a 5–4 opinion written by Breyer, the court held that it was unconstitutional for a jury to use punitive damages to punish a company for its conduct toward similarly affected individuals who are not party to the lawsuit.

This spring, the court will decide the Exxon *Valdez* punitive-damage case, which many consider the culmination of the business community's decades-long campaign against punitive damages. In 1989, the Exxon *Valdez* tanker, whose captain had a history of alcoholism, ran into a reef and punctured the hull; 11 million gallons of oil leaked onto the coastline of Prince William Sound. A jury handed down a $5 billion punitive-damage award.

After the verdict, Exxon began providing money for academic research to support its claim that the award for damages was excessive. It financed some of the country's most prominent scholars on both sides of the political spectrum, including the Nobel laureate Daniel Kahneman and Cass Sunstein, a law professor at the University of Chicago. (Sunstein says he accepted only travel grants, not research support, from Exxon; and Kahneman stresses that the financing had no influence on the substance of his work.) In a 2002 book, *Punitive Damages: How Juries Decide,* Sunstein studied hundreds of mock-jury deliberations and concluded that jurors are unpredictable and often irrational in punitive-damage cases. Jury deliberations, he found, increase the unpredictability, as well as the dollar amount of the final awards. Sunstein concluded that a system of civil fines determined by experts, rather than punitive damages determined by juries, might be more sensible. When Exxon appealed the $5 billion verdict in 2006, it was reduced by an appellate court to $2.5 billion. The reduced verdict is once again being challenged as excessive.

Walter Dellinger, the lawyer now arguing Exxon's case before the Supreme Court, is no Republican activist. Like Sunstein, he is one of the most respected Democratic constitutional scholars, as well as a former acting solicitor general for President Clinton. Last month, in his argument before the court, Dellinger argued that because Exxon has already paid $3.4 billion in fines, cleanup costs and compensation connected with the Exxon *Valdez* spill, and because it didn't act out of malice or greed in failing to monitor the alcoholic captain, additional punitive damages would serve no "public purpose."

During the argument, Breyer noted that the $2.5 billion punitive damage award represents a less than 10-to-1 ratio between punitive damages and compensatory damages, which is in the single-digit range that the Supreme Court has considered acceptable in the past. But Breyer also seemed concerned at other points that punitive-damage awards have not been routine in maritime cases like this one, and that the award might create "a new world for the shipping industry." Alito, who owns Exxon Mobil stock, did not participate, and because a tie would affirm the $2.5 billion punitive-damage award, the plaintiffs who are opposing Exxon need only four votes to prevail. But whether Dellinger gets five votes, a significant triumph is already behind him: he persuaded the court to take the case in the first place.

VI.

Ted Olson and the Chamber of Commerce aren't only trying to persuade the Supreme Court to cut back on large punitive-damage awards; they're also arguing that consumers injured by dangerous or defective medical devices and drugs in some cases shouldn't be able to file product-liability suits at all. Because there is no national product-liability law that allows federal suits for personal injuries, consumers who are injured by, say, defective heart valves or artificial hips have to sue in state courts under state tort law. By asking the Supreme Court to prevent injured consumers from suing in state court, the business community, supported by the Bush administration, is trying to ensure that these consumers often have no legal remedy for their injuries. And the Supreme Court has been increasingly sympathetic to the business community's arguments.

In a Supreme Court case Olson argued in December, he stood before the justices and argued that the manufacturers of defective medical devices—like heart valves, breast implants and defibrillators—should be immune from personal-liability suits because the federal Food and Drug Administration had approved the devices before they were marketed and the manufacturers had complied with all federal requirements. The case involved Charles Riegel, who had an angioplasty in 1996 during which the catheter used to dilate his coronary artery burst. Riegel, who needed advanced life support and emergency bypass surgery, eventually sued the manufacturer of the catheter, Medtronic. The company is colloquially referred to in the business community as "the pre-emption company" because of its practice of arguing that the Food and Drug Administration's "premarket approval" of its products pre-empts product-liability suits in state courts.

The lawyer representing Riegel's estate before the Supreme Court, Allison Zieve of Public Citizen, countered that Congress never intended to ban state product-liability suits when Senator Edward Kennedy sponsored a bill regulating medical devices in 1976. (Kennedy himself filed a brief in the case noting that he indeed intended no such thing.) "Lawyers think this is a close issue, but any time I talk to a nonlawyer about it, they're shocked," Zieve told me after the argument. "People think: of course, if somebody makes a defective product you can sue."

It's one thing to argue that the federal government's "premarket approval" of food, drugs and medical devices should pre-empt clearly inconsistent state laws and regulations. After all, if states imposed safety requirements that conflicted with the federal standard, the resulting regulatory confusion would make a national (and global) market impossible. But Olson's claim that federal regulation of medical devices and drugs should also pre-empt product-liability suits under state tort law is one of the more creative and far-reaching legal arguments of the business groups that litigate before the Supreme Court.

This type of argument arose out of the tobacco litigation of the 1980s and 1990s, which culminated in a $206 billion settlement paid by the top tobacco companies to a consortium of 46 state attorneys general in exchange for dropping tort suits against the companies. The tobacco litigation began modestly: in 1983, Rose Cipollone, a New Jersey woman dying of lung cancer, sued several of the country's largest tobacco companies for their failure to give adequate warnings about the dangers of smoking. After spending tens of millions of dollars fighting the verdict, the companies decided to take their defense to the next level. They argued that because the federal government required cigarette companies to have warning labels, tobacco companies couldn't be subject to tort suits in state courts. Jury verdicts, they argued, are no less a form of regulation than laws explicitly adopted by state legislatures.

In a decision in 1992, the Supreme Court endorsed part of the companies' argument. The decision unleashed a torrent of similar "pre-emption" claims by the manufacturers of dangerous drugs, defective medical devices and cars without air bags. And after the election of President Bush in 2000, the business community's crusade was aggressively supported by the White House. At the same time that the White House was scaling back on federal health-and-safety enforcement, it insisted that consumers should not be able to sue federally regulated industries in state court. Bush appointed as the general counsel of the Food and Drug Administration a former drug- and tobacco-company lawyer named Daniel Troy. With Troy's support, the F.D.A. reversed its position, held for 25 years, and argued for the first time that its premarket approval of medical devices should prevent injured consumers from bringing product-liability suits in state court.

After her Supreme Court argument in the Medtronic case, Zieve told me she wasn't sure what to expect. Until the arrival of Chief Justice Roberts, groups like Public Citizen had found that they had a better chance of winning pre-emption cases before the Supreme Court than in the lower courts. But during the first two years of the Roberts Court, the justices had decided two pre-emption cases in favor of the corporate defendants.

The trend has continued. On Feb. 21, the Supreme Court handed Zieve a crush- ing defeat: an 8–1 opinion immunizing the makers of defective medical devices from product-liability suits. The lone dissent was written by Ruth Bader Ginsburg, who objected that Congress could not have intended such a "radical curtail- ment" of state personal-injury suits when it regulated medical devices in 1976. Ginsburg, who is devoted to liberal judicial restraint, has consistently opposed efforts to second-guess punitive-damage awards or expand federal pre-emption. I called Zieve soon after the Supreme Court issued its opinion, and she sounded shocked. "It's really unfathomable to me," she said. "I wasn't sure that this was a business-friendly court, but now I'm finding it harder not to view it that way." Zieve said that, as a result of the decision, "I think the industry will keep unsafe devices on the market longer and be slower to improve products."

In the eyes of advocates like Zieve and Public Citizen, the public is now caught in a Catch-22: at the very moment that agencies like the F.D.A. are being strongly reproved by critics—including the agency's own internal science board—for being unwilling or unable to protect public health, the court is making it harder for people to receive compensation for the injuries that result. On rare occasions, the Roberts Court has held that the Bush administration's deregulatory efforts circumvent the will of Congress—like the 5–4 decision last year holding that the Environmental Protection Agency acted capriciously when it adopted a rule that said it had no legal authority to regulate greenhouse gases. But by and large, the Supreme Court defers to agencies that refuse to regulate public health and safety. "The industry has a lot of money, and they can routinely hire the biggest names in the biggest firms, while we're doing it on our own," Zieve told me. "We don't charge anything—we're free. It didn't cost $250,000 to get us to write the brief."

VII.

The Supreme Court is unlikely to reconsider its pro-business outlook anytime soon. Nevertheless, there are several currents in American political life that run counter to the court, even if they may not be strong enough, or suitably directed, to reverse it. There are, for example, economic populists in both political parties—John Edwards Democrats and Mike Huckabee Republicans, to cite just two types—who express concern about growing economic inequality and corporate corruption, and blame unchecked corporate power for America's escalating economic problems. These populists tend to be from the working and middle classes rather than the professional classes, and their numbers may be growing. In recent Pew surveys, 65 percent of Americans agreed that corporations make excessive profits—the highest number in 20 years. Moreover, about half the country now asserts that America is divided on economic lines into two groups—the "haves" and "have nots"—up from only 26 percent two decades ago. And the number of Americans who view themselves as "have nots" has doubled to 34 percent today from 17 percent in 1988. Responding to pressures from this demographic, a Democratic Congress—bolstered by states-rights conservatives—might well try to pass legislation to counteract the court's recent decisions barring product-liability suits for defective medical devices.

What about the executive branch? It seems unlikely that John McCain, if he were elected president, would push back against the court: he has already pledged to appoint "judges of the character and quality of Justices Roberts and Alito," rather than justices more devoted to states rights, like Scalia and Thomas. As for Barack Obama and Hillary Clinton, both have sounded increasingly populist notes in an effort to attract union and blue-collar supporters, ratcheting up their attacks on corporate wealth and power, singling out the drug, oil and health-insurance industries and promising to renegotiate the North American Free Trade Agreement. But despite their rhetoric, it is not clear that either candidate would actually appoint justices any more populist than Bill Clinton's nominees. "I would be stunned to find an anti-business appointee from either of them," Cass Sunstein, who is a constitutional adviser to Obama, told me. "There's not a strong interest on the part of Obama or Clinton in demonizing business, and you wouldn't expect to see that in their Supreme Court nominees."

Still, the possibility does exist. If the economy continues to decline and blue-collar voters end up being crucial in the election, a Democratic president might appoint an economic populist to the Supreme Court as a kind of payback. Earlier this month, on the campaign trail in Ohio, Obama mentioned Earl Warren, who served as governor of California before becoming chief justice, as a model of the kind of justice he hoped to appoint. "I want people on the bench who have enough empathy, enough feeling, for what ordinary people are going through," Obama said. He praised Warren for understanding that segregation was wrong because of the stigma it attached to blacks, rather than because of the precise nature of its sociological impact. Appointing a former politician to the court would almost certainly introduce a more populist element: the Supreme Court that in 1954 decided *Brown v. Board of Education* included, in addition to a former governor, three former senators, a former Securities and Exchange Commission member and two former attorneys general. (By contrast, the Roberts court is composed of nine former judges.)

Whatever happens in November, Robin Conrad says the Chamber of Commerce is prepared to lobby as hard as ever for the appointment of pro-business justices. "If we do have a Democrat president, and that president has opportunities to nominate to the court," she said in our meeting as I glanced at her Hillary Clinton action figure, "we want to be able to express ourselves and work with that president." Regardless of how many justices retire in the next presidential term, Conrad is confident that, having helped to transform the Supreme Court in less than 30 years, she and her colleagues can assure American business of a sympathetic hearing for decades to come.

When I told Conrad that Ralph Nader told me that lawyers were leaving Public Citizen because they were tired of losing, she achieved a look of earnest concern. "I hope if they feel they've lost," she said, "they lost for a good reason—not because they've been overpowered or muscled by the big, bad business community, but they've lost because reason won."

Conrad looked at me squarely, and then added, "I guess if Ralph Nader wants to say we did him in"—she paused to weigh her words—"so be it."

Discussion Questions

1. What steps have the Chamber of Commerce and other business groups taken to build a stronger pro-business presence in the American legal system?

2. Rosen calls Theodore Olson an "anti-Nader." Who is Theodore Olson and what is the significance of the term "anti-Nader" in terms of Rosen's overall argument?

3. Who are the winners and losers in the Supreme Court's business decisions? Is the Court saying that what is good for business is good for America?

25 *The Hollow Hope: Can Courts Bring About Social Change?*

Gerald N. Rosenberg

The power of the Supreme Court stems from its power of judicial review, which was acquired in Marbury v. Madison *(1803), when Chief Justice John Marshall declared the Judiciary Act of 1801 unconstitutional. Critics of the Court argue that its power to determine the constitutionality of acts of Congress is too great. Several provisions in the Constitution, however, provide the other branches with means of reining in the Supreme Court. Congress, for example, can increase the number of justices serving on the Supreme Court, even though the number has been set at nine. Congress can also amend the Constitution if it chooses. In the end, the Court rarely exercises its power to overturn national law. Although the Court's power of judicial review is not final, its impact on public policy is great because of a common perception that courts, as the guardians of the Constitution, do have the final say.*

Introduction

The Problem

Justice Jackson: "I suppose that realistically the reason this case is here was that action couldn't be obtained from Congress. Certainly it would be here much stronger from your point of view if Congress did act, wouldn't it?"

Mr. Rankin: "That is true, but . . . if the Court would delegate back to Congress from time to time the question of deciding what should be done about rights . . . the parties [before the Court] would be deprived by that procedure from getting their constitutional rights because of the present membership or approach of Congress to that particular question." (Oral argument in *Briggs v. Elliott,* quoted in Friedman 1969, 244)

Reprinted from *The Hollow Hope: Can Courts Bring About Social Change?* (1991), by permission of University of Chicago Press.

When Justice Jackson and Assistant U.S. Attorney General J. Lee Rankin exchanged these thoughts during oral argument in a companion case to *Brown,* they acknowledged that the Supreme Court is part of a larger political system. As their colloquy overtly demonstrates, American courts are political institutions. Though unique in their organization and operation, they are a crucial cog in the machinery of government. But this exchange rests on a more interesting premise that is all the more influential because it is implicit and unexamined: court decisions produce change. Specifically, both Jackson and Rankin assumed that it mattered a great deal how the Court decided the issue of school segregation. If their assumption is correct, then one may ask sensibly to what extent and in what ways courts can be consequential in effecting political and social change. To what degree, and under what conditions, can judicial processes be used to produce political and social change? What are the constraints that operate on them? What factors are important and why?

These descriptive or empirical questions are important for understanding the role of any political institution, yet they are seldom asked of courts. Traditionally, most lawyers and legal scholars have focused on a related normative issue: whether courts *ought* to act. From the perspective of democratic theory, that is an important and useful question. Yet since much of politics is about who gets what, when, and how, and how that distribution is maintained, or changed, understanding to what extent, and under what conditions, courts can produce political and social change is of key importance.

The answer to the questions raised above might appear obvious if it rests on Rankin's and Jackson's implied premise that courts produce a great deal of social change. In the last several decades movements and groups advocating what I will shortly define as significant social reform have turned increasingly to the courts. Starting with the famous cases brought by the civil rights movement and spreading to issues raised by women's groups, environmental groups, political reformers, and others, American courts seemingly have become important producers of political and social change. Cases such as *Brown* (school desegregation) and *Roe* (abortion) are heralded as having produced major change. Further, such litigation has often occurred, and appears to have been most successful, when the other branches of government have failed to act. While officious government officials and rigid, unchanging institutions represent a real social force which may frustrate popular opinion, this litigation activity suggests that courts can produce significant social reform even when the other branches of government are inactive or opposed. Indeed, for many, part of what makes American democracy exceptional is that it includes the world's most powerful court system, protecting minorities and defending liberty, in the face of opposition from the democratically elected branches. Americans look to activist courts, then, as fulfilling an important role in the American scheme.[1] This view of the courts, although informed by recent historical experience, is essentially functional. It sees courts as powerful, vigorous, and potent proponents of change. I refer to this view of the role of the courts as the "Dynamic Court" view.

As attractive as the Dynamic Court view may be, one must guard against uncritical acceptance. Indeed, in a political system that gives sovereignty to the popular will and makes economic decisions through the market, it is not obvious why courts should have the effects it asserts. Maybe its attractiveness is based on something more than effects? Could it be that the self-understanding of the judiciary and legal profession leads to an overstatement of the role of the courts, a "mystification" of the judiciary? If judges see themselves as powerful; if the Bar views itself as influential, and insulated; if professional training in law schools inculcates students with such beliefs, might these factors inflate the self-importance of the judiciary? The Dynamic Court view may be supported, then, because it offers psychological payoffs to key actors by confirming self-images, not because it is correct.[2] And when this "mystification" is added to a normative belief in the courts as the guardian of fundamental rights and liberties—what Scheingold (1974) calls the "myth of rights"—the allure of the Dynamic Court view may grow.

Further, for all its "obviousness," the Dynamic Court view has a well-established functional and historical competitor. In fact, there is a long tradition of legal scholarship that views the federal judiciary, in Alexander Hamilton's famous language, as the "least dangerous" branch of government. Here, too, there is something of a truism about this claim. Courts, we know, lack both budgetary and physical powers. Because, in Hamilton's words, they lack power over either the "sword or the purse," their ability to produce political and social change is limited. In contrast to the first view, the "least dangerous" branch can do little more than point out how actions have fallen short of constitutional or legislative requirements and hope that appropriate action is taken. The strength of this view, of course, is that it leaves Americans free to govern themselves without interference from non-elected officials. I refer to this view of the courts as weak, ineffective, and powerless as the "Constrained Court" view.

The Constrained Court view fully acknowledges the role of popular preferences and social and economic resources in shaping outcomes. Yet it seems to rely excessively on a formal-process understanding of how change occurs in American politics. But the formal process doesn't always work, for social and political forces may be overly responsive to unevenly distributed resources. Bureaucratic inertia, too, can derail orderly, processional change. There is room, then, for courts to effectively correct the pathologies of the political process. Perhaps accurate at the founding of the political system, the Constrained Court view may miss growth and change in the American political system.

Clearly, these two views, and the aspirations they represent, are in conflict on a number of different dimensions. They differ not only on both the desirability and the effectiveness of court action, but also on the nature of American democracy. The Dynamic Court view gives courts an important place in the American political system while the older view sees courts as much less powerful than other more "political" branches and activities. The conflict is more than one of mere definition, for each view captures a very different part of American democracy. We Americans want courts to protect minorities and defend liberties, *and* to defer to elected officials. We want a robust political life *and* one that is just. Most of the time, these two visions do not clash. American legislatures do not habitually threaten liberties, and courts do not regularly invalidate the acts of elected officials or require certain actions to be taken. But the most interesting and relevant cases, such as *Brown* and *Roe,* occur when activist courts overrule and invalidate the actions of elected officials, or order actions beyond what elected officials are willing to do. What happens then? Are courts effective producers of change, as the Dynamic Court view suggests, or do their decisions do little more than point the way to a brighter, but perhaps unobtainable future? Once again, this conflict between two deeply held views about the role of the courts in the American political system has an obvious normative dimension that is worth debating. But this [article] has a different aim. Relying heavily on empirical data, I ask under what conditions can courts produce political and social change? When does it make sense for individuals and groups pressing for such change to litigate? What do the answers mean about the nature of the American regime?

Political and social change are broad terms. Specifically, conflict between the two views is more sharply focused when courts become involved in social reform, the broadening and equalizing of the possession and enjoyment of what are commonly perceived as basic goods in American society. What are these basic goods? Rawls (1971, 42) provides a succinct definition: "Rights and liberties, powers and opportunities, income and wealth." Later he adds self-respect (Rawls 1971, 440). Fleshed out, these include political goods such as participation in the political process and freedom of speech and association; legal goods such as equal and non-discriminatory treatment of all people; material goods; and self-respect, the opportunity for every individual to lead a satisfying and worthy life. Contributions to political and social change bring these benefits to people formerly deprived of them.

Yet, so defined, social reform is still too broad a term to capture the essence of the difference between the two views. At the core of the debate lies those specific social reforms that affect large groups of people such as blacks, or workers, or women, or partisans of a particular political persuasion; in other words, *policy change with nationwide impact*. Litigation aimed at changing the way a single bureaucracy functions would not fit this definition, for example, while litigation attempting to change the functioning of a whole set of bureaucracies or institutions nationwide would. Change affecting groups of this size, as well as altering bureaucratic and institutional practice nationwide can be called *significant* social reform. So, for example, in the *Brown* litigation, when civil rights litigators sued to end school segregation nationwide, not just in the school systems in which the complaints arose, they were attempting to use the courts to produce significant social reform. Similarly, when abortion activists mounted a constitutional challenge to restrictive abortion laws, aimed at affecting all women, they were attempting to use the courts to produce significant social reform. Although the relevant boundary line cannot be drawn precisely, there is no doubt that the aim of modern litigation in the areas of civil rights, women's rights, and the like, is to produce significant social reform.[3]

This definition of significant social reform does not take much note of the role of the courts in individual cases. Due process and court procedures offer at least some protection to the individual from arbitrary action. Interposing courts and set procedures between government officials and citizens has been a hard fought-for and great stride forward in human decency.[4] However, the protection of individuals, in individual cases, tells us little about the effectiveness of courts in producing nationwide policy change. In addition, there is no clash between the two views in dealing with individuals.

There is good reason to focus solely on the effectiveness of courts in producing significant social reform. Other possibilities, such as courts acting as obstacles to significant social reform, can be excluded because adequate work has been done on them. Studies of the role of the courts in the late nineteenth and early twentieth centuries, for example, show that courts can effectively block significant social reform.[5] Further, since the mid-twentieth century litigants have petitioned American courts with increasing frequency to produce significant social reform. Reform-minded groups have brought cases and adopted strategies that assumed courts could be consequential in furthering their goals. To narrow the focus is to concentrate on an important aspect of recent political activity.

The attentive reader will have noticed that I have written of courts being consequential in effecting significant social reform, of courts producing significant social reform, or of courts being of help to reformers. All of these formulations suggest that courts can sometimes make a difference. The question, then, is whether, and under what conditions, this occurs. When does it makes sense to litigate to help bring about significant social reform? If the judiciary lacks power, as the Constrained Court view suggests, then courts cannot make much difference. Perhaps only when political, social, and economic forces have already pushed society far along the road to reform will courts have any independent effect. And even then their decisions may be more a reflection of significant social reform already occurring than an independent, important contribution to it. But if the Dynamic Court view is the more accurate, if courts are effective producers of significant social reform, then they will be able to produce change. And if each view is partly right, if courts are effective under some conditions and not others, then I want to know when and where those conditions exist.

There is a danger that I have set up a straw man. Given the incremental nature of change in American politics, one might wonder if there is ever significant social reform in the U.S. In fact, if there is not, then asking whether and under what conditions courts produce it won't tell me anything about courts and change. I run the danger of "finding" that courts don't produce significant social reform because it doesn't exist! Fortunately, there are numerous examples of significant social reform in the U.S.: the introduction of social security, medicaid and medicare; increased minority participation in the electoral process; the increasing racial integration of American institutions and society; the increasing breakdown of gender barriers and discrimination against women; enhanced protection of the environment and reduction of pollution; protection for working men and women who organize to improve their lot; and so on. Clearly, then, there is significant social reform in the U.S. And, of course, proponents of the Dynamic Court view claim that both *Brown* and *Roe* produced significant social reform.

In order to determine whether and under what conditions courts can produce significant social reform, . . . this . . . concentrates on two key areas of significant social reform litigation, civil rights and women's rights. These two movements and their leading, symbolic cases (*Brown* and *Roe*) are generally considered the prime examples of the successful use of a court-based strategy to produce significant social reform. Proponents of the Dynamic Court view generally credit *Brown* with having revolutionized American race relations while *Roe* is understood as having guaranteed legal abortions for all. Defenders of the Constrained Court view, however, might suggest that neither interpretation is correct. Rather, they would point to changes in the broader political system to explain such major social and political changes. Clearly, the two views are in conflict.

It should be emphasized that an examination of civil rights, abortion, and women's rights avoids the pitfalls of simple case studies. Each movement spans a sufficient length of time to allow for variance. Covering decades, the debate over these issues has been affected by political, social, and economic variables. Besides the importance of these cases for politics (and for law and social science), they are cases in which claims about court effectiveness should be most clearly highlighted, cases which should most likely falsify one of the two views. . . .

In order to proceed, while not ignoring state and lower federal courts, I will concentrate on the U.S. Supreme Court. Like the Congress and the presidency, the Supreme Court, while not the only institution of its kind in the American political system, is the most visible and important one. It sits atop a hierarchical structure, and decisions of lower courts involving significant social reform seldom escape its scrutiny. Also, because it is the most authoritative U.S. court, it is the most concerned with public policy. Hypotheses that concern the courts and social reform must first deal with the Supreme Court and then turn to the ramifications of its decisions elsewhere in the judiciary.

There remains the question of how to deal with complicated issues of causation. Because it is difficult to isolate the effects of court decisions from other events in producing significant social reform, special care is needed in specifying how courts can be effective. On a general level, one can distinguish two types of influence courts could exercise. Court decisions might produce significant social reform through a *judicial* path that relies on the authority of the court. Alternatively, court influence could follow an *extra-judicial* path that invokes court powers of persuasion, legitimacy, and the ability to give salience to issues. Each of these possible paths of influence is different and requires separate analysis.

The *judicial* path of causal influence is straight-forward. It focuses on the direct outcome of judicial decisions and examines whether the change required by the courts was made. In civil rights, for example, if a Supreme Court decision ordering an end to public segregation was the cause of segregation ending, then one should see lower courts ordering local officials to end segregation, those officials acting to end it, the community at large supporting it, and, most important, segregation actually ending. Similarly, with abortion, if the Court's invalidation of state laws restricting or prohibiting abortion produced direct change, it should be seen in the removal of barriers to abortion and the provision of abortion services where requested. Proponents of the Dynamic Court view believe that the courts have powerful direct effects, while partisans of the Constrained Court view deny this. . . .

Separate and distinct from judicial effects is the more subtle and complex causal claim of *extra-judicial* effects. Under this conception of causation, courts do more than simply change behavior in the short run. Court decisions may produce significant social reform by inspiring individuals to act or persuading them to examine and change their opinions. Court decisions, particularly Supreme Court decisions, may be powerful symbols, resources for change. They may affect the intellectual climate, the kinds of ideas that are discussed. The mere bringing of legal claims and the hearing of cases may influence ideas. Courts may produce, significant social reform by giving salience to issues, in effect placing them on the political agenda. Courts may bring issues to light and keep them in the public eye when other political institutions wish to bury them. Thus, courts may make it difficult for legislators to avoid deciding controversial issues. Indirect effects are an important part of court power in the Dynamic Court view. Evidence for extra-judicial effects might be found in public-opinion data, media coverage, and in public and elite action supporting significant social reform. Both *Brown* and *Roe* are universally credited with producing important extra-judicial effects, from bringing attention to civil rights and sparking the civil rights and women's rights movement to persuading Americans that abortion is acceptable. . . .

Conclusion: The Fly-Paper Court

This study has examined whether, and under what conditions, courts can produce significant social reform. Contrasting two functional and historically derived views of the courts, three constraints and four conditions were developed. They were success-ful in understanding the mostly disappointing results of attempts to use the courts to produce significant social reform in civil rights, abortion, women's rights, the envi-ronment, reapportionment, and criminal rights. Their success, particularly in the paradigmatic cases of *Brown* and *Roe,* suggests general applicability.

The findings show that, with the addition of the four conditions, the constraints derived from the Constrained Court view best capture the capacity of the courts to produce significant social reform. This is the case because, on the most fundamental level, courts depend on political support to produce such reform (Constraint II). For example, since the success of civil rights in fields such as voting and education depended on political action, political hostility doomed court contributions. With women's rights, lack of enforcement of existing laws, in addition to an unwillingness to extend legal protection, had a similar dampening effect. And with abortion and the environment, hostility from many political leaders created barriers to implementation. This finding appears clearly applicable to other fields.

Courts will also be ineffective in producing change, given any serious resistance because of their lack of implementation powers (Constraint III). The structural constraints of the Constrained Court view, built into the American judicial system, make courts virtually powerless to produce change. They must depend on the actions of others for their decisions to be implemented. With civil rights, little changed until the federal government became involved. With women's rights, we still lack a serious government effort, and stereotypes that constrain women's opportunities remain powerful. Similarly, the uneven availability of access to legal abortion demonstrates the point. Where there is local hostility to change, court orders will be ignored. Community pressure, violence or threats of violence, and lack of market response all serve to curtail actions to implement court decisions. This finding, too, appears appli-cable across fields.

Despite these constraints on change, in at least several of the movements exam-ined major legal cases were won. The chief reason is that the remaining constraint, the lack of established legal precedents, was weak (Constraint I). That is, there were precedents for change and supportive movements within the broader legal culture. In civil rights, litigation in the 1930s and 1940s progressively battered the separate-but-equal standard, setting up the argument and decision in *Brown*. In women's rights, the progress of civil rights litigation, particularly in the expansion of the Fourteenth Amendment, laid the groundwork. In the area of abortion, notions of a sphere of privacy in sexual matters were first developed by the Supreme Court in 1965, broadened in 1972, and forcefully presented in several widely read law-review articles. And, by the date of the Supreme Court's abortion decisions, numerous lower courts had invalidated state abortion statutes on grounds that the Supreme Court came to enunciate. Without these precedents, which took decades to develop, it would have been years before even a legal victory could have been obtained. But legal victories do not automatically or even necessarily produce the desired change.

A quick comparison between civil rights and abortion illustrates these points. While both had legal precedents on which to construct a winning legal argument, little else was similar. With civil rights, there was a great deal of white hostility to blacks, especially in the South. On the whole, political leaders, particularly Southerners, were either supportive of segregation or unwilling to confront it as an important issue. In addition, court decisions required individuals and institutions hostile to civil rights to implement the changes. Until Congress acted a decade later, these two constraints remained and none of the conditions necessary for change were present. After congressional and executive actions were taken, the constraints were overcome and conditions for change were created, including the creation of incentives, costs, and the context in which courts could be used as cover. Only then did change occur. In contrast, at the time of the abortion decisions there was much public and elite support for abortion. There was an active reform movement in the states, and Congress was quiet, with no indication of the opposition that many of its members would later provide.[6] Also, the presence of the market condition partially overcame the implementation constraint. To the extent that the abortion decisions had judicial effects, it is precisely because the constraints were weak and a condition necessary for change was present. Civil rights and abortion litigation, then, highlight the existence and force of the constraints and conditions.

Turning to the question of extra-judicial or indirect effects, courts are in a weak position to produce change. Only a minority of Americans know what the courts have done on important issues. Fewer still combine that knowledge with the belief in the Supreme Court's constitutional role, a combination that would enable the Court, and the lower courts, to legitimate behavior. This makes courts a particularly poor tool for changing opinions or for mobilization. As Peltason puts it, "litigation, by its complexity and technical nature and by its lack of dramatic moments, furnishes an ineffective peg around which to build a mass movement" (Peltason 1971, 103). Rally round the flag is one thing but rally round the brief (or opinion) is quite another! The evidence from the movements examined makes dubious any claim for important extra-judicial effects of court action. It strikes at the heart of the Dynamic Court view.

The cases examined show that when the constraints are overcome, and one of the four conditions is present, courts can help produce significant social reform. However, this means, by definition, that institutional, structural, and ideological barriers to change are weak. A court's contribution, then, is akin to officially recognizing the evolving state of affairs, more like the cutting of the ribbon on a new project than its construction. Without such change, the constraints reign. When Justice Jackson commented during oral argument in *Brown,* "I suppose that realistically this case is here for the reason that action couldn't be obtained from Congress" (quoted in Friedman 1969, 244),[7] he identified a fundamental reason why the Court's action in the case would have little effect.

Given the constraints and the conditions, the Constrained Court view is the more accurate: U.S. courts can *almost never* be effective producers of significant social reform. At best, they can second the social reform acts of the other branches of government. Problems that are unsolvable in the political context can rarely be solved by courts. As Scheingold puts it, the "law can hardly transcend the conflicts of the political system in which it is embedded" (Scheingold 1974, 145). Turning to courts to produce significant social reform substitutes the myth of America for its reality. It credits courts and judicial decisions with a power that they do not have.

In contrast to this conclusion, it might be suggested that throughout . . . I have asked too much of courts. After all, in all the cases examined, court decisions produced some change, however small. Given that political action appeared impossible in many instances, such as with civil rights in the 1950s and reform of the criminal justice system more generally, isn't some positive change better than none? In a world of unlimited resources, this would be the case. In the world in which those seeking significant social reform live, however, strategic choices have costs, and a strategy that produces little or no change drains resources that could be more effectively employed in other strategies. In addition, vindication of constitutional principles accompanied by small change may be mistaken for widespread significant social reform, inducing reformers to relax their efforts.

In general, then, not only does litigation steer activists to an institution that is constrained from helping them, but also it siphons off crucial resources and talent, and runs the risk of weakening political efforts. In terms of financial resources, social reform groups don't have a lot of money. Funding a litigation campaign means that other strategic options are starved of funds. In civil rights, while *Brown* was pending in June 1953, Thurgood Marshall and Walter White sent out a telegram to supporters of the National Association for the Advancement of Colored People asking for money, stating "funds entirely spent" (quoted in Kluger 1976, 617). Compare this to the half-million-dollar estimates of the cost of the freedom rides, largely due to fines and bail (Sarratt 1966, 337). Further, the legal strategy drained off the talents of people such as Thurgood Marshall and Jack Greenberg. As Martin Luther King, Jr., complained: "to accumulate resources for legal actions imposes intolerable hardships on the already overburdened" (King 1963, 157).

In the abortion field, reliance on the Court seriously weakened the political efficacy of pro-choice forces. After the 1973 decisions, many pro-choice activists simply assumed they had won and stopped their pro-choice activity. According to J. Hugh Anwyl, at one time executive director of Planned Parenthood of Los Angeles, pro-choice activists went "on a long siesta" after the abortion decisions (quoted in

Johnston 1977, 1). This view was concurred in by a National Abortion Rights Action League activist, Janet Beals: "Everyone assumed that when the Supreme Court made its decision in 1973 that we'd got what we wanted and the battle was over. The movement afterwards lost steam" (quoted in Phillips 1980, 3).[8] Jackson and Vinovskis found that, after the decisions, "state-level pro-choice groups disbanded, victory seemingly achieved" (Jackson and Vinovskis 1983, 73). By 1977, a survey of pro-choice and anti-abortion activity in thirteen states nationwide found that abortion rights advocates had failed to match the activity of their opponents (Johnston 1977, 24). The political organization and momentum that had changed laws nationwide dissipated in celebration of Court victory.

The pro-choice movement was harmed in a second way by its reliance on Court action. The most restrictive version of the Hyde Amendment, banning federal funding even for most medically necessary abortions, was passed with the help of a parliamentary maneuver by pro-choice legislators. Their strategy, as reported the following day on the front pages of the *New York Times* and *Washington Post,* was to pass such a conservative bill that the Court would have "no choice" but to overturn it (Tolchin 1977; Russell 1977).[9] This reliance on the Court was totally unfounded. With hindsight, Karen Mulhauser, former director of NARAL, suggested that "had we made more gains through the legislative and referendum processes, and taken a little longer at it, the public would have moved with us" (quoted in Williams 1979, 12). By winning a Court case "without the organization needed to cope with a powerful opposition" (Rubin 1982, 169), pro-choice forces vastly overestimated the power and influence of the Court.

A further danger of litigation as a strategy for significant social reform is that symbolic victories may be mistaken for substantive ones, covering a reality that is distasteful. Rather than working to change that reality, reformers relying on a litigation strategy for reform may be misled (or content?) to celebrate the illusion of change. . . . In criminal rights, for example, the contribution of the Court's decisions seems more symbolic than substantive, having "more significance as a declaration of intent than as a working instrument of law" (Elsen and Rosett 1967, 645). For some, however, this is meaningful. As Schulhofer puts it, "the symbolic effects of criminal procedural guarantees are important; they underscore our societal commitment to restraint in an area in which emotions easily run uncontrolled" (Schulhofer 1987, 460).[10] . . . There is a danger that symbolic gains cover for actual failings. In strong but colorful language, Tigar sums up this view of the criminal rights revolution, and the dangers of substituting symbolic gain for substantive change more generally: "the constitutional revolution in criminal procedure has amounted to little more than an ornament, or golden cupola, built upon the roof of a structure found rotting and infested, assuring the gentlefolk who only pass by without entering that all is well inside" (Tigar 1970, 7).

It is important to note here that there were options other than litigation in all the cases discussed. With civil rights, massive voter-registration drives could have been started in the urban North and in some major Southern cities. Marches, demonstrations, and sit-ins could have been organized and funded years before they broke out, based on the example of labor unions and the readiness of groups like the Congress of

Racial Equality. Money could have been invested in public relations. Amazingly, in 1957 the NAACP spent just $7,814 for its Washington Bureau operations. Its entire "public relations and informational activities" spending for 1957 was $17,216. NAACP lobbyists did not even try to cultivate the black press or the black church, let alone their white counterparts. And even in 1959 the public relations budget was only $10,135 (Ware 1962, 188–89, 189, 190, 213). When activists succumbed to the "lawyers' vision of change without pain" (Scheingold 1974, 145), a "massive social revolution" was side-tracked into "legal channels" (Horwitz 1979, 184). Because the NAACP failed to understand the limits on U.S. courts, its strategy was bound to fail.[11]

With women's groups, the kinds of political activities and grass-roots organizing that started in the 1980s could have been organized earlier. Organizing around issues such as the earning gap and comparable worth could have been funded. Political activity on behalf of abortion at the state level could have been given greater emphasis. And coalition building, crucial in any ongoing political movement, could have been supported. Only belatedly, after June 1977, did pro-choice forces begin to work together to influence the legislative process (Gelb and Palley 1979, 378). As with civil rights, there was no lack of alternatives for social reform action.[12]

If this is the case, then there is another important way in which courts affect social change. It is, to put it simply, that courts act as "fly-paper" for social reformers who succumb to the "lure of litigation." If the constraints of the Constrained Court view are correct, then courts can seldom produce significant social reform. Yet if groups advocating such reform continue to look to the courts for aid, and spend precious resources in litigation, then the courts also limit change by deflecting claims from substantive political battles, where success is possible, to harmless legal ones where it is not. Even when major cases are won, the achievement is often more symbolic than real. Thus, courts may serve an ideological function of luring movements for social reform to an institution that is structurally constrained from serving their needs, providing only an illusion of change.[13]

While I have found no evidence that court decisions mobilize supporters of significant social reform, the data suggest that they may mobilize opponents. With civil rights, there was growth in the membership and activities of pro-segregation groups such as the White Citizens Councils and the Ku Klux Klan in the years after *Brown*. With abortion, the Right to Life movement expanded rapidly after 1973. While both types of groups existed before Court action, they appeared re-invigorated after it. In addition, in the wake of the Supreme Court's 1989 *Webster* decision, seen by many as a threat to continuing access to safe and legal abortion, pro-choice forces seemed to gain renewed vigor. This interesting and anomalous finding requires further work, but it does suggest that one result of litigation to produce significant social reform is to strengthen the opponents of such change. And that, of course, is far from the aim of those who litigate.

This conclusion does not deny that courts can sometimes help social reform movements. Occasionally, though rarely, when the constraints are overcome, and one of the conditions is present, courts can make a difference. Sometimes, too, litigation can remove minor but lingering obstacles. But here litigation is often a mopping-up operation, and it is often defensive. In civil rights, for example, when opponents of the 1964 and 1965 acts went to court to invalidate them, the courts' refusal to do so allowed change to proceed. Similarly, if there had never been a *Brown* decision, a Southern school board or state wanting to avoid a federal fund cut-off in the late 1960s might have challenged its state law requiring segregation. An obliging court decision would have removed the obstacle without causing much of a stir, or wasting the scarce resources of civil rights groups. This is a very different approach to the courts than one based on using them to produce significant social reform.

Litigation can also help reform movements by providing defense services to keep the movement afloat. In civil rights, the NAACP Legal Defense and Educational Fund, Inc. (Inc. Fund) provided crucial legal service that prevented the repressive legal structures of the Southern states from totally incapacitating the movement. In springing demonstrators from jail, providing bail money, and forcing at least a semblance of due process, Inc. Fund lawyers performed crucial tasks. But again, this is a far cry from a litigation strategy for significant social reform.

The findings of this study also suggest that a great deal of writing about courts is fundamentally flawed. Treating courts and judges as either philosophers on high or as existing solely within a self-contained legal community ignores what they actually do. This does not mean that philosophical thinking and legal analysis should be abandoned. It emphatically does mean that the broad and untested generalizations offered by constitutional scholars about the role, impact, importance, and legitimacy of courts and court opinions . . . must be rejected. When asking those sorts of questions about courts, they must be treated as political institutions and studied as such. To ignore social science literature and eschew empirical evidence, as much court writing does, makes it impossible to understand courts as they are.

American courts, with their power of judicial review, are an important part of the notion of American exceptionalism. Unlike the courts of almost any other country, American courts are vested with the power to declare invalid acts of democratically accountable political actors. From time to time in American history, great debates have flourished about the role of the courts, about whether the exercise of judicial review is consistent with a self-governing democracy. Since the 1950s, the debate has raged anew, with its most recent manifestation the debate over "strict construction" of the Constitution. Its focus has been on the movements I have examined. Yet, while such concerns are of intellectual importance, the analysis presented here has shown that they may be of little practical value. Normative and constitutional concerns about whether courts ought to be used to further social reform are misplaced if the conditions under which they can do so are so rare as to make the production of that change unlikely. Of greater concern are the implications of seeking significant social reform through the courts for political participation, mobilization, and reform. Social reformers, with limited resources, forgo other options when they elect to litigate. Those options are mainly political and involve mobilizing citizens to participate more effectively. The analysis . . . has shown that in assuming that courts can overcome political obstacles, and produce change without mobilization and participation, reformers both reified and removed courts from the political and economic system in which they operate. And while such exercises may make for fine reading in constitutional-law textbooks, they seldom bring reform any closer.

American courts are not all-powerful institutions. They were designed with severe limitations and placed in a political system of divided powers. To ask them to produce significant social reform is to forget their history and ignore their constraints. It is to cloud our vision with a naive and romantic belief in the triumph of rights over politics. And while romance and even naiveté have their charms, they are not best exhibited in courtrooms.

Endnotes

[1] Not everyone, however, thinks such liberal judicial activism is a good thing. It has spawned a wave of attacks on the judiciary ranging from Nathan Glazer's warning of the rise of an "imperial judiciary" to a spate of legislative proposals to remove court jurisdiction over a number of issues. See Glazer (1975); *An Imperial Judiciary* (1979). And, of course, Presidents Nixon and Reagan pledged to end judicial activism by appointing "strict constructionists" to the federal courts.

[2] As McCann (1986, 114) suggests, in the public-interest movement, lawyers are "quite naturally the most ardent spokespersons" for the use of courts to produce change.

[3] A major study of public-interest law takes a similar "focus on policy-oriented cases, where a decision will affect large numbers of people or advance a major law reform objective" (Council for Public Interest Law 1976, 7).

[4] See, for example, Thompson (1975), particularly chapter 10, and Hay et al. (1975). Though the focus of both works is on the role of the criminal law in the eighteenth century in sustaining the hegemony of the English ruling class, both view law as affording some protection to individuals.

[5] A simple example is child labor, where the Supreme Court twice overturned congressional legislation prohibiting it, delaying its eventual outlawing for several decades. For a careful study of the ability of courts to effectively block significant social reform, see Paul (1960). However, it should be noted that given the appointment power, and the general dependence of courts on political elites, such blocking cannot continue indefinitely. On this point, see Dahl (1957).

[6] Comparing the aftermath of the abortion and civil rights decisions, it seems clear that there was substantially less turmoil over abortion than over civil rights. See Friedman (1983, 23); Tatalovich and Daynes (1981, 6–7).

[7] On this point, John Hart Ely's (1980) legislative-failure defense of judicial activism frees the Court to act in precisely those instances where it is most unlikely to be of any help.

[8] Others in agreement with this analysis include Tatalovich and Daynes (1981, 101, 164), and participants in a symposium at the Brookings Institution, noted in Steiner (1983, 84).

[9] See also Gelb and Palley (1979, 376–77); Jaffe et al. (1981, 129).

[10] See also Schulhofer (1981, 883, 892–93).

[11] For an argument that only through violence or its threat can minority groups achieve benefits, see Piven and Cloward (1979).

[12] A similar case can be made with significant social reform of the environment, where continuing and strengthening the movement could have been emphasized. With reform of the criminal justice system, organizations such as those that evolved out of the civil rights movement could have been reinvigorated (. . .). And even with reapportionment, build-

ing political organizations and lobbying for substantive reform could have created pressure (and did in the late 1960s) for significant social reform.

[13]This point was not lost on the nineteenth-century founders of the Legal Aid Society. Their aim was not merely to help the poor but, in the words of Arthur Von Briesen, an early force in the legal aid movement, to "deflect them from anarchy, socialism, and bolshevism." Legal aid was also popular with Vice-President Theodore Roosevelt, who saw it as a "necessary bulwark against 'chaos' and 'violent revolution'" (quotes from Auerbach 1976, 53–55).

> ★ **Gerald Rosenberg** *is professor of political science at the University of Chicago. His main specialty is the judiciary, especially the courts' impact on larger political processes such as school desegregation and abortion rights. He also is director of the American Politics Workshop, a workshop exploring recent work in the sub-disciplines of American politics.*

Questions

1. Explain the origins of the courts' power in national policy making?

2. How are courts constrained in making policy?

3. The public believes that the courts are powerful agents of public policy. Why does Rosenberg argue that this perception is dangerous to groups seeking social justice?

Public Policy Challenges

26   Why Does the Air Stink? Corporate Power and Public Policy

Dan Clawson, Alan Neustadtl, and Mark Weller

How is economic power translated into political influence? Sociologists Dan Clawson, Alan Neustadtl, and Mark Weller examine the impact of corporate political action committees (PACs) on public policy. Uniquely drawing on interviews with PAC directors, they demonstrate how campaign contributions win "access" to members of Congress, resulting in loopholes and regulatory rules favorable to business. Clawson, Neustadtl, and Weller base their analysis of corporate PACs on a "field theory of power." Focus on this concept and consider its usefulness in understanding business "hegemony" in our political system. In a concluding section, the authors itemize the enormous public impact of private corporate power by providing a detailed list of decisions made by business companies in the United States. One implication of this analysis is that even if PACs were banned, business decisions would have a greater impact on our lives than most government decisions have, barring significant change in our economic system.

Everybody wants clean air. Who could oppose it? "I spent seven years of my life trying to stop the Clean Air Act," explained the vice president of a major corporation that is a heavy-duty polluter. Nonetheless, he was perfectly willing to make campaign contributions to members who voted for the Act:

> *How a person votes on the final piece of legislation often is not representative of what they have done. Somebody will do a lot of things during the process. How many guys voted against the Clean Air Act? But during the process some of them were very sympathetic to some of our concerns.*

In the world of Congress and political action committees things are not always what they seem. Members of Congress all want to vote for clean air, but they also want to get campaign contributions from corporations, and they want to pass a law that business will accept as "reasonable." The compromise solution is to gut the bill by crafting

---

dozens of loopholes. These are inserted in private meetings or in subcommittee hearings that don't get much (if any) attention in the press. Then the public vote on the final bill can be nearly unanimous. Members of Congress can reassure their constituents and their corporate contributors: constituents, that they voted for the final bill; corporations, that they helped weaken it in private. Clean air, and especially the Clean Air Act of 1990, can serve as an introduction to the kind of process we try to expose.

The public strongly supports clean air, and is unimpressed when corporate officials and apologists trot out their normal arguments—"corporations are already doing all they reasonably can to improve environmental quality," "we need to balance the costs against the benefits," "people will lose their jobs if we make controls any stricter." The original Clean Air Act was passed in 1970, revised in 1977, and not revised again until 1990. Although the initial goal was to have us breathing clean air by 1975, the deadline has been repeatedly extended—and the 1990 legislation provides a new set of deadlines to be reached sometime in the distant future.

Corporations control the production process unless the government specifically intervenes. Therefore, any delay in government action leaves corporations free to do as they choose; business often prefers a weak, ineffective, and unenforceable law. The laws have not only been slow to come, but corporations have also fought to delay or subvert implementation. The 1970 law ordered the Environmental Protection Agency (EPA) to regulate the hundreds of poisonous chemicals that are emitted by corporations, but, as William Greider notes, "In twenty years of stalling, dodging, and fighting off court orders, the EPA has managed to issue regulatory standards for a total of seven toxics."

Corporations have done exceptionally well politically, given the problem they face: The interests of business are diametrically opposed to those of the public. Clean air laws and amendments have been few and far between, enforcement is ineffective, and the penalties minimal. On the one hand, corporations *have* had to pay billions for clean-ups; on the other hand, the costs to date are a small fraction of what would be needed to actually clean up the environment.

This corporate struggle for the right to pollute takes place on many fronts. The most visible is public relations: the Chemical Manufacturers Association took out a two-page Earth Day ad in the *Washington Post* to demonstrate its concern; coincidentally, the names of many of the corporate signers of this ad appear on the EPA's list of high-risk producers. Another front is expert studies that delay action while more information is gathered. The federally funded National Acid Precipitation Assessment Program took ten years and $600 million to figure out whether acid rain was in fact a problem. Both business and the Reagan administration argued that nothing should be done until the study was completed. Ultimately, the study was discredited: The "summary of findings" minimized the impact of acid rain, even though this did not accurately represent the expert research in the report. But the key site of struggle was Congress. For years, corporations successfully defeated legislation. In 1987 utility companies were offered a compromise bill on acid rain, but they "were very adamant that they had beat the thing since 1981 and they could always beat it," according to Representative Edward Madigan (Republican-Illinois). The utilities beat back all efforts at reform through the 1980s, but their intransigence probably hurt them when revisions finally came to be made.

The stage was set for a revision of the Clean Air Act when George Bush, "the environmental president," was elected, and George Mitchell, a strong supporter of environmentalism, became the Senate majority leader. But what sort of clean air bill would it be? "What we wanted," said Richard Ayres, head of the environmentalists' Clean Air Coalition, "is a health based standard—one-in-1-million cancer risk," a standard that would require corporations to clean up their plants until the cancer risk from their operations was reduced to one in a million. "The Senate bill still has the requirement," Ayres said, "but there are forty pages of extensions and exceptions and qualifications and loopholes that largely render the health standard a nullity." Greider reports, for example, "According to the EPA, there are now twenty-six coke ovens that pose a cancer risk greater than 1 in 1000 and six where the risk is greater than 1 in 100. Yet the new clean-air bill will give the steel industry another thirty years to deal with the problem."

This change from what the bill was supposed to do to what it did do came about through what corporate executives like to call the "access" process. The principal aim of most corporate campaign contributions is to help corporate executives gain "access" to key members of Congress and their staffs. In these meetings, corporate executives (and corporate PAC money) work to persuade the members of Congress to accept a predesigned loophole that will sound innocent but effectively undercut the stated intention of the bill. Representative John D. Dingell (Democrat-Michigan), who was chair of the House Committee, is a strong industry supporter; one of the people we interviewed called him "the point man for the Business Roundtable on clean air." Representative Henry A. Waxman (Democrat-California), chair of the subcommittee, is an environmentalist. Observers had expected a confrontation and contested votes on the floor of the Congress.

The problem for corporations was that, as one Republican staff aide said, "If any bill has the blessing of Waxman and the environmental groups, unless it is totally in outer space, who's going to vote against it?" But corporations successfully minimized public votes. Somehow, Waxman was persuaded to make behind-the-scenes compromises with Dingell so members, during an election year, didn't have to side publicly with business against the environment. Often the access process leads to loopholes that protect a single corporation, but for "clean" air most of the special deals targeted not specific companies but entire industries. The initial bill, for example, required cars to be able to use carefully specified, cleaner fuels. But the auto industry wanted the rules loosened, and Congress eventually incorporated a variant of a formula suggested by the head of General Motors' fuels and lubricants department.

Nor did corporations stop fighting even after they gutted the bill through amendments. Business pressed the EPA for favorable regulations to implement the law: "The cost of this legislation could vary dramatically, depending on how EPA interprets it," said William D. Fay, vice president of the National Coal Association, who headed the hilariously misnamed Clean Air Working Group, an industry coalition that fought to weaken the legislation. As one EPA aide working on acid rain regulations reported, "We're having a hard time getting our work done because of the number of phone calls we're getting from corporations and their lawyers."

Corporations trying to get federal regulators to adopt the "right" regulations don't rely exclusively on the cogency of their arguments. They often exert pressure on a member of Congress to intervene for them at the EPA or other agency. Senators and representatives regularly intervene on behalf of constituents and contributors by doing everything from straightening out a social security problem to asking a regulatory agency to explain why it is pressuring a company. This process—like campaign finance—usually follows rules of etiquette. In addressing a regulatory agency, the senator does not say, "Lay off my campaign contributors or I'll cut your budget." One standard phrasing for letters asks regulators to resolve the problem "as quickly as possible within applicable rules and regulations." No matter how mild and careful the inquiry, the agency receiving the request is certain to give it extra attention; only after careful consideration will they refuse to make any accommodation.

Soft money—unregulated megabuck contributions—also shaped what happened to air quality. Archer Daniels Midland argued that increased use of ethanol would reduce pollution from gasoline; coincidentally, ADM controls a majority of the ethanol market. To reinforce its arguments, in the 1992 election ADM gave $90,000 to Democrats and $600,000 to Republicans, the latter supplemented with an additional $200,000 as an individual contribution from the company head, Dwayne Andreas. Many environmentalists were skeptical about ethanol's value in a clean air strategy, but President Bush issued regulations promoting wider use of ethanol; we presume he was impressed by the force of ADM's 800,000 Republican arguments. Bob Dole, the 1996 Republican presidential candidate, helped pass and defend special breaks for the ethanol industry; he not only appreciated ADM's Republican contributions, but presumably approved of the more than $1 million they gave to the American Red Cross during the period when it was headed by his wife, Elizabeth Dole. What about the post-1994 Republican-controlled Congress, defenders of the free market and opponents of government giveaways? Were they ready to end this subsidy program, cracking down on corporate welfare as they did on people welfare? Not a chance. In 1997, the Republican chair of the House Ways and Means Committee actually attempted to eliminate the special tax breaks for ethanol. Needless to say, he was immediately put in his place by other members of the Republican leadership, including Speaker Newt Gingrich and most of the Senate, with the subsidy locked in place for years to come, in spite of a General Accounting Office report that "found that the ethanol subsidy justifies none of its political boasts." The Center for Responsive Politics calculated that ADM, its executives and PAC, made more than $1 million in campaign contributions of various types; the only thing that had changed was that in 1996, with a Democratic president, this money was "divided more or less evenly between Republicans and Democrats."

The disparity in power between business and environmentalists looms large during the legislative process, but it is enormous afterward. When the Clean Air Act passed, corporations and industry groups offered positions, typically with large pay increases, to congressional staff members who wrote the law. The former congressional staff members who now work for corporations both know how to evade the law and can persuasively claim to EPA that they know what Congress intended. Environmental organizations pay substantially less than Congress and can't afford large staffs. They are seldom able to become involved in the details of the administrative process or to influence implementation and enforcement.

Having pushed Congress and the Environmental Protection Agency to allow as much pollution as possible, business then went to the Quayle council for rules allowing even more pollution. Vice President J. Danforth Quayle's council, technically known as the "Council on Competitiveness," was created by President Bush specifically to help reduce regulations on business. Quayle told the *Boston Globe* "that his council has an 'open door' to business groups and that he has a bias against regulations." During the Bush administration, this council reviewed, and could override, all regulations, including those by the EPA setting the limits at which a chemical was subject to regulation. The council also recommended that corporations be allowed to increase their polluting emissions if a state did not object within seven days of the proposed increase. Corporations thus have multiple opportunities to win. If they lose in Congress, they can win at the regulatory agency; if they lose there, they can try again at the Quayle council (or later equivalent). If they lose there, they can try to reduce the money available to enforce regulations, or tie the issue up in the courts, or plan on accepting a minimal fine.

The operation of the Quayle council probably would have received little publicity, but reporters discovered that the executive director of the Council, Allan Hubbard, had a clear conflict of interest. Hubbard chaired the biweekly White House meetings on the Clean Air Act. He owned half of World Wide Chemical, received an average of more than $1 million a year in profits from it while directing the Quayle council, and continued to attend quarterly stockholder meetings. According to the *Boston Globe,* "Records on file with the Indianapolis Air Pollution Control Board show that World Wide Chemical emitted 17,000 to 19,000 pounds of chemicals into the air" in 1991. At that time the company did "not have the permit required to release the emissions," was "putting out nearly four times the allowable emissions without a permit, and could be subject to a $2,500-a-day penalty," according to David Jordan, director of the Indianapolis Air Pollution Board.

This does not, however, mean that business always gets exactly what it wants. In 1997, the Environmental Protection Agency proposed tough new rules for soot and smog. Business fought hard to weaken or eliminate the rules: hiring experts (from pro-business think tanks) to attack the scientific studies supporting the regulations and putting a raft of lobbyists ("many of them former congressional staffers," the *Washington Post* reported) to work securing the signatures of 250 members of Congress questioning the standards. But the late 1990s version of these industry mobilizations adds a new twist—creating a pseudo grassroots campaign. For example, business, operating under a suitably disguised name (Foundation for Clean Air Progress), paid for television ads telling farmers that the EPA rules would prohibit them from plowing on dry windy days, with other ads predicting the EPA rules "would lead to forced carpooling or bans on outdoor barbecues—claims the EPA dismisses as ridiculous." Along with the ads, industry worked to mobilize local politicians and business executives in what business groups called a "grass tops" campaign.

Despite a massive industry campaign, EPA head Carol Browner remained firm, and President Clinton was persuaded to go along. Of course, industry immediately began working on ways to undercut the regulations with congressional loopholes and exceptions—but business has suffered a defeat, and proponents of clean air (that is, most of the rest of us) had won at least a temporary and partial victory. And who leads the struggles to overturn or uphold these regulations? Just as before, Dingell and Waxman; Republicans "are skittish about challenging" the rules publicly, "so they gladly defer to Dingell as their surrogate." Dingell's forces have more than 130 cosponsors (about one-third of them Democrats) for a bill to, in effect, override the EPA standards.

In business-government relations most attention becomes focused on instances of scandal. The real issue, however, is not one or another scandal or conflict of interest, but rather the *system* of business-government relations, and especially of campaign finance, that offers business so many opportunities to craft loopholes, undermine regulations, and subvert enforcement. Still worse, many of these actions take place beyond public scrutiny.

. . .

What is Power?

Our analysis is based on an understanding of power that differs from that usually articulated by both business and politicians. The corporate PAC directors we interviewed insisted that they have no power:

> If you were to ask me what kind of access and influence do we have, being roughly the 150th largest PAC, I would have to tell you that on the basis of our money we have zero. . . . If you look at the level of our contributions, we know we're not going to buy anybody's vote, we're not going to rent anybody, or whatever the clichés have been over the years. We know that.

The executives who expressed these views clearly meant these words sincerely. Their statements are based on roughly the same understanding of "power" that is current with political science, which is also the way the term was defined by Max Weber, the classical sociological theorist. Power, in this common conception, is the ability to make someone do something against their will. If that is what power means, then corporations rarely have any in relation to members of Congress, nor does soft money give the donor power over presidents. As one senior vice president said to us: "You certainly aren't going to be able to buy anybody for $500 or $1,000 or $10,000— it's a joke." Soft money donations of a million dollars might seem to change the equation, but we will argue they do not: Just as $10,000 won't buy a member of Congress, $1,000,000 won't buy a president. In this regard we agree with the corporate officials we interviewed: A corporation is not in a position to say to a member of Congress, "Either you vote for this bill, or we will defeat your bid for reelection." Rarely do they even say: "You vote for this bill or you won't get any money from us."

This definition of power as the ability to make someone do something against their will is what Steven Lukes calls a "one-dimensional" view of power. A two-dimensional view recognizes the existence of nondecisions: A potential issue never gets articulated or, if articulated by someone somewhere, never receives serious consideration. For example, in 1989 and 1990, one of the major political battles, and a focus of great effort by corporate PACs, was the Clean Air Act. Yet twenty or thirty years earlier, before the rise of the environmental movement, pollution was a nonissue: it simply was not considered, although its effects were, in retrospect, of great importance. In one of Sherlock Holmes stories, the key clue is that the dog didn't bark. A two-dimensional view of power makes the same point: The most important clue in some situation may be that no one noticed power was exercised—because there was no overt conflict.

Even this model of power is too restrictive, however, because it still focuses on discrete decisions and nondecisions. Tom Wartenberg calls these "interventional" models of power, and notes that, in such models "the primary locus of power . . . is a specific social interaction between two social agents." Such models do not recognize "the idea that the most fundamental use of power in society is its use in structuring the basic manner in which social agents interact with one another." Wartenberg argues, instead, for a "field theory" of power that analyzes social power as a force similar to a magnetic field. A magnetic field alters the motion of objects susceptible to magnetism. Similarly, the mere presence of a powerful social agent alters the social space for others and causes them to orient themselves toward the powerful agent. For example, one of the executives we interviewed took it for granted that "if we go see the congressman who represents [a city where the company has a major plant], where 10,000 of our employees are also his constituents, we don't need a PAC to go see him." The corporation is so important in that area that the member has to orient himself in relation to the corporation and its concerns. In a different sense, the very act of accepting a campaign contribution changes the way a member relates to a PAC, creating a sense of obligation, a need to reciprocate. The PAC contribution has altered the member's social space, his or her awareness of the company and wish to help it, even if no explicit commitments have been made.

Business is Different

Power, we would argue, is not just the ability to force someone to do something against their will; it is most effective (and least recognized) when it shapes the field of action. Moreover, business's vast resources, influence on the economy, and general legitimacy place it on a different footing from other campaign contributors. Every day a member of Congress accepts a $1,000 donation from a corporate PAC, goes to a committee hearing, proposes "minor" changes in a bill's wording, and has those changes accepted without discussion or examination. The changes "clarify" the language of the bill, legalizing higher levels of pollution for a specific pollutant, or exempting the company from some tax. The media do not report on this change, and no one speaks against it. On the other hand, if a PAC were formed by Drug Lords for Cocaine Legalization, no member would take their money. If a member introduced a "minor" wording change to make it easier to sell crack without bothersome police interference, the proposed change would attract massive attention, the campaign contribution would be labeled a scandal, the member's political career would be ruined, and the changed wording would not be incorporated into the bill. Drug Lords may make an extreme example, but approximately the same holds true for many groups: At present, equal rights for gays and lesbians could never be a minor and unnoticed addition to a bill with a different purpose.

Even groups with great social legitimacy encounter more opposition and controversy than business faces for proposals that are virtually without public support. One example is the contrast between the largely unopposed commitment of tens or hundreds of billions of dollars for the savings and loan bailout, compared to the sharp debate, close votes, and defeats for the rights of men and women to take *unpaid* parental leave. The classic term for something non-controversial that everyone must support is "a motherhood issue," and while it costs little to guarantee every woman the right to an *unpaid* parental leave, this measure nonetheless generated intense scrutiny and controversy—going down to defeat under President Bush, passing under President Clinton, and then again becoming a focus of attack after the 1994 Republican takeover of Congress. Few indeed are the people publicly prepared to defend pollution or tax evasion. Nevertheless, business is routinely able to win pollution exemptions and tax loopholes. Although cumulatively some vague awareness of these provisions may trouble people, most are allowed individually to pass without scrutiny. No analysis of corporate political activity makes sense unless it begins with a recognition of this absolutely vital point. The PAC is a vital element of corporate power, but it does not operate by itself. The PAC donation is always backed by the wider power and influence of business.

Corporations are unlike other "special interest" groups not only because business has far more resources, but also because its acceptance and legitimacy. When people feel that "the system" is screwing them, they tend to blame politicians, the government, the media—but rarely business. In terms of campaign finance, while much of the public is outraged at the way money influences elections and public policy, the issue is almost always posed in terms of politicians, what they do or don't do. This is part of a pervasive double standard that largely exempts business from criticism. We, however, believe it is vital to scrutinize business as well.

We did two dozen radio call-in shows after the appearance of our last book, *Money Talks*. On almost every show, at least one call came from someone outraged that members of Congress had recently raised their pay to $125,100. (For 1998, it will be about $137,000.) Not a single person even mentioned corporate executives' pay. Business Week calculated that in 1996 corporate CEOs were paid an average of $5.8 million (counting salary, bonuses, and stock option grants), or more than 200 times the average worker's pay, and more than 40 times what members of Congress are paid. More anger is directed at Congress for delaying new environmental laws than at the companies who fight every step of the way to stall and subvert the legislation. When members of Congress do favors for large campaign contributors, anger is directed at the senators who went along, not at the business owner who paid the money (and usually initiated the pressure). The public focuses on the member's receipt of thousands of dollars, not on the business's receipt of millions (or hundreds of millions) in tax breaks or special treatment. It is a widely held belief that "politics is dirty." But little public comment and condemnation is generated when companies get away—quite literally—with murder. This disparity is evidence of business's success in shaping public perceptions. Lee Atwater, George Bush's 1988 campaign manager, saw this as a key to Republican success:

> In the 1980 campaign, we were able to make the establishment, insofar as it is bad, the government. In other words, big government was the enemy, not big business. If the people think the problem is that taxes are too high, and the government interferes too much, then we are doing our job. But, if they get to the point where they say that the real problem is that rich people aren't paying taxes, . . . then the Democrats are going to be in good shape.

We argue that corporations are so different, and so dominant, that they exercise a special kind of power, what Antonio Gramsci called hegemony. Hegemony can be regarded as the ultimate example of a field of power that structures what people and groups do. It is sometimes referred to as a worldview, a way of thinking about the world that influences every action, and makes it difficult to even consider alternatives. But in Gramsci's analysis it is much more than this, it is a culture and set of institutions that structure life patterns and coerce a particular way of life. Susan Harding gives the example of relations between whites and blacks in the South prior to the 1960s. Black inferiority and subservience were not simply ideas articulated by white racists, they were incorporated into a set of social practices: segregated schools, restrooms, swimming pools, restaurants; the black obligation to refer to white men as "Mister"; the prohibition on referring to black men as "Mister"; the use of the term "boy" for black males of any age and social status; the white right to go to the front of any line or to take the seat of any African American, and so on. Most blacks recognized the injustice and absurdity of these rules, but this did not enable them to escape, much less defy, them. White hegemony could not be overthrown simply by recognizing its existence or articulating an ideal of equality; black people had to create a movement that transformed themselves, the South, and the nation as a whole.

Hegemony is most successful and most powerful, when it is unrecognized. White hegemony in the South was strong but never unrecognized and rarely uncontested. White southerners would have denied, probably in all sincerity, that they exercised power: "Why our nigras are perfectly happy that's the way they want to be treated." But many black southerners would have vigorously disputed this while talking to each other. In some sense, gender relations in the 1950s embodied a hegemony even more powerful than that of race relations. Betty Friedan titled the first chapter of *The Feminine Mystique* "The Problem That Has No Name," because women literally did not have a name for, did not recognize the existence of, their oppression. Women as well as men denied the existence of inequality or oppression, denied the systematic exercise of power to maintain unequal relations.

We argue that today business has enormous power and exercises effective hegemony, even though (perhaps because) this is largely undiscussed and unrecognized. *Politically,* business power today is similar to white treatment of blacks in 1959—

business may sincerely deny its power, but many of the groups it exercises power over recognize it, feel dominated, resent this, and fight the power as best they can. At least until very recently, *economically,* business power was more like gender relations in 1959: Virtually no one saw this power as problematic. The revived labor movement is beginning to change this, and there are signs that a movement is beginning to contest corporate power. Nonetheless, if the issue is brought to people's attention, many still don't see a problem: "Well, so what? How else could it be? Maybe we don't like it, but that's just the way things are."

Hegemony is never absolute. African Americans and women both were (and are) forced to live in disadvantaged conditions, but simultaneously fought for dignity and respect. Unusual individuals always violated conventions and tested limits. A hegemonic power is usually opposed by a counterhegemony. Thus, while children in our society are taught to compete with each other to earn the praise of authority figures, and while most children engage in this process much of the time, it is also true that the "teacher's pet" is likely to face ostracism. We hope this book makes a small contribution to weakening business hegemony and to developing a counterhegemony.

. . .

The primary power of the wealthy is not exercised by individuals or even by families. Power in our society is based in institutions, not individuals, and the power of wealth is channeled through corporations. There are more than 200,000 industrial corporations in the United States, but all companies are *not* created equal: The 500 largest industrials control three-quarters of the sales, assets, and profits of *all* industrial corporations. More than 250 of these companies had revenues of more than $5 billion. Similarly, in the service sector, 500 firms control a disproportionate share of the resources. The dominance of these corporations means that a handful of owners and top executives, perhaps one-hundredth of one percent of the U.S. population, or 25,000 individuals, have the power to make decisions that have a huge impact on all of our lives. Collectively these people exercise incalculable power, making decisions with more impact on most of our lives than those made by the entire elected government.

Consider for a moment those decisions that virtually everyone in our society agrees should be made by business. Consider, for this exercise, only those decisions on which there is broad bipartisan political agreement; exclude anything that would generally be considered ethically or legally dubious and anything where a significant fraction of elected officials dispute business's right. Exclude, as well, any actions that are taken only through business's influence on government, and confine your attention to the decisions made in operating businesses. Remember that any decision made by "business" is primarily determined by the 25,000 individuals at the top of the corporate ladder, since their companies control about three-quarters of *all* corporate sales, assets, employees, and profits.

Business Decisions

What are some of these decisions? A brief and partial list indicates their scope:

Decisions about Employment

- the number of people employed.
- when to have layoffs.
- the number of hours people work.
- when work begins in the morning and ends in the afternoon.
- whether to phase out full-time jobs and replace them with part-time, lower-wage, no-benefits jobs. In 1997, UPS workers and the Teamsters Union successfully contested the company's increasingly heavy reliance on part-timers, but it was big news that a union even attempted to raise the issue, much less that they were able to win.
- whether or not there is overtime, and whether it is compulsory.
- whether to allow flextime and job-sharing.
- the skill level of the jobs. Does the company make an effort to use lots of skilled workers paid good wages or is it always trying to de-skill positions and replace skilled workers with unskilled?
- the educational (and other) requirements for employment. Are certain educational levels *necessary* in order to be hired, or are they simply helpful? Are exconvicts or former mental patients eligible for all jobs or only some? What about the handicapped?
- whether the firm *de facto* discriminates in favor of men and whites or makes an active effort to recruit and promote minorities and women.
- workers' rights on the job. For example, do they have free speech? A worker at a Coca-Cola plant was given a three-day suspension (without pay) because his wife brought him a lunch with a soda from Burger King, at a time when Burger King sold Pepsi. It is totally legal to penalize an employee for this or many other such actions.
- job safety. In one of the most extreme examples, a worker was killed while performing a dangerous task. Almost immediately thereafter another worker was ordered to do the same job and refused because he said conditions were unsafe and had not been remedied. The company fired him for this refusal, and the Supreme Court upheld the firing.
- (within limits) whether or not a union is recognized; whether the union and the workers are treated with dignity and respect; how bitterly and viciously the union is resisted.

Investment Decisions

- decisions about whether to expand a plant, and if so, which plant to expand.
- whether to merge the corporation and "downsize" workers. Recently, a number of corporations have laid off thousands of employees, blighting communities and individual lives, at the same time giving huge bonuses to the top executives.
- whether to contract out jobs.
- whether to close down a plant; when and how to do so. Virtually no one questions a company's absolute right (in the United States, not in Europe) to shut down if it chooses to do so, no matter what the effect on the workers and communities.
- where to open new plants. The company has every right to bargain for the best deal it can get. Deals can include tax abatements and implicit agreements to ignore labor or pollution laws.

Product and Marketing

- the products produced, including whether to introduce a new product and whether to discontinue an old stand-by.
- the design, both functional and aesthetic.
- the relative attention to different considerations: in a new car, how important is styling? sex appeal? fuel efficiency? safety? durability?
- the quality of the goods produced. Are they made to last, with high standards throughout, or are they just made to look good in the store and for the first month of use?
- the price for which goods are sold.
- the character of the advertising used to promote the product. Does it stress the significant features of the product, or distract through sex and extraneous symbols?
- the amount spent on advertising—90 percent of the commercials on prime time television are sponsored by the nation's 500 largest corporations.
- the places where ads appear—in left-wing journals? in right-wing journals? on television? on which programs?

Community and Environment

- the level of pollution in the workplace: air, heat, noise, chemicals, and so on.
- the level of pollution in the outside environment. Beginning in the 1970s, for pollution both in the workplace and in the larger community, the government set maximum limits for a few items, but companies are completely free to do better than these standards. No government regulation prevents companies from setting and meeting tougher standards of their own devising. For example, in July 1991, a railroad tanker car derailed, tumbled into the Sacramento River, ruptured, and spilled pesticide. The pesticide was not listed as a regulated substance, and therefore the railroad was not required to carry it in a double-hulled tanker, though it

could have chosen to do so. Though the pesticide was unregulated, it *was* strong enough to kill virtually all the fish in the river, formerly famous for its trout.

• the degree of consideration for the community: Does the company make an effort to be a good neighbor? Does it contribute to local charities? Support local initiatives?

This by no means exhausts the list of decisions that companies are allowed to make. Not only allowed to make, but expected and, in many cases, required to make. There is some regulation of business decisions at the margin, with possible regulation for issues such as: Can a company pull up stakes and leave town with no more than a day's notice? Can it dump raw wastes in the river? Can it make dubious claims in its advertising? For the most part, however, corporations are free to make decisions about their economic operations.

If the government fails to act, big business can do as it wishes.

Discussion Questions

1. Consider the discussion of hidden versus blatant power and relate this to the manner in which business exercised its privileged position through the Clean Air Act negotiations.

2. What comparisons may be drawn, if any, between white hegemony (prior to the 1960s) and corporate hegemony today?

3. If corporations that are so central to the structure of our economy do constitute a "field of power," can their hegemony be reconciled with our "democracy"?

27   *Race, Gender, and Class In U.S. Politics*

Walter Benn Michaels

The battle for the 2008 presidential nomination of the Democratic Party came down to Senators Hillary Rodham Clinton and Barack Obama. What is the significance of a white woman and an African American man seriously contending for the presidential nomination of a major American political party for the first time? Writing while the nomination was still contested, English professor Walter Benn Michaels provides a provocative response. Michaels, the author of a much-debated book The Trouble with Diversity: How We Learned to Love Identity and Ignore Inequality *(2006), argues that struggles for racial and sexual equality have made real progress. Yet paradoxically this progress has been accompanied by greater, not lesser, social and economic inequality. The reason for this, Michaels contends, is that champions of diversity have for the most part accepted the premises of "neoliberal"capitalism, with the inequalities and exploitation it entails. Despite Obama's remark during the campaign about "bitter" workers, class was the great unmentionable in the Obama-Clinton campaigns, in Michaels' view. For him, "Clinton and Obama are the emblems of a liberalism which has made its peace with a political ethics that will combat racist and sexist inequalities, while almost ignoring inequalities that stem not from discrimination but from exploitation."*

There have been two defining moments related to race in the Obama campaign, and more generally in United States progressive politics. The first was in January on the night of the Illinois senator's victory in South Carolina when, in response to comments by Bill Clinton about the size of the black vote, the Obama crowd started chanting: "Race doesn't matter."

"There we stood," said the novelist and Obama activist Ayelet Waldman, "in the heart of the old South, where Confederate flags still fly next to statues of Governor Benjamin Tillman, who famously bragged about keeping black people from the polls ('We stuffed ballot boxes. We shot them. We are not ashamed of it'), chanting race doesn't matter, race doesn't matter. White people and black people. Latinos and Asians, united in our rejection of politics as usual. United in our belief that America can be a different place. United. Not divided."

Reprinted from *Some Democrats are More Equal Than Others* (June 2008), Le Monde Diplomatique

The second moment was in March when, in response to the controversial sermons of his former pastor, the Rev. Jeremiah Wright, Obama gave his "more perfect union" speech, declaring: "Race is an issue this nation cannot afford to ignore right now" and inaugurating what many commentators described as a supposedly much-needed "national conversation on race".

I say supposedly because Americans love to talk about race and have been doing so for centuries, even if today the thing we love most to say is that "Americans don't like to talk about race". What we aren't so good at talking about is class, as Obama himself inadvertently demonstrated when he tried to talk about class on 6 April at a closed-door San Francisco fundraiser ("Bittergate"). He tried to explain the frustrations of some small-town Pennsylvanians: "It's not surprising that they get bitter, they cling to guns or religion or antipathy to people who aren't like them or anti-immigrant sentiment or anti-trade sentiment."

"Change We Can Believe In"

There seems to be an obvious contradiction here. First, the chant of race doesn't matter; then the speech about why race does matter. But after reflection the contradiction fades, since the need for the speech, the history of American racism, is what prompted the promise of the chant: the idea that electing a black man would be a major step toward overcoming that history. Which, of course, it would.

It is the promise of overcoming the long history of racial division, the promise of solving in the twenty-first century what W.E.B. Du Bois described as the overwhelming problem of the twentieth century, the problem of the color line, that gives the Obama campaign its significance. The "change we can believe in" is not ideological, it's cultural (Obama and Clinton are ideologically almost identical; if people had wanted ideological change, we'd be talking about John Edwards). And at the heart of that cultural change is the fact that it cannot be proclaimed. It must be embodied, and only a black person can embody it. We can elect white people who say that race shouldn't matter, but only the election of a black person can establish that it really doesn't.

So the Obama campaign is and has always been all about race, and especially about anti-racism as progressive politics. Whether or not he ultimately wins, and especially if he doesn't, we are still being shown the "progressive" wing of the Democratic Party leading Americans toward an increasingly open and equal society, for African-Americans and also for Asians and Latinos and women and gays.

But the problem with this picture—a problem that is also a crucial part of its attraction—is that it is false. There has been extraordinary, albeit incomplete, progress in fighting racism, but the picture is false because that progress has not made American society more open or equal. In fundamental respects it is less open and equal today than it was in the days of Jim Crow when racism was not only prevalent but was state-sponsored.

The hallmark of a neo-liberal political economy is rising sensitivity about differences of identity—cultural, ethnic, sometimes religious—and rising tolerance for differences of wealth and income. Readers who are familiar with the jargon of economic inequality will have an immediate sense of what it means to say that equality in America has declined when I tell you that in 1947, at the height of Jim Crow and the segregationist laws in the South, the U.S. Gini coefficient was .376 and that by 2006, it had risen to .464. Since on the Gini scale 0 represents absolute equality (everyone makes the same income as everyone else) and 1 represents absolute inequality (one person makes everything), this is significant.

Back then, the U.S. was in the same league as the countries of western Europe, albeit a little more unequal than them; today we're up there with Mexico and China. In 1947, the top 20% of the U.S. population made 43% of all the money the nation earned. In 2006, after years of struggle against racism, sexism and heterosexism, the top 20% make 50.5%. The rich are richer.

Legitimate the Elite

So the struggle for racial and sexual equality—the relative success of which has been incarnated in the race and gender politics of the Democratic Party over the past six months—has not produced greater economic equality, but been compatible with much greater economic inequality, and with the formation of an increasingly elitist society. There is a reason for this. The battles against racism and sexism have never been to produce a more equal society; or to mitigate, much less eliminate, the difference between the elite and the rest; they were meant to diversify and hence legitimate the elite.

This is why policies such as affirmative action in university admissions serve such a crucial symbolic purpose for liberals. They reassure them that no one has been excluded from places like Harvard and Yale for reasons of prejudice or discrimination (the legitimating part) while leaving untouched the primary mechanism of exclusion: wealth (the increasing-the-gap between the rich and everyone else part). You are, as Richard Kahlenberg put it, "25 times as likely to run into a rich student as a poor student" at 146 elite colleges, not because poor students are discriminated against but because they are poor. They have not had the kind of education that makes it plausible for them even to apply to elite colleges, much less attend them.

What affirmative action tells us is that the problem is racism and the solution is to make sure the rich kids come in different colours; this solution looks attractive long after graduation, when the battle for diversity continues to be fought among lawyers, professors and journalists—in fact, any profession with enough status and income to count as elite. The effort is to enforce a model of social justice in which proportional representation of race and gender counts as success.

If what you want is a more diverse elite, electing a black president is about as good as it gets. Electing a woman president would be a close second. But if you want to address the inequalities we have, instead of the inequalities we like to think we have (inequalities produced by inherited wealth and poverty); if you want a political program designed to address the inequalities produced not by racism and sexism, which are only sorting devices, but by neo-liberalism, which is doing the sorting, neither the black man nor the white woman have much to offer.

They are two Democrats who can't even bring themselves to acknowledge publicly, in their last debate in April, that Americans making between $100,000 and

$200,000 a year hardly qualify as middle class. Clinton committed herself "to not raising a single tax on middle-class Americans, people making less than $250,000 a year" and Obama (who was, as a commentator put it, "a lot squishier" about it) also committed himself to not raising taxes on people making under $200,000.

Root of Inequality

But only 7% of U.S. households earn more than $150,000; only 18% earn more than $100,000; more than 50% earn under $50,000. Once you have Democrats who consider people on $200,000 as middle class and in need of tax relief, you don't need Republicans any more. Clinton and Obama are the emblems of a liberalism which has made its peace with a political ethics that will combat racist and sexist inequalities, while almost ignoring inequalities that stem not from discrimination but from exploitation. The candidates' death match prominently features charges of racism and sexism.

In 1967, after the passage of the Civil Rights Act of 1965 and at the beginning of the effort to make the rights guaranteed by that act a reality, Martin Luther King was already asking "where do we go from here?"

King was a great civil rights leader but he was more than that, and the questions he wanted to raise were not, as he pointed out, civil rights questions. They were, he told the Southern Christian Leadership Conference, "questions about the economic system, about a broader distribution of wealth".

There were then, as there are now, more poor white people than poor black people in the U.S. and King was acutely aware of that. He was aware that anti-racism was not a solution to economic inequality because racism was not the cause of economic inequality, and he realized that any challenge to the actual cause, "the capitalistic economy", would produce "fierce opposition".

King did not live to lead that challenge and the fierce opposition he expected never developed because the challenge never did. Instead, not only the anti-racism of the civil rights movement but also the rise of feminism, of gay rights and of all the new social movements proved to be entirely compatible with the capitalistic economy King hoped to oppose.

It is possible but unlikely that Barack Obama or Hillary Clinton might some day take up King's challenge. Neo-liberalism likes race and gender, and the race and gender candidates seem to like neo-liberalism.

Discussion Questions

1. Michaels writes that "The battles against racism and sexism have never been to produce a more equal society; they were meant to diversify and hence legitimate the elite." What does he mean by this statement? Is it too sweeping in your view? How might anti-racism and anti-sexism activists respond?

2. How is it possible for racial and sexual inequality to narrow, while economic inequality widens? What would Michaels say?

28   *Black America and the Dilemma of Patriotism*

Brian Gilmore

Poet and attorney Brian Gilmore explores with sensitivity his complex reactions as a black American to the September 11 attacks. While he is obviously appalled and saddened by the attacks, Gilmore is concerned about the implications for black America of the call to unconditionally "stand by the man" and support the "war on terrorism" launched by President George W. Bush. Reflecting on statements made by the novelist Richard Wright during World War II, Gilmore explains that calls for Americans to close ranks during wartime have often served to remove the problems and grievances of black Americans from the political agenda. In the tradition of scholar and activist W. E. B. Du Bois, Gilmore explores black American "double consciousness" in a way that enables all Americans to comprehend the complexities of national identity. He helps us understand how a ritual like flying the flag has distinct meanings in different communities.

"I pledge my loyalty and allegiance, without mental reservation or evasions, to America. I shall through my writing seek to rally the Negro people to stand shoulder to shoulder with the Administration in a solid national front to wage war until victory is won."

—Richard Wright (December 16, 1941)

On the morning of September 11, I was driving down R Street in Washington on my way to a local foundation where I was working as a writer when I saw a huge cloud of smoke off in the distance. I had already heard that two hijacked planes had crashed into the twin towers of the World Trade Center in New York City. When I saw the huge cloud of smoke rising into the sky, I kind of figured it wasn't someone's house on fire. No more than a minute later, the radio reported that a plane had hit the Pentagon. I immediately pulled over and went inside the Washington Legal Clinic for the Homeless, where I once worked. Everyone there was distraught. Some people began crying. Others were speechless. Then the newscaster announced that the towers had collapsed with possibly thousands of people trapped inside. I told my former co-workers I was leaving.

"Where are you headed?"

"The racetrack," I answered.

My answer was knee-jerk but honest. I wasn't at all surprised at what happened that day because I have always suspected that there are people and nations and factions that do not like America. Oftentimes, Black America does not like America, but, for the most part, many of us remain quiet. We go along for the ride because it is what we are accustomed to doing. Our interests are tied to America. And if you want to know the most poignant truth of all: We really have no choice in the matter. Where are we to go? We are, though some of us forget sometimes, American, perhaps more so than anyone else.

But that is, of course, part of why I was headed to the racetrack. I wanted to pretend that the bombing hadn't happened. I also knew that all of us—every black American—would be called upon (like every other American) from that day forth until we were instructed otherwise, to stand by our man—Uncle Sam. Support the war unconditionally. One shouldn't even question the approach to solving the problem (as if there is only one way to fight this battle). Any other conduct during the war would be deemed un-American.

For black Americans, it has always been that way, no matter our position in society. We would be asked to do what we had always done without any promise of future benefit: to prove our unconditional love and loyalty for America. Drop any grievances or problems we have with our American condition for the time being, or maybe for a generation or so. I didn't want to deal with the bombings, and I definitely didn't want to deal with the culture of violence that the bombings had spawned.

I preferred simply to go look at the horses.

Days after the bombing, with all of those thoughts of my American self still bearing down on me, I read Richard Wright's statement on World War II that appears above. I found it in Michel Fabre's celebrated biography of Wright, *The Unfinished Quest of Richard Wright* (University of Illinois, 1993). I had been in search of statements by authors, black authors in particular, following Pearl Harbor. I wanted to know what they had to say as that attack became part of us. This was war, and that was war back in 1941, and I knew they found themselves in a difficult spot. Before that war, Roosevelt had expressed some interest in being a friend of Black America, but he hadn't really gone that far. Most people even forget that Black America had planned a March on Washington in 1941 that was canceled at the last minute. The argument by black Americans that fighting against tyranny will make democracy for blacks more possible in America was strong even before the Japanese bombed Pearl Harbor; afterwards, it was overwhelming.

Before the September 11 attack, Black America was even more frustrated. The election and subsequent decision by the Supreme Court that propelled George W. Bush into office still burned in the souls of many black folks. In fact, I can't remember a day that went by in the last year that at least one of my black American friends or acquaintances didn't bring up the vote count irregularities among blacks in Florida and how they couldn't wait to vote Bush out of office in 2004.

Even more painfully, our issues, the issues that at least were on the table during the Clinton years (despite his failure to address them), weren't even being discussed anymore. The country was talking tax cuts; we were asking about job cuts. The country was talking education reform; we were asking about just getting an education for our children. Then there were the bigger fish that Clinton turned and ran from for eight years: reparations, racial profiling, police brutality, reforming "drug war" sentencing guidelines, black men disproportionately going to jail.

But when those planes plunged into the World Trade Center and the Pentagon on that blue, blue morning of September 11, 2001, not only was the black agenda taken off the table for the foreseeable future, the table itself was taken down.

That is why Richard Wright's statement struck a chord in me. I finally began to think clearly for the first time about the September 11 bombing. I began to put the attack into some sort of context without being "upset" or "angry" or full of guilt about my initial reaction of wanting to go to the racetrack. I finally knew where I was at that moment, right after I read that quote. I was where the average black American always seems to be in America—in that tragic Duboisian state of double consciousness.

What did the average African American say about the attack and what we should do? This is what I was hearing:

It was an awful thing.

Evil.

Kill the bastards.

Crush them.

Bomb them.

Kill them all.

Profile them Arabs.

Deport them all.

(Note: It was especially vexing to hear black people come on the radio following the bombing and basically call for racial profiling of Arab Americans and deportation. I assure you, this view was rampant. On one radio program based in Washington, D.C., caller after caller, black Americans, stated that "profiling" of Arab Americans was, in fact, needed and had to be done for the good of the nation.)

But that is just one side of the black American experience. Here is the other that I began to hear:

Don't we bomb people all the time?

And look how they treated us for so long.

Slavery.

Lynchings.

Second-class citizenship.

Segregation.

Not to mention the same old bullshit we still got to put up with in daily life.

We are arguing over an apology for slavery.

How can we forget any of it?

We the ones who are going to be over there fighting, too.

And after this war, what then? The same?

Two peoples always, it seems.

I could not get it out of my head that Wright had felt a need to make a statement in support of World War II. For one thing, he was a pacifist. And prior to December 7, 1941, he was badgering America about the need for social justice and equality for the Negro society. He was against any involvement in the war; he was more interested in addressing America's racial policies. Months before the war, on June 6, 1941, at a League of American Writers council meeting, Wright delivered a speech entitled "Not My People's War" that basically stated World War II was not a war black people should participate in because of how they are treated in society. Even after America's entry into that war, Wright remained focused on the improvement of conditions for America's black citizens.

Though he eventually volunteered to contribute to the war effort through writing, Wright's ambivalence was obvious. He supported the war for essentially the same naive reasons Frederick Douglass asked black people to fight with the Union in the Civil War: It was a chance for freedom and democracy. How could they continue to hold us down if we fought beside them against the true oppressors?

But though I was sure something drastic had to be done against terrorism, I couldn't support America's call for war against Afghanistan. I was against terrorism and violence, for sure, with every bone in my body. I abhorred the actions of the suicide bombers, which were so sick and so terribly destructive. Yet, I was sure that bombing a country that is hopelessly stuck in the medieval age would not solve anything. I was sure that as America began dropping bombs, we would become even more unsafe. I was more concerned about civil defense than revenge. I also could not get all that history out of my head about America and its black American people.

But still I wondered: Why wasn't I deeply depressed? This was a tragedy of epic proportions. The loss of human life was unfathomable. We were all attacked that day, too. Black America as well. Osama bin Laden issued a *fatwa* (holy war decree) years ago, and he said all Americans should be killed. Not white Americans, but all Americans. That meant me and my wife and my daughter and the rest of my family and Americans of every race and ethnicity.

This wasn't the Iranian hostage crisis of 1979 and 1980, when the captors, in a clever show of political solidarity, released the black American hostages from the U.S. Embassy. Whoever was responsible for the crashes of September 11 didn't give a damn who you were as a person; this was an attack on America. If the bombers of September 11, 2001, were acting upon bin Laden's *fatwa,* or whoever's order, black America was also a target.

A very good family friend, a schoolteacher, Lizzie Jones, a black American woman who was like a second mother to me, lost one of her best friends in one of the suicide crashes. Her friend was a schoolteacher. They had known each other for more than thirty years and had talked right before the bombing. Her friend was taking a student on a study trip sponsored by *National Geographic.* She told Ms. Jones she would be back on Saturday, and that she would tell her all about it. Her friend did not come back. She is gone. I saw Ms. Jones on television on the news speaking to her lost friend in spiritual phrases. I felt nauseous.

I am afraid for my daughter. She does not need to live in a world that is full of violence, death, and chaos. My sincere hope is that all of us now understand the real horror of mass violence of this magnitude. I know I do. No way should anyone suffer as we did on September 11, 2001. The frantic phone calls looking for friends and family members, the e-mails seeking out answers, the devastation, the catastrophic grief.

Chilean writer Ariel Dorfman refers to America now as "Unique No More." Dorfman says this is so because America has finally experienced what "so many other human beings" in "faraway zones, have suffered." Yes, we have felt it.

I am pretty sure that Richard Wright anguished over writing all the other words he wrote supporting entry into World War II. But he felt America in 1941 was still his country. America is my country, too, but it is much more complex than that. I don't mean just the place where I was born, but a place that is unequivocally my land and the land of my people without the enormous contradictions that create a strange dialogue, which can be summed up like this:

"But we ended slavery."

"But you allowed it to be legal for hundreds of years."

"We conquered Jim Crow and segregation."

"But it was legal for most of the twentieth century, and we had to almost burn the country down to get you to do it."

Today, I marvel at my friends who talk of their families coming to America from India or Nicaragua or my law school classmates who speak about their grandfather or grandmother's journey to America from Italy or Ireland or Greece in search of a better life in America. It is a magical story I don't have. That's why black Americans can never be whole in America, no matter how hard we try. How can we? We don't even have a past that can be defined, and the part that we know, the story that is passed to us regarding our country's relationship to us, is a complete tragedy. America is my country, yet my country, it seems, has never wanted me.

They were blowing their car horn. They were drunk. I was in Georgetown, and several young, white youths were hanging out of the windows of the car with a sign that read: "Honk, If You Love America." It was cute in a way to see such brash patriotism. Drivers began honking in response to the sign. This was September 16, and everyone was still in immense pain. The young drunks were trying to make themselves feel better and everyone else at the same time. I didn't honk my horn. I was in the Georgetown traffic jam, frozen and unable to do anything. I began looking around and realized that no one really would notice because so many cars were honking. Most of the people I saw honking their horns were white. I didn't see any black people around. I didn't honk. It was a disturbing moment for me because I wasn't standing by my man in one of his toughest times. I realized again (as I have been reminded many times since) that though I was and am an American, I didn't have what most Americans feel—that unique sense of belonging. The tragedy was a part of me but it was mostly about the victims, the injured, the dead. I knew I wasn't alone, either.

On the radio in the days after the bombing, I heard many black Americans state that they felt bad for the victims, they felt violated, and they felt that America had to do something, but then some would add at the end of their comments statements about not feeling that deep sense of patriotism that most Americans feel. The kind of emotion that pushes you to put your hand over your heart, take your hat off when the National Anthem is played. The "God Bless America" brand of patriotism. They were Americans, but not quite as American as white Americans. They cried for the victims but not necessarily for America.

In the days following the bombing, I was asked several times with strange looks: "Where is your flag?" I told some people I didn't have a flag. I told others that I simply could not lie to myself. It never dawned on me that I should fly a flag. I felt terrible for the victims. Awful. If the flag was for the victims, it should be flown, but I didn't fly a flag because I remembered the victims in other ways. For me, simply to resign myself to flying the flag was not enough. It was superficial, and it took the focus away from those who had died.

I spent much of my time in the days following the bombing riding through the city, looking at flags. I wanted to see who was flying them, and who wasn't. It would tell me something about America. I rode to upper Northwest first. This is the area of Washington where the affluent live, and I saw the American flag waving on nearly every street. On some streets you could tell that the neighbors probably had talked to each other because nearly every house had a flag out front. There was a pride there that was impressive. Cars had flags, too. It made the streets look like there was going to be a July 4th parade.

Then I rode to my old neighborhood, where I grew up. The families there are less affluent, but they are doing fairly well, at least most of them. They've always wanted to be American. Black Americans live there mostly, some middle class, some working class, but the neighborhood has only small pockets of despair and is usually quiet except on hot summer nights. There were American flags flying up here, too, but not as many as in upper Northwest. My mother, who still lives there, had a tiny flag on her front door. You could barely see it. She said someone gave it to her.

Finally, I rode through the most economically depressed areas of Washington: The Hood—Northwest below Howard University, but above downtown—streets where crack and herion continued to be sold and used as the tragedy unfolded. Drunks were laid out in the gutter, children ran the streets late at nights, addicts came up to my car trying to sell stolen items. There was hardly a flag in sight.

Discussion Questions

1. Why does Gilmore believe that the war on terrorism might in some ways undercut the interests and agenda of black America?

2. Compare Gilmore's reaction to September 11 with Richard Wright's comments about World War II that open this selection. What is it about the black experience in America that leads Gilmore to feel ambivalence about the call to rally around the flag?

29   *Letter From Birmingham Jail*

Martin Luther King, Jr.

"Letter from Birmingham Jail" is a classic statement of the civil rights movement. Written on scraps of paper found in his jail cell, this 1963 essay by the Reverend Dr. Martin Luther King, Jr., crystallizes many of the themes that served as catalysts to the movement for racial equality he helped lead. The letter was written in response to a statement issued by eight white Alabama clergymen who criticized King and other demonstrators for causing violence with their protests against segregation. King's searing moral response in support of nonviolent civil disobedience makes a powerful and impassioned call for democracy and human freedom. Among the many compelling points he makes, King criticizes political moderates— in this case the "white moderate" who, in King's words, "is more devoted to 'order' than to justice." To people who follow the doctrinaire belief that the truth always lies in the middle, his position may be surprising. He suggests that we should question the wisdom of assuming that gradual change and piecemeal reforms are the best way to approach a problem.

April 16, 1963

My Dear Fellow Clergymen:

While confined here in the Birmingham city jail, I came across your recent statement calling my present activities "unwise and untimely." Seldom do I pause to answer criticism of my work and ideas. If I sought to answer all the criticisms that cross my desk, my secretaries would have little time for anything other than such correspondence in the course of the day, and I would have no time for constructive work. But since I feel that you are men of genuine good will and that your criticisms are sincerely set forth, I want to try to answer your statement in what I hope will be patient and reasonable terms.

I think I should indicate why I am here in Birmingham, since you have been influenced by the view which argues against "outsiders coming in." I have the honor of serving as president of the Southern Christian Leadership Conference, an organization operating in every southern state, with headquarters in Atlanta, Georgia. We have some eighty-five affiliated organizations across the South, and one of them is the Alabama Christian Movement for Human Rights. Frequently we share staff, educational and financial resources with our affiliates. Several months ago the affiliate here in

Birmingham asked us to be on call to engage in a nonviolent direct-action program if such were deemed necessary. We readily consented, and when the hour came we lived up to our promise. So I, along with several members of my staff, am here because I was invited here. I am here because I have organizational ties here.

But more basically, I am in Birmingham because injustice is here. Just as the prophets of the eighth century B.C. left their villages and carried their "thus saith the Lord" far beyond the boundaries of their home towns, and just as the Apostle Paul left his village of Tarsus and carried the gospel of Jesus Christ to the far corners of the Greco-Roman world, so am I compelled to carry the gospel of freedom beyond my own home town. Like Paul, I must constantly respond to the Macedonian call for aid.

Moreover, I am cognizant of the interrelatedness of all communities and states. I cannot sit idly by in Atlanta and not be concerned about what happens in Birmingham. Injustice anywhere is a threat to justice everywhere. We are caught in an inescapable network of mutuality, tied in a single garment of destiny. Whatever affects one directly, affects all indirectly. Never again can we afford to live with the narrow, provincial "outside agitator" idea. Anyone who lives inside the United States can never be considered an outsider anywhere within its bounds.

You deplore the demonstrations taking place in Birmingham. But your statement, I am sorry to say, fails to express a similar concern for the conditions that brought about the demonstrations. I am sure that none of you would want to rest content with the superficial kind of social analysis that deals merely with effects and does not grapple with underlying causes. It is unfortunate that demonstrations are taking place in Birmingham, but it is even more unfortunate that the city's white power structure left the Negro community with no alternative.

In any nonviolent campaign there are four basic steps: collection of the facts to determine whether injustices exist; negotiation; self-purification; and direct action. We have gone through all these steps in Birmingham. There can be no gain saying the fact that racial injustice engulfs this community. Birmingham is probably the most thoroughly segregated city in the United States. Its ugly record of brutality is widely known. Negroes have experienced grossly unjust treatment in the courts. There have been more unsolved bombings of Negro homes and churches in Birmingham than in any other city in the nation. These are the hard, brutal facts of the case. On the basis of these conditions, Negro leaders sought to negotiate with the city fathers. But the latter consistently refused to engage in good-faith negotiation. . . .

You may well ask: "Why direct action? Why sit-ins, marches and so forth? Isn't negotiation a better path?" You are quite right in calling for negotiation. Indeed, this is the very purpose of direct action. Nonviolent direct action seeks to create such a crisis and foster such a tension that a community which has constantly refused to negotiate is forced to confront the issue. It seeks so to dramatize the issue that it can no longer be ignored. My citing the creation of tension as part of the work of the nonviolent resister may sound rather shocking. But I must confess that I am not afraid of the word "tension." I have earnestly opposed violent tension, but there is a type of constructive, nonviolent tension which is necessary for growth. Just as Socrates felt that it was necessary to create a tension in the mind so that individuals could rise from the bondage of myths and half-truths to the unfettered realm of creative analysis and objective appraisal, so must we see the need for nonviolent gadflies to create the kind of tension in society that will help men rise from the dark depths of prejudice and racism to the majestic heights of understanding and brotherhood.

The purpose of our direct-action program is to create a situation so crisis-packed that it will inevitably open the door to negotiation. I therefore concur with you in your call for negotiation. Too long has our beloved Southland been bogged down in a tragic effort to live in monologue rather than dialogue.

. . . My friends, I must say to you that we have not made a single gain in civil rights without determined legal and nonviolent pressure. Lamentably, it is an historical fact that privileged groups seldom give up their privileges voluntarily. Individuals may see the moral light and voluntarily give up their unjust posture; but, as Reinhold Niebuhr has reminded us, groups tend to be more immoral than individuals.

We know through painful experience that freedom is never voluntarily given by the oppressor; it must be demanded by the oppressed. Frankly, I have yet to engage in a direct-action campaign that was "well timed" in the view of those who have not suffered unduly from the disease of segregation. For years now I have heard the word "Wait!" It rings in the ear of every Negro with piercing familiarity. This "Wait" has almost always meant "Never." We must come to see, with one of our distinguished jurists, that "justice too long delayed is justice denied."

We have waited for more than 340 years for our constitutional and God-given rights. The nations of Asia and Africa are moving with jetlike speed toward gaining political independence, but we still creep at horse-and-buggy pace toward gaining a cup of coffee at a lunch counter. Perhaps it is easy for those who have never felt the stinging darts of segregation to say, "Wait." But when you have seen vicious mobs lynch your mothers and fathers at will and drown your sisters and brothers at whim; when you have seen hate-filled policemen curse, kick and even kill your black brothers and sisters; when you see the vast majority of your twenty million Negro brothers smothering in an airtight cage of poverty in the midst of an affluent society; when you suddenly find your tongue twisted and your speech stammering as you seek to explain to your six-year-old daughter why she can't go to the public amusement park that has just been advertised on television, and see tears welling up in her eyes when she is told that Funtown is closed to colored children, and see ominous clouds of inferiority beginning to form in her little mental sky, and see her beginning to distort her personality by developing an unconscious bitterness toward white people; when you have to concoct an answer for a five-year-old son who is asking: "Daddy, why do white people treat colored people so mean?"; when you take a cross-country drive and find it necessary to sleep night after night in the uncomfortable corners of your automobile because no motel will accept you; when you are humiliated day in and day out by nagging signs reading "white" and "colored"; when your first name becomes "nigger," your middle name becomes "boy" (however old you are) and your last name becomes "John," and your wife and mother are never given the respected title "Mrs."; when you are harried by day and haunted by night by the fact that you are a Negro, living constantly at tiptoe stance, never quite knowing what to expect next, and are plagued with inner fears and outer resentments; when you are forever fighting a degenerating sense of "nobodiness"—then you will understand why we find it difficult to wait. There comes a time when the cup of endurance runs over, and men are no longer willing to be plunged into the abyss of despair. I hope, sirs, you can understand our legitimate and unavoidable impatience.

You express a great deal of anxiety over our willingness to break laws. This is certainly a legitimate concern. Since we so diligently urge people to obey the Supreme Court's decision of 1954 outlawing segregation in the public schools, at first glance it may seem rather paradoxical for us consciously to break laws. One may well ask: "How can you advocate breaking some laws and obeying others?" The answer lies in the fact that there are two types of laws: just and unjust. I would be the first to advocate obeying just laws. One has not only a legal but a moral responsibility to obey just laws. Conversely, one has a moral responsibility to disobey unjust laws. I would agree with St. Augustine that "an unjust law is no law at all."

Now, what is the difference between the two? How does one determine whether a law is just or unjust? A just law is a man-made code that squares with the moral law or the law of God. An unjust law is a code that is out of harmony with the moral law. To put it in the terms of St. Thomas Aquinas: An unjust law is a human law that is not rooted in eternal law and natural law. Any law that uplifts human personality is just. Any law that degrades human personality is unjust. All segregation statutes are unjust because segregation distorts the soul and damages the personality. It gives the segregator a false sense of superiority and the segregated a false sense of inferiority. Segregation, to use the terminology of the Jewish philosopher Martin Buber, substitutes an "I-it" relationship for an "I-thou" relationship and ends up relegating persons to the status of things. Hence segregation is not only politically, economically and sociologically unsound, it is morally wrong and sinful. Paul Tillich has said that sin is separation. Is not segregation an existential expression of man's tragic separation, his awful estrangement, his terrible sinfulness? Thus it is that I can urge men to obey the 1954 decision of the Supreme Court for it is morally right; and I can urge them to disobey segregation ordinances, for they are morally wrong.

Let us consider a more concrete example of just and unjust laws. An unjust law is a code that a numerical or power majority group compels a minority group to obey but does not make binding on itself. This is *difference* made legal. By the same token, a just law is a code that a majority compels a minority to follow and that it is willing to follow itself. This is sameness made legal.

Let me give another explanation. A law is unjust if it is inflicted on a minority that, as a result of being denied the right to vote, had no part in enacting or devising the law. Who can say that the legislature of Alabama which set up that state's segregation laws was democratically elected? Throughout Alabama all sorts of devious methods are used to prevent Negroes from becoming registered voters, and there are some counties in which, even though Negroes constitute a majority of the population, not a single Negro is registered. Can any law enacted under such circumstances be considered democratically structured?

Sometimes a law is just on its face and unjust in its application. For instance, I have been arrested on a charge of parading without a permit. Now, there is nothing wrong in having an ordinance which requires a permit for a parade. But such an ordinance becomes unjust when it is used to maintain segregation and to deny citizens the First Amendment privilege of peaceful assembly and protest.

I hope you are able to see the distinction I am trying to point out. In no sense do I advocate evading or defying the law, as would the rabid segregationist. That would lead to anarchy. One who breaks an unjust law must do so openly, lovingly, and with a willingness to accept the penalty. I submit that an individual who breaks a law that conscience tells him is unjust, and who willingly accepts the penalty of imprisonment in order to arouse the conscience of the community over its injustice, is in reality expressing the highest respect for law.

Of course, there is nothing new about this kind of civil disobedience. It was evidenced sublimely in the refusal of Shadrach, Meshach and Abednego to obey the laws of Nebuchadnezzar, on the ground that a higher moral law was at stake. It was practiced superbly by the early Christians, who were willing to face hungry lions and the excruciating pain of chopping blocks rather than submit to certain unjust laws of the Roman Empire. To a degree, academic freedom is a reality today because Socrates practiced civil disobedience. In our own nation, the Boston Tea Party represented a massive act of civil disobedience.

We should never forget that everything Adolf Hitler did in Germany was "legal" and everything the Hungarian freedom fighters did in Hungary was "illegal." It was "illegal" to aid and comfort a Jew in Hitler's Germany. Even so, I am sure that, had I lived in Germany at the time, I would have aided and comforted my Jewish brothers. If today I lived in a Communist country where certain principles dear to the Christian faith are suppressed, I would openly advocate disobeying that country's antireligious laws.

I must make two honest confessions to you, my Christian and Jewish brothers. First, I must confess that over the past few years I have been gravely disappointed with the white moderate. I have almost reached the regrettable conclusion that the Negro's great stumbling block in his stride toward freedom is not the White Citizen's Counciler or the Ku Klux Klanner, but the white moderate, who is more devoted to "order" than to justice; who prefers a negative peace which is the absence of tension to a positive peace which is the presence of justice; who constantly says: "I agree with you in the goal you seek, but I cannot agree with your methods of direct action"; who paternalistically believes he can set the timetable for another man's freedom; who lives by a mythical concept of time and who constantly advises the Negro to wait for a "more convenient season." Shallow understanding from people of good will is more frustrating than absolute misunderstanding from people of ill will. Lukewarm acceptance is much more bewildering than outright rejection.

I had hoped that the white moderate would understand that law and order exist for the purpose of establishing justice and that when they fail in this purpose they become the dangerously structured dams that block the flow of social progress. I had hoped that the white moderate would understand that the present tension in the South is a necessary phase of the transition from an obnoxious negative peace, in which the Negro passively accepted his unjust plight, to a substantive and positive peace, in which all men will respect the dignity and worth of human personality. Actually, we who engage in nonviolent direct action are not the creators of tension. We merely bring to the surface the hidden tension that is already alive. We bring it out in the open, where it can be seen and dealt with. Like a boil that can never be cured so long as it is covered up but must be opened with all its ugliness to the natural medicines of air and light, injustice must be exposed, with all the tension its exposure creates, to the light of human conscience and the air of national opinion before it can be cured.

In your statement you assert that our actions, even though peaceful, must be condemned because they precipitate violence. But is this a logical assertion? Isn't this like condemning a robbed man because his possession of money precipitated the evil act of robbery? Isn't this like condemning Socrates because his unswerving commitment to truth and his philosophical inquiries precipitated the act by the misguided populace in which they made him drink hemlock? Isn't this like condemning Jesus because his unique God-consciousness and never-ceasing devotion to God's will precipitated the evil act of crucifixion? We must come to see that, as the federal courts have consistently affirmed, it is wrong to urge an individual to cease his efforts to gain his basic constitutional rights because the quest may precipitate violence. Society must protect the robbed and punish the robber.

I had also hoped that the white moderate would reject the myth concerning time in relation to the struggle for freedom. I have just received a letter from a white brother in Texas. He writes: "All Christians know that the colored people will receive equal rights eventually, but it is possible that you are in too great a religious hurry. It has taken Christianity almost two thousand years to accomplish what it has. The teachings of Christ take time to come to earth." Such an attitude stems from a tragic misconception of time, from the strangely irrational notion that there is something in the very flow of time that will inevitably cure all ills. Actually, time itself is neutral; it can be used either destructively or constructively. More and more I feel that the people of ill will have used time much more effectively than have the people of good will. We will have to repent in this generation not merely for the hateful words and actions of the bad people but for the appalling silence of the good people. Human progress never rolls in on wheels of inevitability; it comes through the tireless efforts of men willing to be co-workers with God, and without this hard work, time itself becomes an ally of the forces of social stagnation. We must use time creatively, in the knowledge that the time is always ripe to do right. Now is the time to make real the promise of democracy and transform our pending national elegy into a creative psalm of brotherhood. Now is the time to lift our national policy from the quicksand of racial injustice to the solid rock of human dignity.

You speak of our activity in Birmingham as extreme. At first I was rather disappointed that fellow clergymen would see my nonviolent efforts as those of an extremist. I began thinking about the fact that I stand in the middle of two opposing forces in the Negro community. One is a force of complacency, made up in part of Negroes who, as a result of long years of oppression, are so drained of self-respect and a sense of "somebodiness" that they have adjusted to segregation; and in part of a few middle-class Negroes who, because of a degree of academic and economic security and because in some ways they profit by segregation, have become insensitive to the problems of the masses. The other force is one of bitterness and hatred, and it comes perilously close to advocating violence. It is expressed in the various black nationalist groups that are springing up across the nation, the largest and best-known being

Elijah Muhammad's Muslim movement. Nourished by the Negro's frustration over the continued existence of racial discrimination, this movement is made up of people who have lost faith in America, who have absolutely repudiated Christianity, and who have concluded that the white man is an incorrigible "devil."

I have tried to stand between these two forces, saying that we need emulate neither the "do-nothingism" of the complacent nor the hatred and despair of the black nationalist. For there is the more excellent way of love and nonviolent protest. I am grateful to God that, through the influence of the Negro church, the way of nonviolence became an integral part of our struggle.

If this philosophy had not emerged, by now many streets of the South would, I am convinced, be flowing with blood. And I am further convinced that if our white brothers dismiss as "rabble-rousers" and "outside agitators" those of us who employ nonviolent direct action, and if they refuse to support our nonviolent efforts, millions of Negroes will, out of frustration and despair, seek solace and security in black-nationalist ideologies—a development that would inevitably lead to a frightening racial nightmare.

Oppressed people cannot remain oppressed forever. The yearning for freedom eventually manifests itself, and that is what has happened to the American Negro. Something within has reminded him of his birthright of freedom, and something without has reminded him that it can be gained. Consciously or unconsciously he has been caught up by the *Zeitgeist,* and with his black brothers of Africa and his brown and yellow brothers of Asia, South America and the Caribbean, the United States Negro is moving with a sense of great urgency toward the promised land of racial justice. If one recognizes this vital urge that has engulfed the Negro community, one should readily understand why public demonstrations are taking place. The Negro has many pent-up resentments and latent frustrations, and he must release them. So let him march; let him make prayer pilgrimages to the city hall; let him go on freedom rides—and try to understand why he must do so. If his repressed emotions are not released in nonviolent ways, they will seek expression through violence; this is not a threat but a fact of history. So I have not said to my people: "Get rid of your discontent." Rather, I have tried to say that this normal and healthy discontent can be channeled into the creative outlet of nonviolent direct action. And now this approach is being termed extremist.

But though I was initially disappointed at being categorized as an extremist, as I continued to think about the matter I gradually gained a measure of satisfaction from the label. Was not Jesus an extremist for love: "Love your enemies, bless them that curse you, do good to them that hate you, and pray for them which despitefully use you, and persecute you." Was not Amos an extremist for justice: "Let justice roll down like waters and righteousness like an ever-flowing stream." Was not Paul an extremist for the Christian gospel: "I bear in my body the marks of the Lord Jesus." Was not Martin Luther an extremist: "Here I stand: I cannot do otherwise, so help me God." And John Bunyan: "I will stay in jail to the end of my days before I make a butchery of my conscience." And Abraham Lincoln: "This nation cannot survive half slave and half free." And Thomas Jefferson: "We hold these truths to be self-evident, that all men are created equal . . . " So the question is not whether we will be extremists, but what kind of extremists we will be. Will we be extremists for hate or for love? Will we be extremists for the preservation of injustice or for the extension of justice? In that dramatic scene on Calvary's hill three men were crucified. We must never forget that all three were crucified for the same crime—the crime of extremism. Two were extremists for immorality, and thus fell below their environment. The other, Jesus Christ, was an extremist for love, truth and goodness, and thereby rose above his environment. Perhaps the South, the nation and the world are in dire need of creative extremists.

I had hoped that the white moderate would see this need. . . .

Before closing I feel impelled to mention one other point in your statement that has troubled me profoundly. You warmly commended the Birmingham police force for keeping "order" and "preventing violence." I doubt that you would have so warmly commended the police force if you had seen its dogs sinking their teeth into unarmed, nonviolent Negroes. I doubt that you would so quickly commend the policemen if you were to observe their ugly and inhumane treatment of Negroes here in the city jail; if you were to watch them push and curse old Negro women and young Negro girls; if you were to see them slap and kick old Negro men and young boys; if you were to observe them, as they did on two occasions, refuse to give us food because we wanted to sing our grace together. I cannot join you in your praise of the Birmingham police department.

It is true that the police have exercised a degree of discipline in handling the demonstrators. In this sense they have conducted themselves rather "nonviolently" in public. But for what purpose? To preserve the evil system of segregation. Over the past few years I have consistently preached that nonviolence demands that the means we use must be as pure as the ends we seek. I have tried to make clear that it is wrong to use immoral means to attain moral ends. But now I must affirm that it is just as wrong, or perhaps even more so, to use moral means to preserve immoral ends. Perhaps Mr. Connor and his policemen have been rather nonviolent in public, as was Chief Pritchett in Albany, Georgia, but they have used the moral means of nonviolence to maintain the immoral end of racial injustice. As T. S. Eliot has said: "The last temptation is the greatest treason: To do the right deed for the wrong reason."

I wish you had commended the Negro sitinners and demonstrators of Birmingham for their sublime courage, their willingness to suffer and their amazing discipline in the midst of great provocation. One day the South will recognize its real heroes. They will be the James Merediths, with the noble sense of purpose that enables them to face jeering and hostile mobs, and with the agonizing loneliness that characterizes the life of the pioneer. They will be old, oppressed, battered Negro women, symbolized in a seventy-two-year-old woman in Montgomery, Alabama, who rose up with a sense of dignity and with her people decided not to ride segregated buses, and who responded with ungrammatical profundity to one who inquired about her weariness: "My feets is tired, but my soul is at rest." They will be the young high school and college students, the young ministers of the gospel and a host of their elders, courageously and nonviolently sitting in at lunch counters and willingly going to jail for conscience' sake. One day the South will know that when these disinherited children of God sat down at lunch counters, they were in reality standing up for what is best in the American dream and for the most sacred values in our Judaeo–Christian heritage, thereby bringing our nation back to those great wells of democracy which were dug deep by the founding fathers in their formulation of the Constitution and the Declaration of Independence.

.   .   .

Yours for the cause of Peace and Brotherhood, Martin Luther King, Jr.

Discussion Questions

1. Explain why Martin Luther King may have come to the conclusion that the white moderate's devotion to order has been "the Negro's great stumbling block" rather than the persecutions of the White Citizen's Counciler or the Ku Klux Klan.

2. In what way does King criticize the white moderate? What does he mean by the statement "justice too long delayed is justice denied"?

3. Why would King object to the pluralist understanding of American politics as explained in the introduction to this reader? How is the kind of action that King calls for viewed in our society today?

30   *Reclaiming the Commons*

Naomi Klein

*One of the most striking developments in U.S. and world politics in recent years has been
the growth of a diverse and broad-based movement against corporate domination of the
global economy. Misleadingly labeled the "antiglobalization" movement, this new wave
of activism reached mass awareness with the protests in Seattle at the meeting of the World
Trade Organization in 1999. One of the most articulate thinkers of the movement is the
Canadian writer and activist Naomi Klein, author of No Logo (2000) and The Shock
Doctrine (2007). In this article Klein clarifies the nature and goals of the movement,
which opposes the privatization and commodification of everyday life rather than globalization as such. She explains that activists have targeted "free-market" trade agreements
as a way of resisting "McGovernment"—the "happy meal" of cutting taxes, privatizing
services, slashing regulations, busting unions, and removing any obstacles to the unfettered
reign of the market which is the hidden agenda of the free trade agenda. Far from seeing
democracy and the free-market as synonymous, Klein asserts that the dominant form of
corporate globalization amounts to "a crisis in representative democracy." For her the spirit
of the oppositional campaigns and movements is one of the "reclaiming the commons"—
acting to create a public sphere in which grassroots democracy can flourish and resist the
boundless drive of the corporate project.*

What is "the anti-globalization movement"? I put the phrase in quote-marks because I
immediately have two doubts about it. Is it really a movement? If it is a movement, is
it anti-globalization? Let me start with the first issue. We can easily convince ourselves
it is a movement by talking it into existence at a forum like this—I spend far too much
time at them—acting as if we can see it, hold it in our hands. Of course, we have seen
it—and we know it's come back in Quebec, and on the U.S.–Mexican border during
the Summit of the Americas and the discussion for a hemispheric Free Trade Area. But
then we leave rooms like this, go home, watch some TV, do a little shopping and any
sense that it exists disappears, and we feel like maybe we're going nuts. Seattle—was
that a movement or a collective hallucination? To most of us here, Seattle meant a kind
of coming-out party for a global resistance movement, or the "globalization of hope,"
as someone described it during the World Social Forum at Porto Alegre. But to everyone else Seattle still means limitless frothy coffee, Asian-fusion cuisine, e-commerce
billionaires and sappy Meg Ryan movies. Or perhaps it is both, and one Seattle bred
the other Seattle—and now they awkwardly coexist.

Reprinted from *New Left Review* 9, May-June 2001.

This movement we sometimes conjure into being goes by many names: anti-corporate, anti-capitalist, anti-free trade, anti-imperialist. Many say that it started in Seattle. Others maintain it began five hundred years ago—when colonialists first told indigenous peoples that they were going to have to do things differently if they were to "develop" or be eligible for "trade." Others again say it began on 1 January 1994 when the Zapatistas launched their uprising with the words *Ya Basta!* on the night NAFTA became law in Mexico. It all depends on whom you ask. But I think it is more accurate to picture a movement of many movements—coalitions of coalitions. Thousands of groups today are all working against forces whose common thread is what might broadly be described as the privatization of every aspect of life, and the transformation of every activity and value into a commodity. We often speak of the privatization of education, of healthcare, of natural resources. But the process is much vaster. It includes the way powerful ideas are turned into advertising slogans and public streets into shopping malls; new generations being target-marketed at birth; schools being invaded by ads; basic human necessities like water being sold as commodities; basic labour rights being rolled back; genes are patented and designer babies loom; seeds are genetically altered and bought; politicians are bought and altered.

At the same time there are oppositional threads, taking form in many different campaigns and movements. The spirit they share is a radical reclaiming of the commons. As our communal spaces—town squares, streets, schools, farms, plants—are displaced by the ballooning marketplace, a spirit of resistance is taking hold around the world. People are reclaiming bits of nature and of culture, and saying "this is going to be public space." American students are kicking ads out of the classrooms. European environmentalists and ravers are throwing parties at busy intersections. Landless Thai peasants are planting organic vegetables on over-irrigated golf courses. Bolivian workers are reversing the privatization of their water supply. Outfits like Napster have been creating a kind of commons on the internet where kids can swap music with each other, rather than buying it from multinational record companies. Billboards have been liberated and independent media networks set up. Protests are multiplying. In Porto Alegre, during the World Social Forum, José Bové, often caricatured as only a hammer of McDonald's, travelled with local activists from the Movimento Sem Terra to a nearby Monsanto test site, where they destroyed three hectares of genetically modified soya beans. But the protest did not stop there. The MST has occupied the land and members are now planting their own organic crops on it, vowing to turn the farm into a model of sustainable agriculture. In short, activists aren't waiting for the revolution, they are acting right now, where they live, where they study, where they work, where they farm.

But some formal proposals are also emerging whose aim is to turn such radical reclamations of the commons into law. When NAFTA and the like were cooked up, there was much talk of adding on "side agreements" to the free trade agenda, that were supposed to encompass the environment, labour and human rights. Now the fight-back is about taking them out. José Bové—along with the Via Campesina, a global association of small farmers—has launched a campaign to remove food safety and agricultural products from all trade agreements, under the slogan 'The World is Not for Sale.' They want to draw a line around the commons. Maude Barlow, director of the Council of Canadians, which has more members than most political parties in Canada, has argued that water isn't a private good and shouldn't be in any trade agreement. There is a lot of support for this idea, especially in Europe since the recent food scares. Typically these anti-privatization campaigns get under way on their own. But they also periodically converge—that's what happened in Seattle, Prague, Washington, Davos, Porto Alegre and Quebec.

Beyond the Borders

What this means is that the discourse has shifted. During the battles against NAFTA, there emerged the first signs of a coalition between organized labour, environmentalists, farmers and consumer groups within the countries concerned. In Canada most of us felt we were fighting to keep something distinctive about our nation from "Americanization." In the United States, the talk was very protectionist: workers were worried that Mexicans would "steal" away "our" jobs and drive down "our" environmental standards. All the while, the voices of Mexicans opposed to the deal were virtually off the public radar—yet these were the strongest voices of all. But only a few years later, the debate over trade has been transformed. The fight against globalization has morphed into a struggle against corporatization and, for some, against capitalism itself. It has also become a fight for democracy. Maude Barlow spearheaded the campaign against NAFTA in Canada twelve years ago. Since NAFTA became law, she's been working with organizers and activists from other countries, and anarchists suspicious of the state in her own country. She was once seen as very much the face of a Canadian nationalism. Today she has moved away from that discourse. "I've changed," she says, "I used to see this fight as saving a nation. Now I see it as saving democracy." This is a cause that transcends nationality and state borders. The real news out of Seattle is that organizers around the world are beginning to see their local and national struggles—for better funded public schools, against union-busting and casualization, for family farms, and against the widening gap between rich and poor—through a global lens. That is the most significant shift we have seen in years.

How did this happen? Who or what convened this new international people's movement? Who sent out the memos? Who built these complex coalitions? It is tempting to pretend that someone did dream up a master plan for mobilization at Seattle. But I think it was much more a matter of large-scale coincidence. A lot of smaller groups organized to get themselves there and then found to their surprise just how broad and diverse a coalition they had become part of. Still, if there is one force we can thank for bringing this front into being, it is the multinational corporations. As one of the organizers of Reclaim the Streets has remarked, we should be grateful to the CEOs for helping us see the problems more quickly. Thanks to the sheer imperialist ambition of the corporate project at this moment in history—the boundless drive for profit, liberated by trade deregulation, and the wave of mergers and buy-outs, liberated by weakened anti-trust laws—multinationals have grown so blindingly rich, so vast in their holdings, so global in their reach, that they have created our coalitions for us.

Around the world, activists are piggy-backing on the ready-made infrastructures supplied by global corporations. This can mean cross-border unionization, but also cross-sector organizing—among workers, environmentalists, consumers, even prisoners, who may all have different relationships to one multinational. So you can build a single campaign or coalition around a single brand like General Electric. Thanks to Monsanto, farmers in India are working with environmentalists and consumers around the world to develop direct-action strategies that cut off genetically modified foods in the fields and in the supermarkets. Thanks to Shell Oil and Chevron, human rights activists in Nigeria, democrats in Europe, environmentalists in North America have united in a fight against the unsustainability of the oil industry. Thanks to the catering giant Sodexho-Marriott's decision to invest in Corrections Corporation of America, university students are able to protest against the exploding U.S. for-profit prison industry simply by boycotting the food in their campus cafeteria. Other targets include pharmaceutical companies who are trying to inhibit the production and distribution of low-cost AIDS drugs, and fast-food chains. Recently, students and farm workers in Florida have joined forces around Taco Bell. In the St. Petersburg area, field hands—many of them immigrants from Mexico—are paid an average $7,500 a year to pick tomatoes and onions. Due to a loophole in the law, they have no bargaining power: the farm bosses refuse even to talk with them about wages. When they started to look into who bought what they pick, they found that Taco Bell was the largest purchaser of the local tomatoes. So they launched the campaign Yo No Quiero Taco Bell together with students, to boycott Taco Bell on university campuses.

It is Nike, of course, that has most helped to pioneer this new brand of activist synergy. Students facing a corporate take-over of their campuses by the Nike swoosh have linked up with workers making its branded campus apparel, as well as with parents concerned at the commercialization of youth and church groups campaigning against child labour—all united by their different relationships to a common global enemy. Exposing the underbelly of high-gloss consumer brands has provided the early narratives of this movement, a sort of call-and-response to the very different narratives these companies tell every day about themselves through advertising and public relations. Citigroup offers another prime target, as North America's largest financial institution, with innumerable holdings, which deals with some of the worst corporate malefactors around. The campaign against it handily knits together dozens of issues—from clear-cut logging in California to oil-and-pipeline schemes in Chad and Cameroon. These projects are only a start. But they are creating a new sort of activist: "Nike is a gateway drug," in the words of Oregon student activist Sarah Jacobson.

By focusing on corporations, organizers can demonstrate graphically how so many issues of social, ecological and economic justice are interconnected. No activist I've met believes that the world economy can be changed one corporation at a time, but the campaigns have opened a door into the arcane world of international trade and finance. Where they are leading is to the central institutions that write the rules of global commerce: the WTO, the IMF, the FTAA, and for some the market itself. Here too the unifying threat is privatization—the loss of the commons. The next round of WTO negotiations is designed to extend the reach of commodification still further. Through side agreements like GATS (General Agreement on Trade and Services) and TRIPS (Trade-Related Aspects of Intellectual Property Rights), the aim is to get still tougher protection of property rights on seeds and drug patents, and to marketize services like health care, education and water-supply.

The biggest challenge facing us is to distil all of this into a message that is widely accessible. Many campaigners understand the connexions binding together the various issues almost intuitively—much as Subcomandante Marcos says, "Zapatismo isn't an ideology, it's an intuition." But to outsiders, the mere scope of modern protests can be a bit mystifying. If you eavesdrop on the movement from the outside, which is what most people do, you are liable to hear what seems to be a cacophony of disjointed slogans, a jumbled laundry list of disparate grievances without clear goals. At the Democratic National Convention in Los Angeles last year, I remember being outside the Staples Centre during the Rage Against the Machine concert, just before I almost got shot, and thinking there were slogans for everything everywhere, to the point of absurdity.

Mainstream Failures

This kind of impression is reinforced by the decentralized, non-hierarchical structure of the movement, which always disconcerts the traditional media. Well-organized press conferences are rare, there is no charismatic leadership, protests tend to pile on top of each other. Rather than forming a pyramid, as most movements do, with leaders up on top and followers down below, it looks more like an elaborate web. In part, this web-like structure is the result of internet-based organizing. But it is also a response to the very political realities that sparked the protests in the first place: the utter failure of traditional party politics. All over the world, citizens have worked to elect social democratic and workers' parties, only to watch them plead impotence in the face of market forces and IMF dictates. In these conditions, modern activists are not so naive as to believe change will come from electoral politics. That's why they are more interested in challenging the structures that make democracy toothless, like the IMF's structural adjustment policies, the WTO's ability to override national sovereignty, corrupt campaign financing, and so on. This is not just making a virtue of necessity. It responds at the ideological level to an understanding that globalization is in essence a crisis in representative democracy. What has caused this crisis? One of the basic reasons for it is the way power and decision-making has been handed along to points ever further away from citizens: from local to provincial, from provincial to national, from national to international institutions, that lack all transparency or accountability. What is the solution? To articulate an alternative, participatory democracy.

If you think about the nature of the complaints raised against the World Trade Organization, it is that governments around the world have embraced an economic model that involves much more than opening borders to goods and services. This is why it is not useful to use the language of anti-globalization. Most people do not really know what globalization is, and the term makes the movement extremely vulnerable to stock dismissals like: "If you are against trade and globalization why do you drink coffee?" Whereas in reality the movement is a rejection of what is being bundled along with trade and so-called globalization—against the set of transformative political policies that every country in the world has been told they must accept in order to make themselves hospitable to investment. I call this package "McGovernment." This happy meal of cutting taxes, privatizing services, liberalizing regulations, busting unions—what is this diet in aid of? To remove anything standing in the way of the market. Let the free market roll, and every other problem will apparently be solved in the trickle down. This isn't about trade. It's about using trade to enforce the McGovernment recipe.

So the question we are asking today, in the run up to the FTAA, is not: are you for or against trade? The question is: do we have the right to negotiate the terms of our relationship to foreign capital and investment? Can we decide how we want to protect ourselves from the dangers inherent in deregulated markets—or do we have to contract out those decisions? These problems will become much more acute once we are in a recession, because during the economic boom so much has been destroyed of what was left of our social safety net. During a period of low unemployment, people did not worry much about that. They are likely to be much more concerned in the very near future. The most controversial issues facing the WTO are these questions about self-determination. For example, does Canada have the right to ban a harmful gasoline additive without being sued by a foreign chemical company? Not according to the WTO's ruling in favour of the Ethyl Corporation. Does Mexico have the right to deny a permit for a hazardous toxic-waste disposal site? Not according to Metalclad, the U.S. company now suing the Mexican government for $16.7 million damages under NAFTA. Does France have the right to ban hormone-treated beef from entering the country? Not according to the United States, which retaliated by banning French imports like Roquefort cheese—prompting a cheese-maker called Bové to dismantle a McDonald's; Americans thought he just didn't like hamburgers. Does Argentina have to cut its public sector to qualify for foreign loans? Yes, according to the IMF—sparking general strikes against the social consequences. It's the same issue everywhere: trading away democracy in exchange for foreign capital.

On smaller scales, the same struggles for self-determination and sustainability are being waged against World Bank dams, clear-cut logging, cash-crop factory farming, and resource extraction on contested indigenous lands. Most people in these movements are not against trade or industrial development. What they are fighting for is the right of local communities to have a say in how their resources are used, to make sure that the people who live on the land benefit directly from its development. These campaigns are a response not to trade but to a trade-off that is now five hundred years old: the sacrifice of democratic control and self-determination to foreign investment and the panacea of economic growth. The challenge they now face is to shift a discourse around the vague notion of globalization into a specific debate about democracy. In a period of 'unprecedented prosperity,' people were told they had no choice but to slash public spending, revoke labour laws, rescind environmental protections—deemed illegal trade barriers—defund schools, not build affordable housing. All this was necessary to make us trade-ready, investment-friendly, world-competitive. Imagine what joys await us during a recession.

We need to be able to show that globalization— this version of globalization—has been built on the back of local human welfare. Too often, these connexions between global and local are not made. Instead we sometimes seem to have two activist solitudes. On the one hand, there are the international anti-globalization activists who may be enjoying a triumphant mood, but seem to be fighting far-away issues, unconnected to people's day-to-day struggles. They are often seen as elitists: white middle-class kids with dreadlocks. On the other hand, there are community activists fighting daily struggles for survival, or for the preservation of the most elementary public services, who are often feeling burnt-out and demoralized. They are saying: what in the hell are you guys so excited about?

The only clear way forward is for these two forces to merge. What is now the anti-globalization movement must turn into thousands of local movements, fighting the way neoliberal politics are playing out on the ground: homelessness, wage stagnation, rent escalation, police violence, prison explosion, criminalization of migrant workers, and on and on. These are also struggles about all kinds of prosaic issues: the right to decide where the local garbage goes, to have good public schools, to be supplied with clean water. At the same time, the local movements fighting privatization and deregulation on the ground need to link their campaigns into one large global movement, which can show where their particular issues fit into an international economic agenda being enforced around the world. If that connexion isn't made, people will continue to be demoralized. What we need is to formulate a political framework that can both take on corporate power and control, and empower local organizing and self-determination. That has to be a framework that encourages, celebrates and fiercely protects the right to diversity: cultural diversity, ecological diversity, agricultural diversity—and yes, political diversity as well: different ways of doing politics. Communities must have the right to plan and manage their schools, their services, their natural settings, according to their own lights. Of course, this is only possible within a framework of national and international standards— of public education, fossil-fuel emissions, and so on. But the goal should not be better far-away rules and rulers, it should be close-up democracy on the ground.

The Zapatistas have a phrase for this. They call it "one world with many worlds in it." Some have criticized this as a New Age non-answer. They want a plan. "We know what the market wants to do with those spaces, what do you want to do? Where's your scheme?" I think we shouldn't be afraid to say: "That's not up to us." We need to have some trust in people's ability to rule themselves, to make the decisions that are best for them. We need to show some humility where now there is so much arrogance and paternalism. To believe in human diversity and local democracy is anything but wishy-washy. Everything in McGovernment conspires against them. Neoliberal economics is biased at every level towards centralization, consolidation, homogenization. It is a war waged on diversity. Against it, we need a movement of radical change, committed to a single world with many worlds in it, that stands for 'the one no and the many yesses.'

Discussion Questions

1. How does Klein characterize the "corporate agenda" in the age of globalization? Why does she think that this agenda is a threat to democracy in any meaningful sense?

2. Contemporary political discourse often speaks of "free market democracy" as an ideal that all countries strive to attain. Why would the movements that Klein discusses take issue with this easy equation of democracy and free markets?

31   *Is Imperial Liquidation Possible For America?*

Chalmers Johnson

In the last few years, a stream of books and articles have appeared that explore critically the nature of U.S. imperialism, militarism, and hegemony early in the twenty-first century, especially in the context of the "war on terrorism." One of the most important contributions has been made by Chalmers Johnson, a longtime foreign policy expert and specialist on Asia who served as a consultant to the CIA in the 1960s and 1970s. In this article written in 2007, Johnson probes beneath the expressed sense of many Americans that the country is going in the wrong direction. He finds that American institutions, including the presidency, the military, and the news media, are jeopardizing American democracy and threatening the Constitutional system. He believes these problems are deeply rooted, and will not be resolved simply by one political party replacing the other party in power. What is needed is a popular movement to rebuild the Constitutional system. For Johnson this will require a project of "imperial liquidation" involving dramatic reductions in military spending, closing of foreign bases, restrictions on covert operations, and rethinking of the dogma of "free trade." While Johnson acknowledges that these changes may appear utopian, he contends that failure to rethink American imperial assumptions poses a threat to democracy itself.

In politics, as in medicine, a cure based on a false diagnosis is almost always worthless, often worsening the condition that is supposed to be healed. The United States, today, suffers from a plethora of public ills. Most of them can be traced to the militarism and imperialism that have led to the near-collapse of our Constitutional system of checks and balances. Unfortunately, none of the remedies proposed so far by American politicians or analysts addresses the root causes of the problem.

According to an NBC News/ *Wall Street Journal* poll, released on April 26, 2007, some 78% of Americans believe their country to be headed in the wrong direction. Only 22% think the Bush administration's policies make sense, the lowest number on this question since October 1992, when George H. W. Bush was running for a second term—and lost. What people don't agree on are the reasons for their doubts and, above all, what the remedy—or remedies—ought to be.

The range of opinions on this is immense. Even though large numbers of voters vaguely suspect that the failings of the political system itself led the country into its

Reprinted from *Tomdispatch.com*, May 15, 1997, by permission of Sheila K. Johnson.

current crisis, most evidently expect the system to perform a course correction more or less automatically. As Adam Nagourney of the *New York Times* reported, by the end of March 2007, at least 280,000 American citizens had already contributed some $113.6 million to the presidential campaigns of Hillary Rodham Clinton, Barack Obama, John Edwards, Mitt Romney, Rudolph Giuliani, or John McCain.

If these people actually believe a presidential election a year-and-a-half from now will significantly alter how the country is run, they have almost surely wasted their money. As Andrew Bacevich, author of *The New American Militarism*, puts it: "None of the Democrats vying to replace President Bush is doing so with the promise of reviving the system of check and balances. . . . The aim of the party out of power is not to cut the presidency down to size but to seize it, not to reduce the prerogatives of the executive branch but to regain them."

George W. Bush has, of course, flagrantly violated his oath of office, which requires him "to protect and defend the constitution," and the opposition party has been remarkably reluctant to hold him to account. Among the "high crimes and misdemeanors" that, under other political circumstances, would surely constitute the Constitutional grounds for impeachment are these: the President and his top officials pressured the Central Intelligence Agency to put together a National Intelligence Estimate (NIE) on Iraq's nuclear weapons that both the administration and the Agency knew to be patently dishonest. They then used this false NIE to justify an American war of aggression. After launching an invasion of Iraq, the administration unilaterally reinterpreted international and domestic law to permit the torture of prisoners held at Abu Ghraib prison in Baghdad, at Guantánamo Bay, Cuba, and at other secret locations around the world.

Nothing in the Constitution, least of all the commander-in-chief clause, allows the president to commit felonies. Nonetheless, within days after the 9/11 attacks, President Bush had signed a secret executive order authorizing a new policy of "extraordinary rendition," in which the CIA is allowed to kidnap terrorist suspects anywhere on Earth and transfer them to prisons in countries like Egypt, Syria, or Uzbekistan, where torture is a normal practice, or to secret CIA prisons outside the United States where Agency operatives themselves do the torturing.

On the home front, despite the post-9/11 congressional authorization of new surveillance powers to the administration, its officials chose to ignore these and, on its own initiative, undertook extensive spying on American citizens without obtaining the necessary judicial warrants and without reporting to Congress on this program. These actions are *prima-facie* violations of the Foreign Intelligence Surveillance Act of 1978 (and subsequent revisions) and of Amendment IV of the Constitution

These alone constitute more than adequate grounds for impeachment, while hardly scratching the surface. And yet, on the eve of the national elections of November 2006, then House Minority Leader, now Speaker, Nancy Pelosi (D-Calif.), pledged on the CBS News program "60 Minutes" that "impeachment is off the table." She called it "a waste of time." And six months after the Democratic Party took control of both houses of Congress, the prison at Guantánamo Bay was still open and conducting drumhead courts martial of the prisoners held there; the CIA was still using "enhanced interrogation techniques" on prisoners in foreign jails; illegal intrusions into the privacy of American citizens continued unabated; and, more than fifty years after the CIA was founded, it continues to operate under, at best, the most perfunctory congressional oversight.

Promoting Lies, Demoting Democracy

Without question, the administration's catastrophic war in Iraq is the single overarching issue that has convinced a large majority of Americans that the country is "heading in the wrong direction." But the war itself is the outcome of an imperial presidency and the abject failure of Congress to perform its Constitutional duty of oversight. Had the government been working as the authors of the Constitution intended, the war could not have occurred. Even now, the Democratic majority remains reluctant to use its power of the purse to cut off funding for the war, thereby ending the American occupation of Iraq and starting to curtail the ever-growing power of the military-industrial complex.

One major problem of the American social and political system is the failure of the press, especially television news, to inform the public about the true breadth of the unconstitutional activities of the executive branch. As Frederick A. O. Schwarz and Aziz Z. Huq, the authors of *Unchecked and Unbalanced: Presidential Power in a Time of Terror*, observe, "For the public to play its proper checking role at the ballot box, citizens must know what is done by the government in their names."

Instead of uncovering administration lies and manipulations, the media actively promoted them. Yet the first amendment to the Constitution protects the press precisely so it can penetrate the secrecy that is the bureaucrat's most powerful, self-protective weapon. As a result of this failure, democratic oversight of the government by an actively engaged citizenry did not—and could not—occur. The people of the United States became mere spectators as an array of ideological extremists, vested interests, and foreign operatives—including domestic neoconservatives, Ahmed Chalabi and his Iraqi exiles, the Israeli Lobby, the petroleum and automobile industries, warmongers and profiteers allied with the military-industrial complex, and the entrenched interests of the professional military establishment—essentially hijacked the government.

Some respected professional journalists do not see these failings as the mere result of personal turpitude but rather as deep structural and cultural problems within the American system as it exists today. In an interview with Matt Taibbi, Seymour Hersh, for forty years one of America's leading investigative reporters, put the matter this way:

"All of the institutions we thought would protect us—particularly the press, but also the military, the bureaucracy, the Congress—they have failed . . . So all the things that we expect would normally carry us through didn't. The biggest failure, I would argue, is the press, because that's the most glaring. . . . What can be done to fix the situation? [long pause] You'd have to fire or execute ninety percent of the editors and executives."

Veteran analyst of the press (and former presidential press secretary), Bill Moyers, considering a classic moment of media failure, concluded: "The disgraceful press reaction to Colin Powell's presentation at the United Nations [on February 5, 2003] seems like something out of Monty Python, with one key British report cited by Powell being nothing more than a student's thesis, downloaded from the Web—with the student later threatening to charge U.S. officials with 'plagiarism.'"

As a result of such multiple failures (still ongoing), the executive branch easily misled the American public.

A Made-in-America Human Catastrophe

Of the failings mentioned by Hersh, that of the military is particularly striking, resembling as it does the failures of the Vietnam era, thirty-plus years earlier. One would have thought the high command had learned some lessons from the defeat of 1975. Instead, it once again went to war pumped up on our own propaganda—especially the conjoined beliefs that the United States was the "indispensable nation," the "lone superpower," and the "victor" in the Cold War; and that it was a new Rome the likes of which the world had never seen, possessing as it did—from the heavens to the remotest spot on the planet—"full spectrum dominance." The idea that the U.S. was an unquestioned military colossus athwart the world, which no power or people could effectively oppose, was hubristic nonsense certain to get the country into deep trouble—as it did—and bring the U.S. Army to the point of collapse, as happened in Vietnam and may well happen again in Iraq (and Afghanistan).

Instead of behaving in a professional manner, our military invaded Iraq with far too small a force; failed to respond adequately when parts of the Iraqi Army (and Baathist Party) went underground; tolerated an orgy of looting and lawlessness throughout the country; disobeyed orders and ignored international obligations (including the obligation of an occupying power to protect the facilities and treasures of the occupied country—especially, in this case, Baghdad's National Museum and other archaeological sites of untold historic value); and incompetently fanned the flames of an insurgency against our occupation, committing numerous atrocities against unarmed Iraqi civilians.

According to Andrew Bacevich, "Next to nothing can be done to salvage Iraq. It no longer lies within the capacity of the United States to determine the outcome of events there." Our former ambassador to Saudi Arabia, Chas W. Freeman, says of President Bush's recent "surge" strategy in Baghdad and al-Anbar Province: "The reinforcement of failure is a poor substitute for its correction."

Symbolically, a certain sign of the disaster to come in Iraq arrived via an April 26th posting from the courageous but anonymous Sunni woman who has, since August 2003, published the indispensable blog Baghdad Burning. Her family, she reported, was finally giving up and going into exile—joining up to two million of her compatriots who have left the country. In her final dispatch, she wrote:

"There are moments when the injustice of having to leave your country simply because an imbecile got it into his head to invade it, is overwhelming. It is unfair that in order to survive and live normally, we have to leave our home and what remains of family and friends. . . . And to what?"

Retired General Barry McCaffrey, commander of the 24th Infantry Division in the first Iraq war and a consistent cheerleader for Bush strategies in the second, recently radically changed his tune. He now says, "No Iraqi government official, coalition soldier, diplomat, reporter, foreign NGO, nor contractor can walk the streets of Baghdad, nor Mosul, nor Kirkuk, nor Basra, nor Tikrit, nor Najaf, nor Ramadi, without heavily armed protection." In a different context, Gen. McCaffrey has concluded: "The U.S. Army is rapidly unraveling."

Even military failure in Iraq is still being spun into an endless web of lies and distortions by the White House, the Pentagon, military pundits, and the now-routine reporting of propagandists disguised as journalists. For example, in the first months of 2007, rising car-bomb attacks in Baghdad were making a mockery of Bush administration and Pentagon claims that the U.S. troop escalation in the capital had brought about "a dramatic drop in sectarian violence." The official response to this problem: the Pentagon simply quit including deaths from car bombings in its count of sectarian casualties. (It has never attempted to report civilian casualties publicly or accurately.) Since August 2003, there have been over 1,050 car bombings in Iraq. One study estimates that through June 2006 the death toll from these alone has been a staggering 78,000 Iraqis.

The war and occupation George W. Bush unleashed in Iraq has proved unimaginably lethal for unarmed civilians, but reporting the true levels of lethality in Iraq, or the nature of the direct American role in it was, for a long time, virtually taboo in the U.S. media. As late as October 2006, the journal of the British Medical Association, *The Lancet*, published a study conducted by researchers from Johns Hopkins University in Baltimore and al-Mustansiriya University in Baghdad estimating that, since March 2003, there were some 601,027 more Iraqi deaths from violence than would have been expected without a war. The British and American governments at first dismissed the findings, claiming the research was based on faulty statistical methods—and the American media ignored the study, played down its importance, or dismissed its figures.

On March 27, 2007, however, it was revealed that the chief scientific adviser to the British Ministry of Defense, Roy Anderson, had offered a more honest response. The methods used in the study were, he wrote, "close to best practice." Another British official described them as "a tried and tested way of measuring mortality in conflict zones." Over 600,000 violent deaths in a population estimated in 2006 at 26.8 million—that is, one in every 45 individuals—amounts to a made-in-America human catastrophe.

One subject that the government, the military, and the news media try to avoid like the plague is the racist and murderous culture of rank-and-file American troops when operating abroad. Partly as a result of the background racism that is embedded in many Americans' mental make-up and the propaganda of American imperialism that is drummed into recruits during military training, they do not see assaults on unarmed "rag heads" or "hajis" as murder. The cult of silence on this subject began to slip only slightly in May 2007 when a report prepared by the Army's Mental Health Advisory Team was leaked to the *San Diego Union-Tribune*. Based on anonymous surveys and focus groups involving 1,320 soldiers and 447 Marines, the study revealed that only 56% of soldiers would report a unit member for injuring or killing an innocent noncombatant, while a mere 40% of Marines would do so. Some militarists will reply that such inhumanity to the defenseless is always inculcated into the properly trained soldier. If so, then the answer to this problem is to ensure that, in the future, there are many fewer imperialist wars of choice sponsored by the United States.

The Military-Industrial-Congressional Complex

Many other aspects of imperialism and militarism are undermining America's Constitutional system. By now, for example, the privatization of military and intelligence functions is totally out of control, beyond the law, and beyond any form of Congressional oversight. It is also incredibly lucrative for the owners and operators of so-called private military companies—and the money to pay for their activities ultimately comes from taxpayers through government contracts. Any accounting of these funds, largely distributed to crony companies with insider connections, is chaotic at best. Jeremy Scahill, author of *Blackwater: The Rise of the World's Most Powerful Mercenary Army*, estimates that there are 126,000 private military contractors in Iraq, more than enough to keep the war going, even if most official U.S. troops were withdrawn. "From the beginning," Scahill writes, "these contractors have been a major hidden story of the war, almost uncovered in the mainstream media and absolutely central to maintaining the U.S. occupation of Iraq."

America's massive "military" budgets, still on the rise, are beginning to threaten the U.S. with bankruptcy, given that its trade and fiscal deficits already easily make it the world's largest net debtor nation. Spending on the military establishment—sometimes mislabeled "defense spending"—has soared to the highest levels since World War II, exceeding the budgets of the Korean and Vietnam War eras as well as President Ronald Reagan's weapons-buying binge in the 1980s. According to calculations by the National Priorities Project, a non-profit research organization that examines the local impact of federal spending policies, military spending today consumes 40% of every tax dollar.

Equally alarming, it is virtually impossible for a member of Congress or an ordinary citizen to obtain even a modest handle on the actual size of military spending or its impact on the structure and functioning of our economic system. Some $30 billion of the official Defense Department (DoD) appropriation in the current fiscal year is "black," meaning that it is allegedly going for highly classified projects. Even the open DoD budget receives only perfunctory scrutiny because members of Congress, seeking lucrative defense contracts for their districts, have mutually beneficial relationships with defense contractors and the Pentagon. President Dwight D. Eisenhower identified this phenomenon, in the draft version of his 1961 farewell address, as the "military-industrial-congressional complex." Forty-six years later, in a way even Eisenhower probably couldn't have imagined, the defense budget is beyond serious congressional oversight or control.

The DoD always tries to minimize the size of its budget by representing it as a declining percentage of the gross national product. What it never reveals is that total military spending is actually many times larger than the official appropriation for the Defense Department. For fiscal year 2006, Robert Higgs of the Independent Institute calculated national security outlays at almost a trillion dollars—$934.9 billion to be exact—broken down as follows (in billions of dollars):

Department of Defense: $499.4 Department of Energy (atomic weapons): $16.6 Department of State (foreign military aid): $25.3 Department of Veterans Affairs (treatment of wounded soldiers): $69.8 Department of Homeland Security (actual *defense): $69.1 Department of Justice (1/3rd for the FBI): $1.9 Department of the Treasury (military retirements): $38.5 NASA (satellite launches): $7.6 Interest on war debts, 1916-present: $206.7*

Totaled, the sum is larger than the combined sum spent by all other nations on military security.

This spending helps sustain the national economy and represents, essentially, a major jobs program. However, it is beginning to crowd out the civilian economy, causing stagnation in income levels. It also contributes to the hemorrhaging of manufacturing jobs to other countries. On May 1, 2007, the Center for Economic and Policy Research released a series of estimates on "the economic impact of the Iraq war and higher military spending." Its figures show, among other things, that, after an initial demand stimulus, the effect of a significant rise in military spending (as we've experienced in recent years) turns negative around the sixth year.

Sooner or later, higher military spending forces inflation and interest rates up, reducing demand in interest-sensitive sectors of the economy, notably in annual car and truck sales. Job losses follow. The non-military construction and manufacturing sectors experience the largest share of these losses. The report concludes, "Most economic models show that military spending diverts resources from productive uses, such as consumption and investment, and ultimately slows economic growth and reduces employment."

Imperial Liquidation?

Imperialism and militarism have thus begun to imperil both the financial and social well-being of our republic. What the country desperately needs is a popular movement to rebuild the Constitutional system and subject the government once again to the discipline of checks and balances. Neither the replacement of one political party by the other, nor protectionist economic policies aimed at rescuing what's left of our manufacturing economy will correct what has gone wrong. Both of these solutions fail to address the root cause of our national decline.

I believe that there is only one solution to the crisis we face. The American people must make the decision to dismantle both the empire that has been created in their name and the huge (still growing) military establishment that undergirds it. It is a task at least comparable to that undertaken by the British government when, after World War II, it liquidated the British Empire. By doing so, Britain avoided the fate of the Roman Republic—becoming a domestic tyranny and losing its democracy, as would have been required if it had continued to try to dominate much of the world by force.

For the U.S., the decision to mount such a campaign of imperial liquidation may already come too late, given the vast and deeply entrenched interests of the military-industrial complex. To succeed, such an endeavor might virtually require a revolutionary mobilization of the American citizenry, one at least comparable to the civil rights movement of the 1960s.

Even to contemplate a drawing back from empire—something so inconceivable to our pundits and newspaper editorial writers that it is simply never considered—we must specify as clearly as possible precisely what the elected leaders and citizens of the United States would have to do. Two cardinal decisions would have to be made. First, in Iraq, we would have to initiate a firm timetable for withdrawing *all* our military forces and turning over the permanent military bases we have built to the Iraqis. Second, domestically, we would have to reverse federal budget priorities.

In the words of Noam Chomsky, a venerable critic of American imperialism: "Where spending is rising, as in military supplemental bills to conduct the wars in Iraq and Afghanistan, it would sharply decline. Where spending is steady or declining (health, education, job training, the promotion of energy conservation and renewable energy sources, veterans benefits, funding for the UN and UN peacekeeping operations, and so on), it would sharply increase. Bush's tax cuts for people with incomes over $200,000 a year would be immediately rescinded."

Such reforms would begin at once to reduce the malevolent influence of the military-industrial complex, but many other areas would require attention as well. As part of the process of de-garrisoning the planet and liquidating our empire, we would have to launch an orderly closing-up process for at least 700 of the 737 military bases we maintain (by official Pentagon count) in over 130 foreign countries on every continent except Antarctica. We should ultimately aim at closing all our imperialist enclaves, but in order to avoid isolationism and maintain a capacity to assist the United Nations in global peacekeeping operations, we should, for the time being, probably retain some 37 of them, mostly naval and air bases.

Equally important, we should rewrite all our Status of Forces Agreements—those American-dictated "agreements" that exempt our troops based in foreign countries from local criminal laws, taxes, immigration controls, anti-pollution legislation, and anything else the American military can think of. It must be established as a matter of principle and law that American forces stationed outside the U.S. will deal with their host nations on a basis of equality, not of extraterritorial privilege.

The American approach to diplomatic relations with the rest of the world would also require a major overhaul. We would have to end our belligerent unilateralism toward other countries as well as our scofflaw behavior regarding international law. Our objective should be to strengthen the United Nations, including our respect for its majority, by working to end the Security Council veto system (and by stopping using our present right to veto). The United States needs to cease being the world's largest supplier of arms and munitions—a lethal trade whose management should be placed under UN supervision. We should encourage the UN to begin outlawing weapons like land mines, cluster bombs, and depleted-uranium ammunition that play particularly long-term havoc with civilian populations. As part of an attempt to right the diplomatic balance, we should take some obvious steps like recognizing Cuba and ending our blockade of that island and, in the Middle East, working to equalize aid to Israel and Palestine, while attempting to broker a real solution to that disastrous situation. Our goal should be a return to leading by example— and by sound arguments—rather than by continual resort to unilateral armed force and repeated foreign military interventions.

In terms of the organization of the executive branch, we need to rewrite the National Security Act of 1947, taking away from the CIA all functions that involve sabotage, torture, subversion, overseas election rigging, rendition, and other forms of clandestine activity. The president should be deprived of his power to order these types of operations except with the explicit advice and consent of the Senate. The CIA should basically devote itself to the collection and analysis of foreign intelligence. We should eliminate as much secrecy as possible so that neither the CIA, nor any other comparable organization ever again becomes the president's private army.

In order to halt our economic decline and lessen our dependence on our trading partners, the U.S. must cap its trade deficits through the perfectly legal use of tariffs in accordance with World Trade Organization rules, and it must begin to guide its domestic market in accordance with a national industrial policy, just as the leading economies of the world (particularly the Japanese and Chinese ones) do as a matter of routine. Even though it may involve trampling on the vested interests of American university economics departments, there is simply no excuse for a continued reliance on an outdated doctrine of "free trade."

Normally, a proposed list of reforms like this would simply be rejected as utopian. I understand this reaction. I do want to stress, however, that failure to undertake such reforms would mean condemning the United States to the fate that befell the Roman Republic and all other empires since then. That is why I gave my book *Nemesis* the subtitle *The Last Days of the American Republic*.

When Ronald Reagan coined the phrase "evil empire," he was referring to the Soviet Union, and I basically agreed with him that the USSR needed to be contained and checkmated. But today it is the U.S. that is widely perceived as an evil empire and world forces are gathering to stop us. The Bush administration insists that if we leave Iraq our enemies will "win" or—even more improbably— "follow us home." I believe that, if we leave Iraq and our other imperial enclaves, we can regain the moral high ground and disavow the need for a foreign policy based on preventive war. I also believe that unless we follow this path, we will lose our democracy and then it will not matter much what else we lose. In the immortal words of Pogo, "We have met the enemy and he is us."

Discussion Questions

1. According to Johnson, what policies and actions of the United States in the context of the "war on terrorism" have endangered the American constitutional system?

2. How would you assess Johnson's specific proposals for "imperial liquidation" as laid out in the last section of his article? How deeply rooted in U.S. politics, society, and culture are these imperial patterns?